Her Own Voice

Her Own Voice

EIGHT WOMEN WHO REWROTE LIFE AND ART

Anne E. Fernald

BEACON PRESS
BOSTON

BEACON PRESS
24 Farnsworth Street
Boston, Massachusetts
www.beacon.org

Beacon Press books
are published under the auspices of
the Unitarian Universalist Association of Congregations.

Printed in the United States of America

29 28 27 26   8 7 6 5 4 3 2 1

This book is printed on acid-free paper that meets the uncoated paper
ANSI/NISO specifications for permanence as revised in 1992.

Text design and composition by Kim Arney

Library of Congress Cataloging-in-Publication
Data is available for this title.

Names: Fernald, Anne E. author
Title: Her own voice : eight women who
rewrote life and art / Anne E. Fernald.
Description: Boston : Beacon Press, 2026. | Includes bibliographical
references and index. | Summary: "Tells the stories of eight radical
women who responded to social oppression and helped create
the modernist movement"—Provided by publisher.
Identifiers: LCCN 2026007734 (print) | LCCN 2026007735 (ebook) |
ISBN 9780807021330 hardcover | ISBN 9780807021347 ebook
Subjects: LCSH: Literature—Women authors—History and
criticism | Modernism (Literature)—English-speaking countries |
Women authors—Social conditions—20th century |
Women and literature—History—20th century
Classification: LCC PN471 .F48 2026 (print) | LCC PN471 (ebook)
LC record available at https://lccn.loc.gov/2026007734
LC ebook record available at https://lccn.loc.gov/2026007735

The authorized representative in the EU for product safety
and compliance is Easy Access System Europe 16879218, Mustamäe tee 50,
10621 Tallinn, Estonia: https://beacon.org/eu-contact.

CONTENTS

INTRODUCTION

Imagine a young woman born into a middle-class family sometime between 1880 and 1920. At birth, her parents may have been disappointed to learn she was a girl. Girls are a drain on the family budget; girls worry their parents. Will she be pretty enough to marry well—or at all? Pretty or not, parents might have consoled themselves with the hope that she would be helpful by managing the household accounts or caring for family members in illness or old age. Even if her brothers attended university, her parents might feel relieved not to have that expense before them. Her parents likely expected her to marry, and, once married, they hoped for her to have children. They would not have wanted their daughter to have an extramarital affair, and they never would have imagined her having an affair with a woman.

Sports would be an acceptable diversion. A woman in the early twentieth century could walk, ride horses, play cricket, tennis, or even ride a bicycle. But, even in those pursuits, the layers of heavy cotton and wool clothing required to keep her young body covered and appropriately modest might discourage her. Still, tennis is a social game, and parents might take comfort in the opportunity that it could afford their daughter to come in the way of a suitable partner. Music, too, would be encouraged. With pianos in most homes, and radios and phonographs still rare, a young woman who could play a few songs would be a welcome part of any gathering. Needlework, reading, painting, drawing, speaking a bit of French—all of the "accomplishments" that Elizabeth Bennet and Mr. Darcy bantered about in *Pride and Prejudice* in the early nineteenth century would still, a hundred years later, mark the limits of mainstream womanhood. In short, much of her life was defined by constraint.

In her 1929 book *A Room of One's Own*, Virginia Woolf considered what it might mean for a woman to have an ambition to be something more than a good woman. Responding to a widespread argument that women must be less capable than men because, for centuries, women had achieved so little, Woolf invented a sister for Shakespeare, calling her Judith. She imagines Judith's parents trying to distract her from her dreams of learning. But, when she goes to London, as William did, disaster strikes. Turned away from theater after theater, a man finally "takes pity on her," which, to him, means sleeping with her. Pregnant, she commits suicide. As Woolf writes, "That, more or less, is how the story would run . . . if a woman in Shakespeare's day had had Shakespeare's genius."[1] We can still find stories like Judith Shakespeare's today, but, starting with the women profiled in this book, Judith's is no longer the only or most likely fate for the young woman who wants more. Despite the familiar and limiting horizons, by 1880 activists and pioneers had achieved reforms that meant the next generation's horizons could be wider.

From the late nineteenth century into the first decades of the twentieth, social and legal changes opened a broad array of choices for women in the arenas of economic independence, marriage choice, sexuality and birth control, education, and work. The women in *Her Own Voice*, born between 1882 and 1920, came into a world of rapidly and unevenly changing laws that had dramatic effects on their rights. Most of these women were born without the right to vote; college education was just emerging as a regular option for middle-class families; birth control became more widespread, but was still tightly controlled and often illegal; World War I needed women's labor to aid the devastating scale of destruction, and in war work many women found new independence; the professions opened, uneasily and with tension, to women; even married women gained the right to keep control of the money they earned; divorce became more common and less socially sanctioned; taboos around homosexuality reached a fever pitch before falling away somewhat, ushering in new possibilities for lesbian and queer women to live less secretively. In England, the Married Women's Property Act was passed in 1870, allowing women to keep £200 of their own earnings, rights that were extended in 1884.

In China, the Republican era (1912–1949) gave widows some control over property; the Communist victory in 1949 simultaneously utterly transformed Chinese people's relation to property and introduced a sudden sea change in gender roles and possibilities. In 1918, women over thirty attained the right to vote in England; propertied women could vote in Jamaica by 1919, offering some rights while excluding almost all Black women; in 1920, women in the United States won the vote, although racist laws effectively prohibited Black and other nonwhite women from voting.

The first birth control clinic opened in the United States in 1916; Britain got one in 1921. Although the Mount Holyoke Female Seminary was founded in 1837 and chartered as a college in 1888, and Girton College was founded in England in 1866, many highly educated, progressive parents did not consider sending their daughters to college for decades after these schools were founded. Well into the twentieth century, many families persisted in the assumption that higher education was only for unmarriageable daughters, and paid work was for the unfortunate. The world changed, but women experienced those changes variably. Be it education, labor, suffrage, or birth control, the women in this book experienced revolutionary cultural change in their lifetimes.

As a result of these changes, for the first time a large group of women faced the choice that many men have faced for centuries: What do you want to do with your life? All those conventional hopes and expectations that parents harbor for daughters—that they will be "accomplished" rather than professional, that they need not get an education—presented challenges. Women had choices.

Such choices come, as they always have, with obstacles and constraints. Some are important and worth heeding; others need to be ignored. Deciding which is which is a difficult and uncertain task. The women in this book all wrote about what it feels like to be faced with those choices and to live through the experience of trying to take a role in shaping their life path. The century that saw the introduction of radio, film, television, barbed wire, the machine gun, and the automobile was also one in which half of the population suddenly had the chance to exercise a significant control over their lives. These inventions all pale next to the changes experienced by women—changes with consequences that resonate a century later.

Her Own Voice tells the story of women's dreams of independence, the changes that made them possible, and how those changes affected the choices that individual women made. A hundred years ago, women born into economically secure families—what Woolf called the "daughters of educated men"—were expected to become little more than wives.[2] Many of us have forgotten, or never knew, that little girls, including Virginia Woolf, used to act as chaperones for their unmarried sisters; that even those few women who worked outside the home had no control over the money they earned—if their work was paid at all; that even prosperous families did not send girls to college; that a young lady might be horrified to realize she had left the house without gloves, because a woman walking alone was often assumed to be a sex worker; or that parents often felt free to call working daughters back home, even from war.

Around the turn of the last century, these constraints were beginning to fall away. While there had long been room for one or two singular women of ambition, suddenly there was a cohort of creative and ambitious women with new opportunities, beyond what had been available just a generation before. These opportunities created both freedom and strain. They completely changed the story of a woman's life in unexpected ways, and they exposed women to some of the same risks and disappointments that men seeking careers and success have long confronted. Alongside these new risks, women had to navigate the unknown terrain of pursuing a career while remaining in a family that still might expect them to pour the tea, dress for dinner, or care for an ailing relation.

Each of the eight women in *Her Own Voice* experienced these changes and dramatized them in her work: Margaret Wise Brown, best known for *Goodnight Moon*, who invented a new way of writing children's books; Eileen Chang, who wrote essays, fiction, and screenplays in 1940s occupied Shanghai; the World War I nurse Vera Brittain; the poet Muriel Rukeyser, who witnessed the opening shots of the Spanish Civil War; the novelist and musicologist Sylvia Townsend Warner; the poet, playwright, and radio host Una Marson; the Harlem Renaissance novelist and editor Jessie Fauset; and, finally, Dorothy Arzner, the only woman film director who made the transition from silents to talkies, the first director to cast Katharine Hepburn in a starring role, and the inventor of the boom mic. Through their lives and their art, they changed the world.

A young woman's decision to leave home can be climactic. As many early twentieth-century novels show, it is also dangerous. In Jessie Fauset's *Plum Bun*, Angela Murray leaves her home in Philadelphia with the intention of moving to New York to pursue her career as an artist, planning to pass for white so she can have access to better artistic training. Her departure is carefully choreographed: she sets rumors in motion that she is going to visit a relative out west, and she leaves from the north Philadelphia train station, rather than the Union Station, so as to avoid running into any acquaintances who work as Pullman porters. The precautions pale, however, next to the difficulty she faces leaving her beloved sister: "Yet when the taxi stood rumbling and snorting outside, Angela, her heart suddenly mounting to her throat, her eyes smarting, put her arm tightly about her sister who clung to her frankly crying. But she only said: 'Now, Jinny, there's nothing to cry about.' . . . She ran down the steps, glanced happily back. But her sister had already closed the door."[3] That pang of regret at the very last moment is familiar to most travelers. For all the love the sisters bear each other, Angela's departure shows the seeds of her eventual betrayal. Too overcome by emotion to show it, she makes light of her sister's tears only to find the door shut in her face.

The decision to leave is pivotal in *Plum Bun*, but it is just one part of the process of leaving home, of taking charge of your life. Hope changes to fear, fear gives way to exhilaration, and exhilaration can fade. In leaving, a young woman seizes new opportunities, impossible to pursue under the gaze of her parents, but she also faces the often-unpleasant reality of life in public, including street harassment, public shame, and assault. These consequences force an ongoing reassessment of the original decision to leave: each setback brings with it second thoughts, and occasionally a visit from a well-meaning sister, aunt, or mother, ready to welcome the prodigal daughter back home if she will just give up her foolish notions of independence.

What becomes of the women who hear, and worry about, the controlling admonishments of others and decide to cross the threshold anyway? In the 1970s, the sociologist Mark Granovetter studied how people decide to participate in a large public event. He was especially interested in the psychology of crowds, and especially when a crowd turns violent, such as when a demonstration becomes a riot. He observed that different people have different thresholds for action. The most violent person—the committed revolutionary—is going to throw a rock no matter what; such people are rare. Slightly less rare is the person who joins in after the first rock has been thrown, or after three, four, or five people have begun rioting. Some people will act only once they see many others act, and some very few will never act at all. Without weighing the morality of these decisions, Granovetter created a model to describe the variation in people's response to a situation, observing that "different individuals require different levels of safety before entering a riot and also vary in the benefits they derive from rioting. The crucial concept for describing such variation among individuals is that of 'threshold.'"[4] In every crowd, each person brings their specific threshold for action that combines in unpredictable ways with the particular makeup of that crowd. A crowd full of revolutionaries will act differently than a crowd full of pacifists.

In *Plum Bun*, it takes being kicked out of art school for Angela to move to New York, and her departure paves the way for her sister to follow suit a few months later. Angela's threshold is lower than her sister's. *Her Own Voice* is about women like Fauset's heroines: ordinary women who witness something that compels them into action, sometimes in ways that take even them by surprise. These women find in the social changes around them the courage to choose an unpredicted life.

Her Own Voice is not only about that first decision. It is also about how women sustain the courage to remain in public, even in the face of ongoing taunts, threats, and challenges. The young speaker in Una Marson's "Black Is Fancy" finds that her courage in public is drained by a picture of a pretty white woman hanging on her wall. Constantly comparing her reflection to the picture and finding herself wanting, she finally decides to act: "Maybe I will be more proud / Of my black skin if I don't see her / I will remove her picture."[5] This decision, private and seemingly small, comes after rejecting a Black lover and falling for an unattainable light-skinned one. Freeing herself from the offending image allows her to imagine it possible that her boyfriend loves her after all. When Sylvia Townsend Warner's eponymous heroine Lolly Willowes decides, at the age of forty-seven, to move out of her brother's London house and seek an independent life in the country, "the rest of the family thought the whole scheme was nothing more than one of Lolly's odd jokes."[6] She has to announce her intention again in the morning and stand up to her brother, who at first does not believe her and later refuses to assent to her wish. It takes twenty years for her to summon this courage, and, when she does, she has to assert and reassert herself. One of the most dramatic examples of attempted departure comes in Eileen Chang's *Aloeswood Incense*. Frustrated and disappointed with her life as a guest in her aunt's house, Weilong decides to leave Hong Kong and return home to Shanghai, but, after she books her passage, she falls ill and misses the ship. In bed and feverish for days, she is tortured by indecision: "Suddenly, she decided not to leave—no matter what, she would not leave. Then she went on changing her mind every five minutes: leave, don't leave, leave, don't leave. Lying on her bed, she rolled back and forth between the two extremes, her heart frying in hot oil. Seeking relief from the pain, she rushed off the moment she was well enough to leave the house, and booked her passage."[7] This definitive gesture, so narratively satisfying, is immediately undone. George, her faithless lover, passes her in his fine car on the long, humid, uphill walk from the booking office. She accepts a ride and her fate is sealed: Weilong is not strong enough to resolve, once more, to leave.

Virginia Woolf, whose essay "Street Haunting" celebrates female *flânerie*—the art of wandering the city streets without purpose—is also an expert in describing the hazards of crossing thresholds. In *Mrs. Dalloway*, in a few deft sentences, we are introduced to Maisie Johnson, only nineteen, who has just come to London from Edinburgh. Sitting in the park, she sees Rezia Warren Smith trying to manage her shell-shocked husband. The public scene unnerves Maisie so much, Woolf tells us, that she will remember it fifty years from now. It makes her doubt her ability to survive in the big city.

Stories like these help us understand our ability to change even within the often-crushing contingencies of our lives. We tell young people that they can be whatever they want to be, but again and again we see how conditioning limits choices, and how circumstances narrow opportunities. Early in my career, when I was teaching a survey of British literature, I casually mentioned in class one day that I did not think the women in that week's text were particularly interesting. My comment intrigued my students, so I elaborated, suggesting that the way you live your life depends on the kind of story you imagine yourself to be in: if you see yourself as a princess awaiting the arrival of your prince, you approach your education very differently than if you see yourself as the main character who must make her own way in the world. To me, this was common sense, but I could see that, for some of my students, it had the force of a revelation. The atmosphere in the room quickened. Most of them were cherished by parents who called them little princesses. They had never stopped to consider how little agency princesses have. Some of them even treated college as a period of waiting for the next part of life to happen to them. As their professor, I thought I was offering them a set of stories out of which to shape a life; they were waiting for an enchanted kiss. To their credit, when I pointed this out, they listened and reconsidered. My students, like many of us, were hungry for a richer set of models.

After that, I was on the lookout for such stories. This book is the result of that search. The women in this book lived lives and made art that not only responded to the complexities of these new opportunities, it also changed what is possible for all of us who have come after them. These women worried about how their talent and ambition might upset their family members; they weighed the cost of taking a risk and took it anyway. *Her Own Voice* is about the bravery of ordinary women. The stories at its heart are of women writers who, late into adolescence—and even into adulthood—show every sign of obeying a conventional social script, and then, their lives take a turn: they change jobs, take a leap into political activism, commit to earning a living, leave a male lover for a woman. What combination of social change, family context, and personal bravery makes such change possible?

The women in this book are paired according to four strategies that they deploy as they navigate this modern landscape: as wanderers, rebels, explorers, and mentors. These are not necessarily conscious ways of moving about the world so much as patterns that emerge retrospectively. Because naming these patterns as strategies might help understand others' responses to challenges as well as our own, each pairing begins with a short reflection on the strategy, both on how it works and where it can fall short. The wanderers, Brown and Chang, are two of the youngest writers in the group, and both had mothers who went to college. They take their time in finding what they want to do with their lives, but in doing so they make themselves vulnerable to elders and others who would decide for them. The rebels, Brittain and Rukeyser, are the boldest, and they often seem to have been born brave; nevertheless, if we listen, we find those moments in which they reflect on the cost of their brash actions. Explorers Warner and Marson are expert at pivoting when circumstances go against them; their multi-chaptered careers are difficult to summarize. Their lives contain moments in which they were prevented from pursuing a dream, and those blockages became junctures where they summoned the strength to find a different dream and pursue it otherwise. Mentors like Fauset and Arzner are beloved figures, admired for the care they pour into the lives of the next generation. However, both of these mentors' careers stalled completely when they reached their forties and, at the peak of their powers, the men around them decided they were too old or too threatening to have any more support.

Woolf's words form a common thread; her reflections on the challenges of women's lives bring these stories together, since she wrote about almost every aspect of being a woman in the twentieth century. Discussion of these women's art—mostly novels, but also essays, poems, plays, and film—blends with discussion of their lives. All of these women lived bravely. In their art, each of them dramatizes the inner conflicts, the moments of shaky confidence, the courage, and the desire that women need to make the choice to be the main character of their own lives.

More women can find satisfaction working outside the home when there are fewer obstacles to women working for pay. And a world in which more women defer marriage and motherhood, where some women live openly with female partners, is one in which being a wife and a mother ceases to be the limit of possibility. A world in which women have the chance to explore and experiment is one in which some women may discover whole new avenues of creativity and contribution. The world changes when women are offered more than one kind of story. The women at the heart of *Her Own Voice*, in their lives and the stories they tell, document the ways new possibilities clash with the fear of change, making it hard for individual women to take control of the choices available to them.

Woolf said of *A Room of One's Own*, "I wanted to encourage the young women—they seem to get fearfully depressed."[8] *Her Own Voice*, too, means to encourage women through telling the stories of other women's uneven, individual experiences of huge social and cultural transformations. Through the lens of today's feminism, *Her Own Voice* looks at the literature these women wrote and how it uncovers their own stories—and ours. Through their writing, we can see how their choices were shaped by the social revolutions of the century and the people in their lives and, equally importantly, see how their examples can expand what we see as possible.

PART 1
Wanderers

Wandering has long been recognized as a key part of the creative process. Books on productivity and creativity often counsel a walk—even a brief one—to renew energy and welcome in new thoughts and perspectives. The change of air, the new sights, the physical pleasure of walking all return us to the ordinary rhythms of breath and movement: these things crack open our stuckness and forge new paths. A free path in the world encourages a freer path in the mind. William Wordsworth composed poetry during long rambles in the Lake District, and Virginia Woolf could be seen conducting imaginary dialogues on long walks across the Sussex Downs. But women who enjoy solitary walks are often suspect. In *Pride and Prejudice*, when her sister Jane falls ill and Elizabeth Bennet walks several miles to the Bingley estate to be with her, the muddy hem of her dress is mocked by the fashionable Bingley sisters. In *Wuthering Heights*, Catherine's love of wandering across the moors is one of the chief signs of her independence and eccentricity. Readers have loved these heroines from the time of the novels' publication down to today, but part of our affection for them resides in the ways in which they stood out from the crowd, and that takes courage. A wandering woman outside a novel risked being labeled odd—or worse—by her neighbors.

While country rambles pose obstacles for women, wandering in the city has proven equally if not more dangerous. From at least the 1870s, men explored the city on long meandering walks. This was such a fruitful creative habit that the men who enjoyed it got a name—they were *flâneurs*, from the French verb *flâner*, meaning "to lounge"—and the practice of walking, especially by a bourgeois or aristocratic man walking in a poorer neighborhood in search of adventure, gained a name: *flânerie*. This practice was essential to the thinking of a wide range of men: sociologists such as Jacob Riis and W. E. B. Du Bois, painters such as Edgar Degas and Gustave Caillebotte, and writers including Charles Baudelaire, Edgar Allan Poe, and Oscar Wilde. However, women's experience of wandering the streets was typically imagined as the object of male attention, for "women's walking is often construed as performance rather than transport," as Rebecca Solnit puts it.[1] While sophisticates borrowed "flâneur" from the French, our lexicon abounds with words that associate women pedestrians with sex workers: for example, "Among the terms for prostitutes are streetwalkers, women of the streets, women on the town, and public women (and of course phrases such as public man, man about town, or man of the streets mean very different things than do their equivalents attached to women)."[2] Only in the 1980s did critics coin the word *flâneuse*, a feminine version of the noun that should have been obvious from the start but was, it turns out, unthinkable for over a century. The social stigma and real danger around women's solitary wandering is yet another damper to women's creativity. If wandering is essential to creativity, but wandering as a woman is construed as sex work, how are women to wander?

It is a privilege to be a little bit vague, to not know where you are going, to take time for discernment: all of these are crucial to developing big ideas, to becoming an artist, to being creative. This is a privilege that men have long had. Woolf notes that even a man of modest means like John Keats, who had no university education and apprenticed as an apothecary, was able to scrape together funds to travel on the continent. This privilege has been denied women, who were expected to pass directly from their father's home to their husband's. Up and down the class hierarchy, women have struggled to gain the right to wander the streets. For middle- and upper-middle class women in the Victorian and Edwardian world, the simple act of daring to leave home without gloves could produce exhilaration. For these women, walking down the street with bare hands was brave.

Woolf's *A Room of One's Own* offers one of the most well-known accounts of the creative frustrations of wandering as a woman. It makes its argument about women and fiction by telling the story of how hard it is to write. Woolf invents a persona who, like herself, is trying to write a lecture on the topic of "Women and Fiction." This figure walks through the fictional town of Oxbridge, puzzling out her lecture, when, suddenly she has the glimmer of an idea: "Thought—to call it by a prouder name than it deserved—had let its line down into the stream. . . . But however small it was, it had, nevertheless, the mysterious property of its kind—put back into the mind, it became at once very exciting, and important."[3] She starts walking quickly—matching her pace with the speed of thought, only to be interrupted by a beadle—a kind of campus security officer—demanding that she get off the grass. The abrupt demand startles her. It also makes her lose track of what she was thinking. As she wryly notes, "The only charge I could bring against the Fellows and Scholars of whatever the college might happen to be was that in protection of their turf, which has been rolled for 300 years in succession, they had sent my little fish into hiding."[4] Losing track of a thought is at once nothing and everything. What Woolf does not need to say here, what she did not need to clarify in 1929, is that the beadle knows from afar that she is trespassing because, by definition, a woman could not be a fellow or a scholar except at one of the few women's colleges. However intelligent or worthy she is, her very status as a woman means she cannot, and does not, walk on that grass. Women only got the right to earn degrees at Oxford in 1920; Cambridge followed decades later, in 1948. A beadle, glancing across the quad at a person in a skirt, would immediately know that she did not belong there.

Woolf's argument is only half embedded in her essay's title. To write fiction, Woolf proposes, a woman must have a room of her own, preferably with a lock and key, where she can write without interruption. But she must also have the right and freedom to explore the world unmolested. For Woolf, creativity depends on the interchange between these two states—the ability to be in the world, independent and unfettered, and the ability to withdraw from it into a privacy that is uninterrupted by family demands.

One way around these prohibitions at the time was to have a chaperone. When women left home, they often had to be accompanied, permitting *walking* but discouraging *wandering*, which is, ideally, a solitary activity. Perversely, chaperones need not have been either older or male. In fact, Woolf served as a chaperone as a very little girl, accompanying her much older half-sister, Stella, on calls: "She was nineteen when I was six or seven; and as a girl could not then go about London alone, I used as a small child to be sent with her, as chaperone. Among my earliest memories is the memory of going out with her perhaps to shop or pay some call; and, the errand done, she would take me to a shop and give me a glass of milk and biscuits sprinkled with sugar on a marble table."[5] This is a lovely reminiscence of girlhood and her love for Stella, but it also describes a remarkably sheltered life, one designed to prevent independence. The Victorian imagination was fertile in its strategies for keeping young women from going astray. Saddling a nineteen-year-old with a six-year-old companion is an inventive way to ensure she stays out of trouble and is publicly marked as "respectable."

In *Flush*, a mock-biography of Elizabeth Barrett Browning's dog, Woolf explores the way the Victorian invalid finally breaks out of this pattern of chaperonage. When Flush is kidnapped, Elizabeth (then still Barrett) must venture to a part of London previously unknown and off-limits to her to pay the ransom and secure his return. That escapade, in which the terrified poet remains in her carriage, proves the catalyst that allows her to accept Robert Browning as a suitor and eventually elope with him to Italy and to freedom. The comically extraordinary effort it takes Elizabeth to make this journey across town indexes the intensity of the prohibition on leaving home unaccompanied and the limitations of chaperoned excursions as a way out.

If chaperones and carriages offered only a very limited solution to the prohibitions on women's wandering, shopping presented an alternative. Women could wander arcades and department stores, which were late nineteenth-century developments designed for the occupation and amusement of middle-class women who claimed to be just looking, and, in doing so, they could have a taste of what it might mean to wander. But shopping brings its own hazards; after all, in most households, men still controlled the money. Moreover, malls and arcades offer a pale simulacrum of real wandering; while shopping, the only danger is going over budget, and the only possible adventure is a bargain.

Woolf's 1927 essay "Street-Haunting" thinks its way to using the pretext of shopping to embark on a larger excursion. It opens with Woolf's narrator manufacturing an errand to justify a city walk: "No one perhaps has ever felt passionately toward a lead pencil," Woolf writes. "But there are circumstances in which it can become supremely desirable to possess one; moments when we are set upon having an object, a purpose, an excuse for walking half across London between tea and dinner."[6] In these opening lines, Woolf's anonymous narrator aligns herself as much with the men whom she seems to imagine as her readers, recommending an oblique strategy in which the errand is a cover for a deeper purpose—here, not just the delight of walking in the street, but the preservation of that delight for others; "as a foxhunter hunts in order to preserve the breed of horses," so the wanderer walks to preserve the practice of walking.[7] What Woolf's essay hints at but never quite says is how new this practice of walking, of wandering through the streets, was for women in her time.

Although these obstacles are considerable and the strategies for overcoming them imperfect, it is still easier to describe these physical and external obstacles than the internal ones. Woolf admits this in her 1931 talk "Professions for Women." But that essay also offers one of the best descriptions of two of the internal obstacles that make it difficult for women to allow themselves to fully use their imaginations: the specter of the angel in the house, and the internal prohibition against speaking the truth about their bodies.

The angel in the house is a Victorian ideal celebrated in a poem by Coventry Patmore that describes the perfect wife, a phantom who urges women to "be sympathetic; be tender; flatter; deceive; use all the arts and wiles of our sex. Never let anybody guess that you have a mind of your own."[8] While Patmore emphasizes self-sacrifice and the art of pleasing others, Woolf shows the incompatibility of this project with the work of writing. Having a mind of your own is the first necessity of writing. Ideals like that of the angel in the house are offered to women instead of an actual image of a horizon of a rich and diverse future, a world full of possibilities. Parents, elders, and mentors present the idea that to be a good woman means being someone who has no desires, someone who is willing to sacrifice, someone who, "if there was chicken, she took the leg; if there was a draught she sat in it."[9] Instead of asking herself, "What do I want? do I know what I want and, if not, how can I figure it out?," she asks, "How can I help?" Helping is good, and the world is better with helpful people in it, but one of the easiest and cruelest divisions of labor is to decide that a certain class of people (here, women) is created to *help* while another class (men) is created to pursue their desires and explore their potential.

This is how the angel in the house works: if you follow the doctrine, you believe that men are created to wander, explore, and conquer, and women are created to please. The contemporary critic Sara Ahmed encourages people to break out of the illusions that, a century ago, Woolf identified and worked to destroy—to become instead what she calls "feminist killjoys," dedicated to continuing Woolf's work of destroying these ideals.[10] Once you recognize others are pulling you to understand your own desires in terms of what would be easiest or most helpful for *them*, you can begin to resist (although powerful forces conspire against this recognition).

A second internal obstacle to wandering, however, is more difficult to destroy or evade. For Woolf, creative wandering requires a kind of self-forgetting: "A novelist's chief desire is to be as unconscious as possible."[11] The artist requires this sacred silence to be able to imagine and wander freely in mind. Unfortunately, so powerful are these cultural ideas of pleasing others and of not shaming yourself that they creep into even these most private moments of imagination and creation. Here is how Woolf describes it, figuring the young writer lost in thought as a woman fishing, dropping her line deep into the pool of imagination:

> She was letting her imagination sweep unchecked round every rock and cranny of the world that lies submerged in the depths of our unconscious being. Now came the experience that I believe to be far commoner with women writers than with men. The line raced through the girl's fingers. Her imagination had rushed away. . . . And then there was an explosion. . . . The imagination had dashed itself against something hard. . . . To speak without figure, she had thought of something . . . which it was unfitting for her as a woman to say. Men, her reason told her, would be shocked. . . . The trance was over. Her imagination could work no longer.[12]

This is not the external interruption of a knock on the study door, but an internal interruption. The mind works against itself, dashing itself against the rocks of convention just when it should be rushing free. In "Professions for Women," Woolf personifies the figure of self-sacrifice and then kills her, but she finds herself unable to personify the figure of the shocked man. Woolf does, however, kill a version of that figure in *A Room of One's Own*, when she scribbles the image of the imaginary misogynist Professor Von X, or, later, when she destroys the young male novelist. In fact, once you begin to look, there is a lot of violent imagery, a lot of anger, in Woolf's depictions of those critics who seek to oppose and limit her scope. The anger indicates the power of the struggle, even for a Virginia Woolf.

Where Woolf struggled to find strategies to overcome these blocks to the imagination, Ahmed offers some maxims. She admits they are difficult to follow, but she encourages solidarity. One of her consistent pieces of advice is to "stop the world from making sense": that is, do not accept as true a practice that limits or harms women. Stopping automatic acceptance of such strategies is bound to lead to accusations of being willful, but, again, Ahmed counsels: "If you are charged with willfulness, accept and mobilize the charge." In fact, she encourages women to "become monstrous" rather than give in to those who would tame them. She offers one of the hardest exhortations for those of us who have been socialized to get along: "When it is not funny, do not laugh!"[13]

Wandering matters. Of all the strategies for facing the modern world, it is the riskiest and the most luxurious. The wanderer, having no clear aim at the outset of the journey, can offer no explanation for why she must go. She depends on her ability to trust herself, and on those around her not to set up obstacles so great that she cannot move. Greatness requires time, and wandering as a strategy has the highest risk and the highest potential reward. It is not surprising that the two wanderers in this book are two of the youngest; we see in each of them the fruits of the advantages of having watched a few more women paving the path before them.

The women wanderers in this section—Margaret Wise Brown (1910–1952) and Eileen Chang (1920–1995)—write about the precious value of wandering, and how swiftly others seek to impose their vision, ideas, and control on a woman who takes her time to choose a path. Margaret Wise Brown's writing for very young children celebrates empowered wandering. Bold, joyous books such as *Goodnight Moon* and *The Runaway Bunny* emerged from the imagination of a woman who enjoyed privileges few women before her ever had. Brown's false starts, failed attempts, and the taunts of others leave barely a trace in her spirited and adventurous classics. Her books celebrate the adventures of wandering without limitations, and they do so often without assigning gender to the wanderer.

Even so, her boldest adventurer is clearly a boy. The posthumously published *The Sailor Dog* tells the story of a dog whose dream is to sail the world. Rejecting all other forms of transport, he sticks to his desires, only to find himself shipwrecked. Alone on the shore, he happens upon treasure, a box of tools and some wood, and builds himself a shelter. Then, he has the thought that saves him: "If he could build the house, he could mend the hole in the ship."[14] Sailor Dog's is not a strategy of anger, but of changing perspective: if I can do this, I can do that. Brown offers the child an uncomplicated vision of confidence and analogic thinking, encouraging them to believe that their every success has the additional power to increase the child's belief in her ability to take on the next challenge.

The women in Eileen Chang's fiction know the risks of leaving home and see with clear eyes the social cost and possibilities of wandering. They are sexual beings, attracted to men and desirous of romance. They also clearly perceive what it means to attach themselves to a man, and they make choices based in hard truths. In her essays, however, Chang comfortably inhabits the persona of a modern, urban sophisticate. This works in an essay because, there, the writer takes on a universal persona, and in the early twentieth century that persona was presumed to be male. Writing in drag, as it were, Chang could assume the imaginative freedom that men have always had; Woolf frequently indulged in this performance in her literary essays, too. Sometimes playing with and taking on the male persona, Woolf and Chang can take the chance to stretch their limbs and wander as freely as men.

More than other women in this book, these wanderers encounter barriers: hard challenges to their own desires, obstacles that force them, their characters, and us to consider who gets the right to wander. Taken together, these writers have much to teach us about the importance of wandering and how essential wandering is for women, for all of us.

Margaret Wise Brown
1910–1952

IN THE GREAT GREEN ROOM

It might seem strange to take *Goodnight Moon* seriously or even to consider its author, Margaret Wise Brown, an author at all. Perhaps it is hard to think of *Goodnight Moon* as writing because it is written for children too young to read. Its formula is so soothing and familiar that it is possible to read it even in the sleep-deprived fog of those early months of parenthood, when reading seems impossible. From the beginning, admirers asked readers to pause over the art of this simple prose. A *Life* magazine profile from December 1946 cautions against thinking that these books, so easy to read, were easy to write: baby books may be short—often less than three hundred words—but they have to interest babies, creatures who care little about saving face by feigning an interest, as well as their caregivers, adults who long ago learned their colors and what sound a cow or a car horn makes. On this measure, Brown's books are "a rollicking success."[1] There is something about *Goodnight Moon* that makes the book, simple as it is, bearable—and even interesting—to both babies and adults. Somehow, that little bunny in its magical nursery offers comfort and interest when other things do not. Brown invented a new kind of book: writing for people who cannot yet read, writing that is intended to be read aloud. However, her path to creating *Goodnight Moon*, *The Runaway Bunny*, and many other books was long and indirect, and those closest to her often doubted her ability to succeed.

Writing in *Parents* magazine, John Fleischman remembers a noisy cocktail party. When one guest said, "In the great green room . . .," he picked up with "there was a telephone," and other guests joined in, reciting the text, as one recites a beloved poem.[2] Leonard Marcus, one of Brown's biographers, hears the poetry, too—the poetry that drew him to write about her. He did not grow up with *Goodnight Moon*, but when he discovered it in a bookshop he immediately recognized the text as poetry "of a kind I prized: accessible, but not predictable, emotional but purged of sentiment, vivid but so spare that every word felt necessary."[3] Novelist Aimee Bender describes her "*literary* excitement" in reading *Goodnight Moon* to her infant twins, and how, even after a hundred readings "the unexpected choices . . . keep my interest."[4] I grew up with *Goodnight Moon*, and I raised my children on it. For me, as for Bender, Marcus, and Fleischman, the text remains bearable, charming, and even compelling after many, many readings. I wanted to find out why.

One year, when my children were still very young, I went from reading *Goodnight Moon* to them at night to teaching Gertrude Stein's *Tender Buttons* to my college students the next morning. In the midst of making an argument for Stein's radical experiments with language, I was struck by how familiar it all seemed. Instead of Stein's break with tradition, I noticed how much her work had in common with the books I was reading to my children: a love of color, prose that takes joy in the ordinary things in a home, repetition with unexpected variation. This dovetailed with another observation: that my students were not as puzzled by Stein as I expected them to be. They read Stein's "Glazed Glitter. Nickel, what is nickel, it is originally rid of a cover" and found it weird but not radically disorienting.[5] Stein's language does not tell a story but just wonders about an ordinary thing. That is familiar to them—to us—in part because we have been raised on the lists that originated with *Goodnight Moon*. This is no accident: Stein was Brown's favorite writer.

Reading (or hearing) "In the great green room there was a telephone. And a red balloon. And a picture of a cow jumping over the moon" over and over, first as children and again as parents, has taught generations of Americans to see a list of things as, in itself, comforting.[6] The experiments with forms and sounds that Stein initiated have come to seem familiar thanks, in part, to Brown. So we accept, and even can be soothed by, "Glazed Glitter. Nickel, what is nickel": glitter is shiny, so is nickel—so far, Stein's associations are no weirder than the order of Brown's list. By the time Stein's text stops making sense ("it is originally rid of a cover"), the effect of wonder may have blunted our insistence on *sense*.[7] Even if today's students did not grow up with *Goodnight Moon*, they have grown up in a world where writing for the very youngest children builds on the lessons of modernism that Brown learned from and transformed into art for the very young.

The story of Margaret Wise Brown's life is as compelling and surprising for adults as *Goodnight Moon* is for babies. Her opportunities and what she made of them play a large part in how she was able to transform the project of writing for babies into art. She was born in 1910, the second of three children. Her mother, Maude Brown, had abandoned a dream of acting for the conventional life of marriage and motherhood; her father, Robert, worked in the family business and eventually rose to become treasurer and vice president of American Manufacturing, a rope and bagging company. Theirs was a conventional, conservative, upper-middle-class childhood. In the large family home in Greenpoint, Brooklyn, "Margaret and [her sister] Roberta's large second-floor bedroom was heated by means of a gas grate framed with decorative ceramic tiles depicting nursery rhyme characters—the Three Little Bears and the Cow that Jumped Over the Moon."[8] Later, on Long Island, the sisters "preferred action toys like [their brother's] train set" to dolls, and the children used his allowance, larger because he was a boy, to buy pets, including the rabbits that would become central to Brown's personal mythology: "Once, when one of the rabbits died, Margaret . . . skinned the carcass for its fur.'"[9] Brown loved bunnies, but she was a pragmatist: they were equally valuable to her as pets, food, literary characters, and fur coats.

For secondary school, Brown went to Dana Hall in Wellesley, Massachusetts, where she was called "Tim" for her hair, blonde as timothy grass. (She would later adopt "Timothy Hay" as one of her pseudonyms.) After Dana Hall, she and her sister spent a few years in a Swiss boarding school, where she became fluent in French. Margaret's mother, who had gone to college, supported her daughters' desire to go to college, despite their father's strong objections. He eventually relented and, in funding their education, granted access to new worlds that might not otherwise have been open to either of the sisters. (Roberta did graduate work in physics at Yale and became a physics professor.) At Hollins College, a women's college in Southern Virginia, Margaret "acquired a reputation around campus as an individualist. . . . She quoted from *Winnie the Pooh* and gave parties to celebrate unbirthdays and the arrival of asparagus at the local market."[10] She and her best friend "read to each other from Proust, Virginia Woolf, and Gertrude Stein, writers for whom the typical Hollins student cared little, and they shared a theory that they and a fortunate few others had remained children in spirit."[11] At the time, Hollins was not a radical place; it mainly educated young women to become cultured, upper-middle-class wives, but there she encountered the writers who would inspire her career.

After graduation, Brown moved to New York, and in September 1934 she enrolled in a fiction-writing workshop at Columbia University. Her Greenwich Village apartment building housed other aspiring artists, including the painter Ines Camprubi. Camprubi and Brown spent time together talking about life, art, and Gertrude

Stein. That fall, Brown reread Woolf and Chaucer, listened to Stein on the radio, and attended Stein's lectures at BAM, the Brooklyn Academy of Music. That lecture tour came at the apex of Stein's fame; *The Autobiography of Alice B. Toklas* had been a bestseller the year before. To admire Stein in 1934 was to be absolutely in the swim of modern culture.

Camprubi was already affiliated with Bank Street, and, in the fall of 1935, at her urging, Brown applied to be a teacher in training. Her financial independence—her father sent her a monthly allowance—meant that she was under no great pressure to earn a living. Nonetheless, she wanted something to do, and, until her hoped-for writing career began, she drifted toward teaching. Outwardly, Brown must have seemed very like many young women with college degrees. Teaching children was an uncontroversial pastime until marriage and generally agreed to be good preparation for motherhood. In Brown's case, this activity provided her the time she needed to discover her talents. She had no prior teaching experience and did not seem particularly interested in teaching. In her application, she mentions postgraduate writing classes at Columbia and the University of Virginia. As for teaching experience, she briefly mentions a child in Connecticut whom she had tutored privately: "The child had an interesting mind and I enjoyed her company. Also there was the continuous problem of getting her to work since she had a peculiar hatred of taking time for studying away from her horse and dogs."[12] Brown's charge sounds not very different from Brown herself. Her description echoes her own interest in children not as an undifferentiated class but as young individuals who are occasionally interesting. This specificity, this interest in one child's individuality, and even the slightly ironic but sympathetic understanding of a child's love for her animals were present from the beginning and remained consistent elements of her work.

Brown's taste for Stein connected her to Camprubi, as it had connected her to a select few classmates and teachers at Hollins. So, too, did it distinguish her when she enrolled at the Bank Street

College of Education (still then the Bureau of Educational Experiments) in the fall of 1935. A report in her student file noted that she was "steeped in the modern."[13] And, in landing at Bank Street and attracting Lucy Sprague Mitchell's attention, Brown had hit upon the perfect place to continue her interest in the modern. Like Stein, Mitchell had studied with William James at Radcliffe. And, while Stein turned her intelligence to art, Mitchell's commitment to American pragmatism had taken her to John Dewey (a friend and correspondent) and educational reform. At Bank Street, Brown found a community of writers, educators, and artists who were inspired by the relevance of modern ideas (if not always modernist art) to early childhood education. Modernism's interest in finding new ways to represent sensory impressions suggested exciting methods to enact the principles of allowing children to explore the world through their senses. Bank Street enacted that in a lively, open, exciting atmosphere where psychologists, writers, artists, dancers, toymakers, and teachers collaborated on new approaches to educating the very young.

Even so, Brown's start at Bank Street was rocky. She was deeply interested in the individual child, but she was indifferent to the management of a classroom of children. This became a problem almost right away. In her progress reports, one teacher noted that from the start she "seemed to contribute a somewhat disorganizing influence to the class"; another observed that "much of the time Miss Brown seems to be in a day-dream"; still another suspects that her "interest in children is no more real than interest in all types of personality,"and that she lacks an understanding of how whims and desires need to come into check in order for a child "to function in a cooperative society." Most damningly for a future preschool teacher, she left the art closet messy, "with two pots of glue spilled." Her "casualness about practical things" did not inspire confidence.[14]

The classroom held no interest for Brown. While Brown struggled there, and although her analytic writing was only fair, she excelled in Mitchell's language class. In December, Mitchell had already noticed her "real flair for language." By April, Mitchell could see that she had potential to be a real writer. "She is waking," she wrote in a report. Moreover, employing one of her favorite images, Mitchell is "still inclined to think our content for children as limited and of 'spinach' variety."[15] Perhaps, Mitchell thought, Brown could become the writer Bank Street needed. It took Brown longer to accept that her gift was to write for babies.

During the early 1930s, Brown was writing fiction for both adults and children, but it was a children's story that was first accepted for publication. And while it was Bank Street that led her to write for children, her first solo book, in 1937, *When the Wind Blew*, told a story, thus already containing the seed of a small protest against the Bank Street philosophy, which opposed narrative. When her royalty check came, she cashed it. On the way home, she hailed a horse-drawn flower cart, still a common sight in the Village, and bought all the flowers on the cart. She had them delivered to her door and called all her friends over for a party to celebrate.

The exuberance of this gesture characterizes Brown. She delighted in sharing her good fortune with friends, and her open-handed relationship with money is a reminder of what financial stability can engender: the royalties became a way for her to share joy. Few people have the audacity to make such a bold gesture as to buy out a whole flower cart, and flowers themselves are always a luxury purchase. No one needs flowers, and yet flowers are also essential. The opening line of Woolf's *Mrs. Dalloway*—"Mrs. Dalloway said she would buy the flowers herself"—is memorable in part because of its recognition of female agency: she declares she will do it, and she does. In buying *all* the flowers on that cart, in filling her apartment with ephemeral abundance, Brown expressed her confidence that this good fortune was only the beginning—as indeed it was.

By the fall of 1937, Brown was meeting regularly with Mitchell and a few other colleagues forming the Bank Street Writer's Laboratory. She was also reading Virginia Woolf's latest novel, *The Years*, and finding significance in one of the characters, who says, "But you must come and see it for yourselves."[16] That sentiment—that it must be seen to be understood—spoke to her delight in the life she was making for herself, as a single woman, living in the city, earning money as a writer. It also echoed some of the main tenets of the Writer's Laboratory and Bank Street's "here and now" philosophy of children's literature.

In late 1939, Brown had enough prominence that she played a small role in inviting Gertrude Stein to work on a children's book (which became *The World Is Round*), but that collaboration was mostly disappointing. The advent of World War II dampened prospects for further collaboration—or even a meeting—between Brown and her hero. Stein spent the war in France, improbably surviving the Holocaust, but she died of stomach cancer in 1946. Brown never met her. News of Virginia Woolf's death in the spring of 1941 closed another hoped-for encounter.

Throughout the war, Brown kept publishing, with *The Noisy Book* series and *The Runaway Bunny*. Brown's less-well-known work is full of delights and surprises. *The Seven Little Postmen* combines the onomatopoeia of *The Noisy Books*—"Stamp, stamp, clickety click"—with the child's pleasure at having a little bit of news: "A boy had a secret. It was a surprise. / He wanted to tell his grandmother. / So he sent his secret through the mail."[17] She depicted her summers in Maine in *The Little Island*, a book in which the island itself is the main character, and the only plot is the changing season and the various animals who come to visit. Little kittens try to mix colors in *The Color Kittens*, but, unlike other books that teach the colors, these kittens have a vision of green that exceeds simply mixing yellow and blue. They long for a green that is "green as cats' eyes / Green as grass / By streams of water / Green as glass. / So they tried to make some green paint."[18]

In November 1950, Brown's longtime partner, the poet and actress Michael Strange, died. Shortly thereafter, Brown fell in love with James Stillman "Pebbles" Rockefeller Jr. and they became engaged to marry. She traveled to France, where he would join her later. There, she fell ill and had to have an operation. It was a success, but she was told to remain in bed for days to recover. Unbeknownst to her or her doctors, a blood clot developed in her leg, and, in demonstrating to a visiting friend that she felt fine, she did a can-can kick in her bed, causing almost instant death. She was forty-two.

Brown's work at Bank Street was central to the development of her art. There she learned about how children pay attention, whether walking in the neighborhood or sitting still in a circle, and absorbed the importance of children understanding the concrete facts of their world over fairy tales and religious moralizing. One of the school's most important techniques was transcribing children's speech. Teachers recorded children at play and took them aside to write down the stories and poems they told. This helped confirm their belief in the importance of the here and now for young children. It also developed a strong sense of how children's interests grow and develop as they mature. In the school's documents, children are referred to by age, and, in everything the school produced, from minutes of committee meetings through official publications for parents and other educators, Bank Street teachers demonstrate a clear sense of what is typical for "fours" (that is four-year-olds), as opposed to "fives" or "threes."

In 1939, Brown wrote a twenty-one-page typed paper, "Writing for Five-Year-Olds." In it, she displays her familiarity with how very young children develop and how that development is reflected in language. "When a child reaches the age of five he is the sum total of all his younger experiences and discoveries in a brand new world," she begins, and goes on to summarize the child's development so far: "He carries with him . . . the glamor of the two-year-old's own small self; the three-year-old's humor and love of pattern . . . and four-year-old's first playful flights into the humor of incongruous things . . .; and finally, the five-year-old's . . . careful watching of his own eyes and ears."[19] Already, in this opening page, we can glimpse the writer that Brown was becoming, for, even as she details with precision the child's development, she is attracted to the elements of that development that characterize her own work: glamour, play, love of pattern, and careful observation.

Commenting on a transcription from a young child, Brown writes, "There is enough rhythm of rough water in this song to get sea-sick on."[20] Even in an internal academic report, Brown shows herself a writer, recognizing and delighting in a child's happy turn of phrase. She fully enters the child's world and grasps the thrill of language. Marcus details her continuing efforts, never very successful, to write for adults. He recounts how Brown's friends and her partner, Michael Strange, taunted her about her so-called baby books. However, in her study of five-year-olds, we see the strength of her conviction that writing for the very young could be truly great:

> Here is an audience sensitive to the sheer elements of the English language. Here is the playful audience of James Joyce and Edith Sitwell and Gertrude Stein, the audience of Virginia Woolf and Swinburne and the King James version of the Bible. Translate their playfulness and serious use of the sheer elements of language into the terms and understandings of a five-year old and you have as intelligent an audience in rhythm and sound as the maddest poet's heart could desire.[21]

Her practical experience at Bank Street taught her how to translate modernist poetry into the language and world of the very young. And her understanding of early childhood education taught her to value children as an audience, against the current of mockery from her lover and others.

Bank Street teachers emphasized neighborhood walks for small children. When they returned, the children were encouraged to talk about all they had seen and heard as a way of reinforcing their memories and developing their ability to tell a story. Their descriptions helped Brown, Mitchell, and others at Bank Street in their writing curriculum. Books such as *The Noisy Book* capture Bank Street's philosophy of letting children see the world for themselves and building on that to teach them. This philosophy must have been especially liberating for little girls accustomed to "Mary Had a Little Lamb" and "Little Miss Muffet."

Illustrations are central to Brown's work, and her books represent close collaboration with artists who, like Brown herself, were steeped in the modern. In 1938, she met the American painter Clement Hurd. He was just back from Paris, where he had studied with Fernand Léger, and on his return he and his friends chartered a train car to see the production of Stein and Virgil Thomson's opera, *Four Saints in Three Acts*, in Hartford, Connecticut. As admiration for Stein had been a basis for Brown's friendship with Camprubi, a mutual admiration for Stein helped cement Brown's bond with Hurd. She looked at his portfolio and, attracted to a painting of an octopus, invited him to show his work to the children at Bank Street. During his visit he participated in an intimidating ritual that was central to the school's success:

> The classroom teacher instructed the visitor to arrange his paintings on the floor and step back while the children examined them. The waiting period that followed was unnerving. When the children finally dispersed with what seemed like a killing indifference to the work laid before them, Hurd's heart sank. The teacher's cheerful verdict soon revived him. "Congratulations!" she said. "You held their attention for five minutes!"[22]

The Bank Street kindergartners' critique must have been more intimidating than that of the most ferocious painting professor, but Hurd passed with flying colors. His paintings with their bold lines, clear colors, and flattened shapes—learned from his lessons with Léger—were ideal for conveying the sensory experiences at the heart of Brown's prose. The first of their many collaborations was a 1938 book, *Bumble Bugs and Elephants*; when Hurd returned from serving in World War II, worried about restarting his career, Brown welcomed him home with the manuscript of *Goodnight Moon* to illustrate.

Brown worked with another key collaborator, Leonard Weisgard, on *The Important Book*. In it, Brown describes ordinary things that matter to young children, using the formula "The important thing about" a spoon or grass or whatever familiar object "is / that," going on to describe other attributes, but concluding with a repetition of that singular important thing. For this project, Brown returned to Bank Street's preference for non-narrative language. *The Important Book* takes up everyday objects with a child's wonder and curiosity, assuming no prior knowledge of the reader. Brown gently guides children to perceive the main function of each thing—so, a spoon is important because you eat with it. Each page has its own little poem about importance until we end with "you": "The important thing about you is / that you are you."[23] A sweet and powerful message about self-love, made even more delightful by coming after a surprisingly bossy and eccentric catalog of what makes spoons and grass and other ordinary things important, all accompanied by Leonard Weisgard's spiky, geometric illustrations.

Without any figurative images of reference to a single identity category, in a book that avoids gender altogether, Brown, with Weisgard's drawings, celebrates the individuality of every child reader. *The Important Book* is not about achievement or aspiration. Here, she returns to the Here and Now curriculum of her Bank Street roots and, in doing so, reaches a soaring conclusion with an unsentimental message about our fundamental humanity. Initially, another illustrator (Charles Shaw) got the job, but he moved her text around and played with her line breaks to suit his drawing. Enraged, Brown wrote to Shaw:

> The important thing about the break in typesetting is
> That you break here
> It is true that you might want to break els[e]where
> And breaking elsewhere makes a pretty picture
> And that you for[g]et the break is for the reader
> And that the break is to make a pause
> In which the child will chime in
> And that is the purpose of the book
> So that the important thing about the break is—
> That you break here.[24]

Shaw lost the job.

However far Brown may have moved from Bank Street and the "here and now" school, texts like *The Important Book* continued to avoid metaphor and to insist on the poetry intrinsic to the thing itself. A rose is a rose is a rose to the last. This conviction fueled her mockery of the slogan for the 1946 Children's Book Week, "Books Are Bridges." Brown wrote:

> If I were a child, and saw [on posters] "Books are Bridges" I'd go out and make channels of diverted water from a stream through the sand and stretch the Books across the little streams for my imaginary armies to march across. . . . If I were a child and read "Books are Bullets" I and other children would throw them at each other. If I were a child and read "Books Around the World" I would wish that I had gone myself—If I read "Friendship Through Books" I would have wished the Book weren't there between us. Therefore for next year I propose "Books are Books" for the Book Week slogan. A fact any child would recognize with relief.[25]

While still at Bank Street, Brown was also on the staff at William Scott's new publishing house, working to develop a group of children's books in keeping with the experiments at Bank Street. Brown, Scott, and John McCullough, another editor, invited several writers, including Ernest Hemingway, John Steinbeck, and Stein, to submit children's manuscripts. This invitation to Stein was the culmination of much that Brown had hoped for, but Stein's acceptance was clouded when McCullough and Scott cut Brown out of communication with her hero. Although she drafted the correspondence, only McCullough signed the letters. Brown was excluded from the correspondence and denied the credit for commissioning Stein. One of the downsides of a wandering approach to new opportunities is the way it robs you of professional recourse when things do not work out. As a staffer at Scott and a woman, Brown was not treated as a full partner.

Stein was enthusiastic and wrote that she had a project already underway, a story that expanded upon and played with her most famous sentence, "Rose is a rose is a rose," while paying homage to a young French friend called Rose. When Stein accepted, she asked how long a manuscript could be and still be of interest to children, and if the book could be printed on rose-colored paper, and if Scott would hire her friend Francis Rose as the book's illustrator. Two of her three requests were granted: Scott allowed the book to be much longer than is ordinary, found a way to print on rose paper, but vetoed Rose's art. Rose's name was an apt coincidence for Stein's "rose" theme, but Scott wanted to use one of their own illustrators. An in-house competition was set; Clement Hurd emerged the winner and, in the end, his drawings, in blue and white on the rose paper, charmed everyone. The result was *The World Is Round*.

The World Is Round tells the story of Rose. Rose has a large dog, Pépé, and calls a small dog hers, too, though it is not hers at all. She loves to sing, though singing makes her cry. Her melancholy is both existential and childish: the revelation that the world is a sphere fills her with terror and wonder, setting her off on a quest to climb to the top of a mountain and see for herself. Rose takes her favorite blue chair with her. Her climb is long, arduous, and solitary. At one point, afraid and lonely, Rose climbs on her chair and, to assure herself of her own being, carves "Rose is Rose is Rose is Rose" high up around the trunk of a tree. Eventually, she arrives, sings, questions her place in the world and then, in a strange fairy-tale ending, spots her cousin Willie on another peak and realizes he is not her cousin at all. Some appropriate time later, they marry.

When the typescript arrived, McCullough and Scott brought it to Brown's apartment, where they drank wine, ate a cake in the shape of a boat, and read the book aloud, to much general merriment. Adding to the holiday atmosphere, the electricity went out during their celebration: Brown, never very careful with money, had neglected to pay the bill. However much the manuscript delighted the adults, they still put it through the usual Bank Street test of reading it aloud to children. Over many sessions with children of different ages, observers noted which passages provoked confusion or restlessness. In the end, the publishers sent Stein a forty-page, single-spaced letter, suggesting revisions. At the same time, the children of Bank Street were critiquing *The Noisy Book*, too, telling Brown "that car horns did not go 'honk honk,' as she had written in her first draft, but 'awurra awurra.'"[26] In the fall of 1939, both books were published. Stein's, on lovely rose paper with illustrations by Hurd, never sold well, but *The Noisy Book*, with illustrations by Weisgard, quickly rose to the top of Scott's list.

The World Is Round is not a good children's book. It does not take more than a few moments to see that it is far too long and far too dense for a child to love or a parent to read aloud. Even with multiple illustrations, large font, and widely spaced text, at over sixty pages, *The World Is Round* is many times longer than the 130 *words* of *Goodnight Moon*. Still, there are moments when Stein is delightful, and one can see anew why Brown, Stein herself, and others guessed she might be able to pull it off. Many small moments in *The World Is Round* could be extracted as books or little poems for toddlers in their own right. Rose thinks about thinking in ways that seem in tune with childhood existential thoughts. She wonders if she would still be Rose if she was called something else; she wonders "if the world is round, would a lion fall off."[27] Stein's writing for children did not work, but Stein taught other writers, Brown first among them, a crucial lesson about *how* to write for children.

Brown only gained confidence to write to Stein in 1940, first with a long, rambling fan letter and, a second time, with a letter about her pet dogs, the power of folktales, and some of the reservations about Stein's second manuscript. No reply exists to the first. Stein sent only a postcard in response to the second, and that one mainly congratulates Brown on her new puppies. Discouraged, Brown let go of her hope that Stein might become a mentor. Much as we might want to speculate on what might have come of a meeting between them—the conversations they might have enjoyed about dogs, Paris, cakes, and Hemingway—Brown still learned much about art from her careful reading of and delight in Stein's work.

Many of Brown's children's books celebrate movement, travel, and wandering. Brown spent the summer of 1941 in her rustic cottage on an island off the coast of Maine, where she began adapting a Provençal folk song into what would become *The Runaway Bunny*. Brown spoke French, having spent several years in secondary school in Switzerland, and admired French music greatly. As a reader of modern literature, she would have known how much Provençal poetry was admired among the modernists. Ezra Pound began his career with a series of lectures on the genre; he, Eliot, and others celebrated the poetry as among the earliest vernacular literature in Europe. Rather than look to medieval poetry, Brown took her inspiration from a folk song, "O Magali." Brown must have loved that Magali is a Provençal version of her own name, Margaret. (You can perhaps hear that "Magali" and "Marguerite" have similar sounds, particularly if you don't stress the R.)

The song was collected by the poet Frédéric Mistral in the nineteenth century; his memoirs describe the worker from whom he learned it. It was incorporated into Charles Gounod's 1864 opera, *Mireille*, based on Mistral's poem "Mireo." In the opera, Mireille is a poor girl who determines to marry for love. In the opening of act 2, she and her beloved, a basket-maker, pledge their undying love in a duet based on the folk song "O Magali." In the duet, Vincent suggests escape, but Mireille resists, suggesting that she will turn into a swallow as a result, and if she becomes a swallow, he will become a hunter. Mireille sings: "In vain do you think me caught, I am a cloud." Vincent responds: "And I am the breeze, and carry you away on a sunbeam."[28] As a love song, it's a flirtation and a test: How much do you love me? How far will you go to be mine? In addition to the appearance of "O Magali" in *Mireille*, the song was recorded separately by Adrien Legros in 1933.

Brown borrowed the song's pattern of metamorphoses, escapes, and captures for *The Runaway Bunny*. In turning to a literary inspiration, Brown turned her back on the "here and now" of Bank Street and toward her literary side. In the book, she changed the story from a testament of a *lover's* devotion to a *mother's* devotion. It's a favorite of many, but it has its detractors. Some love it and the reassurance it offers. Others find the insistence on chasing the little bunny-child to the ends of the earth a little worrying, even smothering: the bunny's mom as helicopter parent. *The Runaway Bunny* can seem overly committed to quashing the runaway's efforts to get away from mother and home. Even so, Brown depicts a powerful tension between the desire to run away and the power of love to pull the runaway back home.

The more deeply you look, the stranger the story and its connection to Brown becomes. The choice of a bunny as protagonist reflects her lifelong love of rabbits. She loved them completely but unsentimentally. She identified with the animal, keeping many rabbits as pets, even as she loved to hunt. An avid runner, Brown spent many weekend mornings on Long Island running to hounds with the Buckram Beagles, a cross-country running club based on British rabbit-hunting traditions. Her home in New York City was full of fur throws, and, when she ghost-wrote the text for a children's photography book by the African explorer Osa Johnson, she took a pair of leopard slacks as part of her payment. At her house in Maine, she polished her dining room table with cooking grease, mixing the fat of her dinner with the table itself.

Brown's emotional life is another source for *The Runaway Bunny*. Her parents' marriage ended in 1941, a change that a friend recalled as devastating to Brown. She had broken an engagement as a young woman. An affair with William Gaston, a married neighbor whose summer cottage in Maine was very near her own, also ended. Since 1940, she had been involved in a long, difficult, nonmonogamous relationship with the poet and performer Michael Strange. Strange, born Blanche Oelrichs, had been married to the actor John Barrymore as well as two other men (her first husband, Leonard Thomas, and her third, Harrison Tweed). She transformed herself into a writer and traveled the country, performing the poetry of Shakespeare and Tennyson, as well as her own original works. During the early years of their tempestuous romance, Brown maintained her own apartment. (They lived together from 1943 until Strange's death from leukemia in 1950.) A chief source of tension between them was Strange's mockery of Brown for being a mere author of "baby books." Where Brown might have written that the youngest readers can offer all that "the maddest poet's heart could desire," having a lover frequently deride one's work might well make one dream of running away.[29] All of this suggests Brown's equal ability to identify with the hunter and the hunted, the runaway bunny and the mother/lover who continually chases it down.

The stories of Strange's taunting abuse are painful to read. They speak to another difficulty for the wanderer. The creative person, like Brown, who is unostentatiously, gradually discovering a new path often appears to be wasting their time. Unlike a bolder adventurer, who sets off in a direction or begins work with a clear goal, wanderers may not be able to explain what they are doing for a long time, exposing themselves to ridicule such as Brown endured from her girlfriend. Today, Strange's career of traveling the country offering "An Evening with Michael Strange" at which she would recite the poems of great English poets alongside her original compositions seems at least as unlikely as Brown's career writing so-called baby books.

A second, less well-known book about a little traveling child, *The Little Fur Family* (1946), was manufactured with a fur cover, another pioneering innovation in children's publishing. From the first, Brown had insisted on sturdy pages and solid bindings, understanding that very small children were rough on their books, and that books for the very young needed to hold up to that treatment. But with *The Little Fur Family*, she introduced a new complication and a new possibility of delight: fur covers. Like *Pat the Bunny*, another interactive book of the postwar boom in children's literature, *The Little Fur Family* invites children to touch the book. But where *Pat the Bunny* insists on gender norms—try on Mommy's wedding ring, feel Daddy's scratchy beard—the little fur child barely even has a gender. Like *The Runaway Bunny*, *Peter Rabbit*, and many other children's books, *The Little Fur Family* tells the story of a small, well-loved furry creature taking its first steps outside the immediate circle of its mother's care.

The little fur child puts on a huge fur hat and takes a walk in the forest. His grandfather says, "Bless you," to the child when it sneezes. The child walks on, finding creatures that fly and swim—they don't have fur—and a tiny, tiny fur creature that does. After this minor adventure, the child's parents offer a lullaby:

Sleep, sleep, our little fur child,
Out of the windiness,
Out of the wild.
Sleep warm in your fur
All night long,

In your little fur family.
This is a song.[30]

The little fur child's adventure is thus framed back into safety. The family's song has the ring of amateur verse, the kinds of ditties barely worth the name of song that parents concoct to get through the day's routine. The rhymes may be obvious, but the pattern is unconventional. There are seven lines; lines one and three rhyme with each other, as do lines five and seven, but the even-numbered lines do not have rhymes at all. The last line, too, is unusual. To rhyme "long" with "this is a song" might seem like a cheat. However, that kind of identification characterizes both the speech of young children, still anchoring themselves to the world through constant naming, and Stein's experiments. Just when songs and roses seem like the most familiar clichés, we have Brown and Stein to remind us of what can be special about being little and being loved and having parents make a song up just for you, a song that places you safely in the vast world. In fact, one of Mitchell's main recommendations was to take time, after any excursion, to help a young child turn that excursion—to the post office or to the wild—into a little story-song.

One of the first of Brown's books to be published after her death was *The Sailor Dog*, at once a sequel to the delightful *Mister Dog: The Dog Who Belonged to Himself* and a tribute to "Pebbles" Rockefeller, her fiancé, who was embarking on a sail around the world. Like Rockefeller, Sailor Dog dreams of adventure and sets off to sea. *The Sailor Dog* is explicitly about adventure, and its protagonist, a young dog, is definitively male. Even so, the book's lessons are universal and tenderly empowering. His little boat wrecks, and he is washed onto a deserted beach. With great ingenuity, luck, and energy, Sailor Dog gathers driftwood on the beach and builds himself a house with a working fireplace. The shaggy dog (charmingly rendered in illustrations by Garth Williams) settles into his home only to dream a dream that calls him back to adventure: "If he could build a house, he could mend the hole in the ship."[31] Brown shows Scuppers figuring things out on his own, coming to believe in his ability because he sees what he can do by himself, and, in doing so, he remembers what he wanted—not to be safe, but to explore—and he adjusts and sets off again.

It is difficult to imagine a better lesson in what we might today call "resilience." The adventure of the final pages repays Scuppers's wandering, and, again, although he is male, what he does is ungendered: like many happy tourists with a little ready cash in his pocket, he gets himself a snazzy new outfit and enjoys the local oranges. *The Sailor Dog* is a fantasy of the ways the traveling can go right, a celebration of the best kind of wandering, and a story whose conflict—the dramatic shipwreck—resolves in a most satisfying way, into a lesson in Scuppers's abilities. As with *The Little Fur Family*, Brown seems to know just the right amount of adventure to fire a child's imagination.

As World War II ended, Brown wrote the work for which she is best known today, *Goodnight Moon*, a celebration of the objects in a wonderful, enormous nursery, furnished with some of the features of Brown's own childhood room. In this text, objects are celebrated for themselves. A rose is a rose is a rose, and a little toy house is a little toy house. The book itself is little more than an inventory. The structure echoes Stein in following a personal logic, ordering itself through rhyme and repetition, with a symmetry that is not entirely precise, gesturing toward the overwhelming feeling of one's smallness in the universe ("Goodnight stars / Goodnight air"), even toward the void ("Goodnight nobody"), while ultimately offering the reassurance, in the form of the quiet old lady and the final lines that cocoon our little sleeper in "noises everywhere." These noises, if not understood, are introduced as a normal feature of the atmosphere of the great green room. This last gesture seems particularly astute in a book for the very young. Since misunderstood noises often keep us from sleep, the final line of *Goodnight Moon* seems to anticipate them, incorporating them into the lulling final words as if to reassure the youngest listener that the complaint she is about to make is unnecessary, that those noises are just another thing to placidly bid goodnight.

The order in which we hear about the objects in the room follows the child's own interests: in the fanciness of a telephone, the thrill of a helium balloon, in the nursery rhyme pictures before the little animals, and in the mouse's existence not as a pest but as a creature of equal stature to the little kittens. In the book's second half, the bears and the chairs are bid goodnight as much as if they were in the room, causing us to wonder which moon it is that the little bunny sees and bids goodnight: the one the cow jumps over in the picture, or the one that rises in the window as the narrative progresses? As for the utilitarian clocks and the socks, they do not rank in the first inventory, but they do get bid goodnight. It is, as a friend and children's book author wrote, "the perfect list," and it is perfect in part because it is so wholly in the perspective of the child who surveys this wonderful nursery.[32]

It may be useful to compare one of Stein's rooms with the great green room. In "Rooms," the third and final section of *Tender Buttons*, Stein writes: "A little lingering lion and a Chinese chair, all the handsome cheese which is stone, all of it and a choice, a choice of a blotter. If it is difficult to do it one way there is no place of similar trouble. None. The whole arrangement is established. The end of which is that there is a suggestion, a suggestion that there can be a different whiteness to a wall. This was thought."[33] The passage begins with a list. The objects here are not from a nursery but from Stein's home with Alice B. Toklas on the rue du Fleurus in Paris. Then, things shift in a way that no one could expect. The list is odd and delightful, playing with /ch/ and /l/ sounds, but what follows offers none of the comfort of a list. Stein's language games derive their energy and their delight from lingering in that space where young children often dwell, but she is not thinking about or talking to children. "This was thought," ends the paragraph and breaks us out of the puzzle of language for a brief comment on what has come before. Suddenly, Stein brings self-consciousness to the page. She labels the moment, as one might in an art gallery or a laboratory, "thought," much as the little fur child's parents label the lullaby for him: "This was a song."

In *Goodnight Moon*, the wandering happens not in the world—the little bunny child is safely tucked into bed and its magnificent nursery, though he does briefly venture out from under the covers. The eye and the mind do wander, and, in tiptoeing into the void, bidding goodnight and backing off to contemplate safer, more ordinary objects, Brown knits the fact of nighttime fears and nightmares back into the comforting fabric of a bedtime story.

Goodnight Moon was published in 1946. That January, *Life* magazine published a full-length celebrity profile of Brown. The children's folk singer Burl Ives recorded her books. Sales of the book were strong, if not extraordinary. No one predicted it would become a classic. Its sales only began to take off in 1953, a year after its author's premature death, growing steadily and then astonishingly. Sales have mounted ever since. Now, the book is a fixture of American parenting and inspires praise, think pieces, and parodies. It sold half a million copies in 2013, making it the fifth-highest seller on the children's hardcover backlist. In 2011, *Goodnight iPad* made fun of the gap between the idealized nursery of *Goodnight Moon* and the distractions of modern technology. Aimee Bender, Elisabeth Egan, and Anna Holmes have each written on *Goodnight Moon* and its author in the *New Yorker* and the *New York Times*.[34]

By 1990, sales were at $4 million. Brown left many unpublished manuscripts at her death. Posthumous publications continue to appear to this day, amid the recent revelation that Brown wrote not just poems but songs for children. We have yet to fully reckon with the rich legacy she left us or with how it has changed our relationship to language and to childhood. One of the first publications to appear after her death was *The Four Fur Feet*, about a little furry creature's travels. In it Brown wrote:

> And as he slept
> he dreamed a dream,
> dreamed a dream,
> dreamed a dream.
> And as he slept
> he dreamed a dream
> that all the world was round—O.[35]

Eileen Chang
1920–1995

FASHION AND LOVE IN SHANGHAI

The novelist Eileen Chang's career was at its height in the 1940s, when she was a very young woman living in Japanese-occupied Shanghai. In the decades after that heady beginning, moving amid Shanghai, Hong Kong, Taiwan, and the United States, Chang worked to recapture the magic that made her a celebrated writer of wartime China. One such attempt was the novella *Lust, Caution*, which she began in the 1950s but did not publish until 1979. Ang Lee made it into a film of the same name in 2007. This taut erotic thriller tells the story of Chia-Chih, a college actress, who enters a patriotic scheme to entrap Mr. Yee, a wealthy Chinese spy passing information to the Chinese puppet regime during the Second Sino-Japanese War (1937–45). Taking place over just twenty-four hours, the story begins and ends with a sinister table of bourgeois matrons or "tai-tais" playing mah-jongg in diamond rings and gold brooches. The honorific "tai-tai" means more than just "wife" or "missus"; it connotes a specific kind of bourgeois wife, comfortable in her material success and conscious of the compromises and ruses she has used to marry well. These tai-tais prove formidable, passive witnesses to the unfolding drama. On this day, Chia-Chih must deliver Yee to a jewelry store, where her collaborators plan to assassinate him, but at the very last moment she imagines they love each other and, throwing over the plan, whispers to him, "Run."[1] It takes Yee just a moment to recognize the danger he is in. He races down the steps, and, "as soon as he'd reached safety, he'd immediately telephoned to get the whole area sealed off. By ten o'clock that evening they'd all been shot."[2] Yee's is a shocking, brutal act: Chia-Chih loses her life for acting on her feelings.

Like many of Chang's heroines, Chia-Chih is an intelligent young woman, hoping for more from life, navigating wartime China, while also experiencing—and often getting derailed by—sexual desire. What sets *Lust, Caution* apart is its explicit politics: Chia-Chih and her associates are actively resisting Japanese occupation and the Chinese puppet regime—a political position that Chang could not have articulated in the 1940s. Chang's translator says that in many ways the novella "reads like a long-considered riposte to . . . those who dismissed her as a banal boudoir realist."[3] Despite the text's clear contempt for collaboration and admiration for Chinese patriotism, Chia-Chih's own politics falter in the crucial moment. She wanders, fatally, both in act and in thought.

As she sits in a café, waiting for Mr. Yee, Chia-Chih reflects anxiously on how she arrived in this situation: "She felt a kind of chilling premonition of failure, like a long snag in a silk stocking, silently creeping up her body."[4] This metaphor, drawn from imagining intimate embarrassment—a run in one's stocking, with the hope that no one else will notice something you are keenly conscious of—is typical of Chang, who has a powerful feeling for clothing and a gift for vivid metaphors drawn from nearby domestic items.

As she waits, Chang offers, in flashback, the story of the plot to entrap Yee. Chia-Chih had been the star of her college's drama troupe in Canton. War closes their university, and the troupe relocates to Hong Kong. There, she has her first encounter with the group that makes the plan to set a honey trap and assassinate Mr. Yee:

> The drama troupe had given one last public performance. Overexcited, unable to wind down after the curtain had fallen, she had gone for a bite to eat with the rest of the cast. But even after almost everyone else had dispersed, she still hadn't wanted to go home. Instead, she and two female classmates had ridden through the city on the deserted upper deck of a tram as it swayed and trundled down the middle of the Hong Kong streets, the neon advertisements glowing in the darkness outside the windows.[5]

Chia-Chih loves the thrill of wandering city streets in darkness. This restless feeling, the jangling, thrilling excitement that abates only slowly after a performance, proves disastrous. In those moments when she still vibrates with energy, she is vulnerable and makes her worst decisions. She thinks of joining up with the radicals as a sacrifice, but Chang does not give her any other political thoughts. Instead, we see her nervous energy, her need to keep moving. She has a similar keyed-up feeling after her first meeting with Yee. Proud that she has played the role of a wealthy young wife so flawlessly, she is eager to go out and celebrate: "None of the male students were dancers, but a bowl of soup at one of those small, all-night restaurants and a long walk through the damp night would do just as well. Anything to avoid bed."[6] She knows this nerdy group will not go dancing with her, so she pivots quickly to soup: an abrupt and sorry compromise for a night out dancing, but, as she thinks, "anything to avoid bed." Unfortunately for her, bed is precisely what she must face: a virgin, she cannot proceed with the plan without any experience, so she must sleep with one of her coconspirators. It is an embarrassing necessity, and, once accomplished, disaster strikes: their rich benefactor loses parental favor, the plan comes apart, Hong Kong falls, and everyone else relocates to Shanghai. Two years pass, when, unexpectedly, a nationalist Chinese agent asks them to revive the scheme.

Now Chia-Chih is living with the Yees in Shanghai, taking advantage of Mrs. Yee's desire for an inside line on black market luxuries, playing mah-jongg and running out of time: "If they didn't finish it off today, she couldn't stay on at the Yee's—not with all those great bejeweled cats watching her every move."[7] These "bejeweled cats," the other tai-tais with their gold jewelry and diamond rings, are key to her plan: she has convinced Yee that she needs a ring as big as theirs and lures him into a shabby jewelry store just off a main road. As she examines a huge pink diamond, she realizes how little time she has had to think about what she has been doing: "The two occasions she had been with Yee, she had been so tense, so taken up in saying her lines that there had been no opportunity to ask herself how she actually felt."[8] Knowing that this plot, two years in the planning, is about to come to fruition, time slows to a standstill on the second-floor balcony of the shop. "Almost dizzy with the precariousness of her situation," she feels "a numb chill creeping up the back of her head; the display windows downstairs and the glass door between them seemed to be broadening out, growing taller."[9] In this suspended moment, it is not just that time stops; space also expands. The window that stands between them and the street, the pane of glass separating the lovers from their fate, expands outward, as if beckoning her to an alternative reality where they both might survive. In this suspended moment, Chia-Chih's mind wanders:

> Only now, as this last tense moment of calm stretched infinitely out, on this cramped balcony, the artificial brightness of its lamplight contrasting grubbily with the pale sky visible through the door and windows downstairs, could she permit herself to relax and inquire into her own feelings. Somehow, the nearby presence of the Indian, bent over his writing desk, only intensified her sense of being entirely alone with her lover. But now was not the moment to ask herself whether he loved him; instead, she needed to—[10]

And her thought breaks off precisely at the moment when politics ought to enter. Chang draws this moment out with expert tension, and, in it, we see how ill prepared Chia-Chih has been to perform her role. Instead of thinking of how Yee has "to be nailed," as she had earlier, she sees him as "her lover."[11] The presence of an inattentive clerk makes their intimacy more poignant. She realizes that she has never been in love before, having spent her teenaged years fending off unwanted attention, and, examining whether she loves Yee, "she found herself unable to refute the notion entirely."[12] Her thought breaks off, and Chang has the lovers continue to communicate telepathically. For the first time, we have Mr. Yee's internal monologue. He is awash in a delicious realization: "He had never dared dream such happiness would come his way in middle age."[13] In response, again, without speaking, but as if they are reading each other's minds, Chia-Chih makes her fatal decision, mistaking the satisfaction of being loved with love itself:

> He really loves me, she thought. Inside, she felt a raw tremor of shock—then a vague sense of loss.
>
> It was too late.
>
> The Indian passed the receipt to him. He placed it inside his jacket.
>
> "Run," she said softly.[14]

And, with that, the uneasy dance of lust and caution comes to an end. Yee escapes. He orders the assassination of Chia-Chih and her coconspirators. The next day, Liao Tai-tai, another matron, takes Chia-Chih's spot at the mah-jongg table.

Chia-Chih pays with her life for her lapse of attention. Her mind wanders, her desire overcomes her patriotic intent, and, in saving her "lover" (a traitor), he has her executed. Her keyed-up post-performance mood earlier in the story and the accidental way in which that energy led her into espionage is characteristic of Chang's writing on women and wandering. Her perspective is unusual, for, unlike Margaret Wise Brown, she was not a wanderer in her vocation. Though caught in the events' history, Chang had no uncertainty about what to do with her life: she was determined to be a writer. Her wandering was either the urban wandering of a writer in search of material or the wandering of the political immigrant and refugee, forced by history to relocate. By contrast, Chang's characters are both caught by history and uncertain of what they want, unable, in the chaos of politics and war, to find their way, and coming up against the ways that desire gets in the way of other plans. In this way, Chang exposes the precarious position of the woman who wanders.

Interwar China, especially Shanghai and Hong Kong, where most of Chang's work is set, was chaotic and unstable. The overlapping conflicts of the Chinese Civil War, the Sino-Japanese War, and World War II divided families, interrupted plans, and altered lives. Indeed, World War II's impact on China was subsumed under two more pressing ongoing regional conflicts, the Chinese Civil War (1927–1949), which pitted nationalists against communists, and the second Sino-Japanese War, in which Japan invaded mainland China in an act of imperial aggression, installing a puppet leader in Manchuria and attempting to take more Chinese territory from there.

The Qing Dynasty collapsed in 1912, but the young republic splintered quickly. When World War I ended, negotiators in Versailles ignored Chinese concerns, transferring the Shandong Peninsula from German to Japanese control, thus giving Japan a foothold on the mainland. In 1925, Chiang Kai-Shek took control of the republic, but his power was almost immediately challenged by the Communist Party, sparking the civil war that persisted until the party's victory in 1949. At the same time, the conflict between China and Japan continued, and, in 1937, Japan invaded, taking territory as far south as Nanjing, less than two hundred miles from Shanghai. During this time, the Japanese carried out the Nanjing

Massacre, brutally raping, torturing, and killing several hundred thousand civilians in Nanjing and the surrounding area. Thus, by the time World War II was declared, Japan had already occupied parts of China for eight years, and the Second Sino-Japanese War was two years underway. From 1937 through Japan's surrender at the end of World War II, the tensions between the nationalists and communists were somewhat in check under the necessity of fighting Japan, but civil war resumed after Japan's surrender at the end of World War II.

Eileen Chang (1920–1995) was born into this chaotic and unstable atmosphere, the child of Zhang Zhiyi (張志沂, 1896–1953), a traditional Qing-dynasty intellectual who was also a womanizer and an opium addict, and Huang Suqiong (黃素瓊, 1893–1957), a cosmopolitan mother with a degree from University College London. Thus, her parents represented two versions of China at the beginning of the twentieth century: the cosmopolitan modern intellectual China and the classical dynastic China. However, neither of her parents' outlooks were political, and neither aligned with communism or with nationalism. Thus, Chang was disconnected from modern politics, divided in her allegiances, and poised to enter a modern China with a complex, highly individual perspective.

The year Chiang Kai-Shek took power, Chang's mother, Huang, went to France for two years, traveling with her sister-in-law; Chang was five. Huang returned two years later, lured by her husband's promises to stop smoking opium and to be faithful. The affairs and the opium continued, and the couple divorced in 1930. The clash in cultures represented by their marriage extends to Chang's name. Chang was born Zhang Ying (張煐), around the time of the divorce, her mother renamed her Eileen Chang, changing Zhang to Chang, Ying to Eileen, and flipping her given and family name in the English style. Then, registering her for school, her mother renamed her again as Zhang Ai-ling, Ai-ling being a Sinicization of Eileen. As an adult, Chang was understandably self-conscious about her name, writing, "I myself have an unbearably vulgar name, am well aware of the fact, and have no plans to change it. Even so, I remain extremely interested in people's names."[15]

Despite her mother's frequent absences, Chang adored her and took her side. She was "entirely in favor" of the divorce and relieved "the agreement stipulated that I could still see my mother on a regular basis."[16] Moreover, she wrote with characteristic wry irony, "it was in her apartment that I saw a built-in porcelain bathtub and gas stove for the first time, which made me very happy and came as something of a consolation."[17] Shortly after that, with Chang in boarding school, her mother moved to France. Of that parting, Chang writes:

> My mother was gone, but something of her atmosphere lingered in my aunt's house: an exquisitely carved table with an interlocking "puzzle-piece" mosaic on top, gentle pastel colors, wonderful people whose lives were beyond my ken constantly bustling in and out the front door. All the best things I knew, be they spiritual or material, were contained in those rooms. And that is why spiritual and material virtues have always seemed intermeshed to me.[18]

Cataloging the contents of her mother's apartment, tenderly lingering over beautiful objects, becomes a way of remembering. Mixed in with beautiful colors are "wonderful people," undifferentiated, out of reach, and sophisticated. This autobiographical essay vibrates with her memories of that intense childhood, longing to be a part of that sophisticated world, barely understood and desired all the more because it belonged to her beloved but often absent mother.

Chang spent her teenaged years with her father and stepmother. There, she was severely abused and neglected. At one point, she was imprisoned in a room for months and starved to such an extent that she developed dysentery. During these hard years, she attended St. Mary's Hall in Shanghai, a prestigious girl's school founded in 1851 by Emma Jones, an American Episcopalian. There, she became fluent in English and deepened her love of Chinese literature. An episode in "Jasmine Tea" may offer a clue of to the scorn she endured in this hostile home: "All that English you're doing—why bother? A donkey can jounce along after the horses, jounce till his legs break, and still it won't amount to anything!"[19] Bookish young people confronted by elders who mock the value of learning turn up often in Chang's works. Unsurprisingly, Chang longed to leave this uncongenial and abusive atmosphere.

Upon graduation, Chang was admitted to University College London, where she hoped to follow in her mother's footsteps. However, World War II made that impossible. Instead, Chang enrolled at Hong Kong University, where she was a strong student. She studied literature, both classical Chinese and English, and nurtured her love of classic texts such as *The Dream of the Red Chamber*, as well as modern masterpieces including *The Sing-Song Girls of Shanghai*, which she would later translate into English. Her student identification shows a young woman in glasses with a center part, looking directly at the camera. While at university, she transformed herself from this bespectacled schoolgirl into a chic young woman, but her maturation collided with the war. British-occupied Hong Kong was under threat, and, in December 1941, simultaneous with the attack on Pearl Harbor, Japan attacked Hong Kong.

When the Battle of Hong Kong began, the university sent most of its students home; those who stayed, including Chang, needed to be trained as air wardens, a role for which Chang was ill-suited. Even so, "there was no way to solve the problem of room and board save to join the defense effort."[20] On the way home from their first training session, Chang and several classmates ran into an air raid, jumping "off the tram we had been riding and . . . flattening ourselves against a doorway, wondering whether we had fulfilled our duties as Air-Raid Precaution volunteers in the process. (Before I had managed to find out what the duties of an Air-Raid Precaution volunteer might be, the battle was already over and done)."[21] Practical, detached, and keenly ironic, Chang understands the absurdity of the role she has been assigned and is not sorry to see it come to an end. At one point, she gets assigned to guard the library: "I finished reading *An Exposé of the Bureaucrats* during an artillery barrage. I had read it when I was little, before I was able to appreciate its virtues, and had always wanted to read it again. As I read, I worried whether I would be allowed to finish the book. The print was miniscule, and the light poor, but if a bomb were to fall, what would I need my eyes for anyway?"[22]

Still pragmatic, here Chang also reveals the depth of her love for literature and how it feeds her urgent need to write. Under threat of bombardment, Chang uses the anxious hours to read. Her engagement with the war was detached. As she writes, "What we did not have to pay attention to we managed to ignore."[23] Even so, the violence affected her. Her beloved history teacher, Professor France, was shot and killed by friendly fire: "A good teacher, a good man. The waste of humanity."[24]

Facing death, she wondered what it would be like to die before getting to the end of the book she was reading. Chang was undoubtedly glamorous, as attested by the most widely circulated photograph of her, hips cocked, hair bobbed, wearing a slim silk tunic of her own design, but this representation of her wartime experiences illustrates an easily overlooked aspect of her character. In addition to all the fashion and the wry, knowing stories of frustrated desire, Chang was a passionate writer and reader.

She moved home to Shanghai in the winter of 1942 and began writing. Despite the war, the 1940s were Chang's most prolific decade, both in terms of the quantity and quality of her work. She was avid for success, and she found it. In the preface to the second edition of *Written on Water*, a collection of her essays, she wrote: "Make yourself famous as early as you can! If success comes too late, the pleasure of it isn't as intense. . . . Hurry! Hurry! Otherwise it will be too late! Too late!"[25] In Shanghai, she quickly connected with three editors who helped her career: Zhou Shoujuan (1895–1968), a novelist and translator who first published Chang's Chinese writing; Klaus Mehnert (1906–1984), the editor of an Axis-aligned, German-funded English-language magazine, *The XXth Century*, who published her essays and movie reviews; and Hu Lancheng (1906–1981), a writer and politician who was among the first to praise Chang in print.

Of these, her connection to Hu was the most consequential and controversial. Reviled to this day as a traitor, Hu's history as a thinker and writer are even trickier than Chang's to untangle, though some critics, especially in Taiwan, have begun to reassess his writing. He had been a supporter of Chiang Kai-Shek, but, as Japan's military strength grew, he joined the Chinese puppet regime, believing it to be the best way to resist Western imperialism. He advocated resistance to the West, but this entailed a tolerance for Japan; as David Der-Wei Wang reminds us, "at a time when millions of Chinese were being coerced, exiled, and slaughtered by the invaders, Hu Lancheng's lyrical appreciation of Oriental civilization could not have sounded more disturbing."[26] Hu was imprisoned in Nanjing for criticizing Wang's collaborationist government, but he was released thanks to the intervention of Japan, and he traveled to Shanghai in 1944.

In Shanghai, Hu read Chang's "Sealed Off," a perfect short story about a flirtation on a stopped tram between a young college teacher and a businessman. Dazzled by her writing, he sought to meet her and in her found an irresistible intellectual peer: "When he first saw Chang, he was so enchanted by her as to feel that 'the whole cosmos shattered.' . . . Chang had an intriguing character—both innocent and cynical, awkward and smart—that exuded an irresistible charm. Their rendezvous, as Hu puts it, was as much an amorous engagement as an intellectual rivalry."[27] They began an affair. Hu, who was eighteen years Chang's senior, was married to his third wife at the time, but they divorced within a few months, and Hu and Chang had a secret wedding with only one witness, Chang's friend Fatima.

What was an exciting affair for him, however, was traumatic for her. Hu, who never acknowledged his betrayals, political or sexual, cheated on Chang from the start. Moreover, he was financially dependent on her. When Japan was defeated in the war, Hu was on the run, having an affair with another woman, and still taking money from Chang. After the war, her association with the collaborationist Hu created complications—to say the least—for her career. They divorced in 1947 after just three years of marriage, and Hu escaped to Japan in 1950. During these years, the civil war in China between nationalists and communists resumed in force, but Chang remained in Shanghai. Although blacklisted from publishing, she found success as a screenwriter, putting her lifelong love of the cinema into practice. She spent several months in the countryside, participating in the land reform movement that she would go on to criticize. In 1952, she returned to Hong Kong, then still a British territory, and worked for the American News Agency, translating American classics into Chinese.

In 1955, she immigrated to the United States and wrote her first novel in English, *The Rice Sprout Song*, a book that was critical of communist land reform and produced for the US Information Service. With this commission, Chang seemed "poised to become a leading international figure, seemingly destined to be mentioned alongside Chinua Achebe and Derek Walcott as the most widely recognized writers from decolonizing areas. Her timing, it would appear, could not have been better."[28] She had a fellowship to the prestigious MacDowell artist residency program in 1956. With time to write and the support of an anticommunist US government, Chang did indeed seem positioned for success.

At MacDowell, she met and fell in love with Ferdinand Reyher, who became her second husband. Reyher is best remembered today as the writer and German emigré who secured Bertold Brecht's successful emigration from Nazi Germany. If a Japanese-sympathizing husband was inconvenient in communist China, a communist-sympathizing husband was only slightly less inconvenient in 1950s America. Still, this was a much happier marriage, despite the fact that Chang was once again married to a politically inconvenient older man who depended on her financially. When she got pregnant soon into their relationship, he made clear he did not want children. She traveled from New England to New York City for an illegal abortion. In her autobiographical novel, *Little Reunions*, she tells a fictionalized version of the story, including the horrifying experience of seeing a fetus in the toilet bowl. Terrified by the sight of the face and the recognition that it had been a boy, she flushes the toilet in haste and is haunted by the memory. In her novel of the Cultural Revolution, *Naked Earth*, one of the protagonists dies at the hands of an underground abortionist.

Chang became a US citizen in 1960 and relocated briefly to Taiwan, from 1961 to 1962, in search of work, before returning to the United States, where she remained until her death. Her years there were marked by continued efforts to find her footing at a university—she held several visiting positions, including one at Berkeley—and to make a living as a novelist. After two novels sponsored by USIS, she published a third novel in English, *The Rouge of the North*, a return to "The Golden Cangue," a celebrated novella from the 1940s. She continued to write screenplays throughout the early 1960s; at least thirteen of her screenplays were made into films.

Reyher died in 1967. From 1972 until her death in 1995, Chang lived in increasing isolation in Los Angeles. She translated *The Sing-Song Girls of Shanghai*, Han Bangqing's 1892 picaresque classic about late Qing dynasty concubines and their clients, offering a tour of the brothels of Shanghai, from the luxurious to the squalid. The translation, however, was not a success and was only published, much revised by Eva Hung, in 2005. The Chinese American scholars Stephen Soong and C. T. Hsia worked hard to help her find an audience, but to little personal benefit to Chang. She died alone and unknown. Even so, scholars continue to praise her, translators work to make her work available in English, and in the 1990s filmmakers began adapting Chang's fiction. These films, including *Lust, Caution* (2007), alongside the New York Review of Books translations and reissues of her English-language works, have done much to keep her reputation alive.

Chang's essays celebrate modern urban wandering, especially window-shopping. A distinctly modern phenomenon, window-shopping emerged as material prosperity and the widespread availability of mass-produced goods spread across much of the developed world. As people—especially women—increasingly became consumers, shopkeepers developed department stores and shopping arcades to lure women inside. For women especially, these stores became acceptable sites of wandering and daydreaming. Writers, including Chang, were quick to notice the narrative potential of these additions to the urban scene, in which a woman gazing into a shop window provides an occasion for meditations on desire, money, and the self, as women compare their reflections to the clothes they long for. But Chang's version of window-shopping is hers alone.

In her essays, Chang explores Shanghai with dash and enthusiasm, resembling—but not precisely the same as—the European flâneur. The closest cousins to these essays are Woolf's depictions of her own urban wanderings, especially the essay "Street Haunting," where Woolf makes up a minor errand as an excuse to wander: "Getting up we say, 'Really I must buy a pencil,' as if under cover of this excuse we could indulge safely in . . . rambling the streets of London."[29] Unlike Woolf, Chang feels no need for a pretext. Her delight in city life is unmixed with the anxiety of the wandering woman, but it is shadowed by the twin threats of Japanese occupation and the rising pressure to conform to communist orthodoxy. Both threats are acknowledged and blithely brushed off, unequal, Chang asserts, to the persistent strength, interest, and variety of ordinary Chinese people.

Chang's essay "Seeing with the Streets" opens with an anecdote about an incurious foreigner who spends two years in China, visiting none of the great sites but developing a keen love for how cute and round little Chinese children look in their padded winter clothes—she could just sweep them up and take them home! Chang notes the remark and, without denying it, proceeds to observe that strangers and tourists sometimes show us things about ourselves that we have failed to notice. Waddling children in padded clothes are, indeed, cute, and distinctively Chinese, and if you have never left China, you may not have taken the time to notice them. Noticing, "we could not help looking anew at Chinese children, for we had never thought there was anything particularly remarkable about them before!"[30]

This anecdote of the tourist's silly colonialist rapture introduces a key idea for the remainder of the essay: the aspiration, to paraphrase Henry James, to be a person upon whom nothing is lost. This wanderer's credo stands in tension with the more sinister connotation of the title, for, as the translator's note makes clear, seeing with the streets refers to surveillance: "'Seeing with the Streets' is a literal translation of an idiom (*daolu yimu*) . . . refer[ring] to the harsh rule of a Zhou king, during which passersby on the street, too scared to speak, could only signal their mutual understanding with their eyes."[31] Chang considers the wonders we might find, and the distances we would travel, if we added up every day's brief journey out of the house to work and home again: "After ten or twenty years, we will have covered several thousand miles."[32]

Noticing a mannequin in a state of undress, but criticizing its crude form, she sees that in its nakedness it is too crude to elicit sympathy:

> A shop has long since closed, the lights are off, and the wooden mannequin's leather coat has been stripped away. She stands with her shoulders exposed, facing away from the street. But her modesty is wasted, for even if she were facing outward, she would hardly move passersby to beautiful dreams. She was manufactured a little too cheaply and too clumsily, and there is nothing to recommend even the face or the hands or the feet that would have been exposed even with the benefit of the coat.[33]

Her keen eye dismisses it as beneath our pity, but it does lead to a broader consideration of shop windows and capitalism. Just as she veers toward controversy—and orthodoxy—she swerves away.

Chang describes the cycle of consumerist desire that keeps people dissatisfied, longing for more money, more things: "The purpose of shop windows is to stimulate one's desire to buy things. . . . In desiring to buy items they do not need, they naturally want more money than they can earn and proceed to do whatever it takes to get it. Shop windows are thus the irrational by-product of an irrational society."[34] We can imagine where the argument might go from here—something about human fallibility or the predations of capitalism—but Chang pivots away from the expected. Displays of Western fashion interest her, as lovely museum display cases do. They are interesting, they delight, they kindle the imagination, but they are not for her; they do not tempt.

Shop windows are not just about shopping. They are also art, little free displays that perhaps ought to be considered "a form of public service" for "dispensing delight and visual pleasure free of charge." Chang remembers a particularly beautiful display of hats years ago with great fondness, adding, "I don't wear Western suits and had no need to wear a hat to match and no desire to buy one, but I could still gaze at the display with appreciation."[35] Here, being committed to Chinese fashion inoculates her against temptation. And, with that, Chang has released window-shopping from some of its usual constraints: she can find the fashion beautiful without wondering about her own beauty or worthiness, or even her bank balance.

This celebration of noticing moves beyond fashion to domestic life. Even eggplants and spinach leaves in a basket can inspire. In "Notes on Apartment Life," she offers a cheerful celebration of an aspect of apartment living: the unexpected freedom of not living with servants. In this long passage, Chang moves from the awkwardness of being watched—not by the government, the military, or their spies, but by servants—to the joys of shopping for food and cooking it, to a knowing but joking denial of the politics of these observations:

> Not having to have a maid is one of the best things in life. Leaving any notions of the ideal of equality aside, it's terribly annoying, if not utterly ruinous in terms of one's appetite, to have someone who has not yet eaten standing over you and watching as you eat at mealtimes, always at the ready to give you more rice. There are so many little chores that are inherently pleasurable to perform. If you can't see eggplants growing in a garden, it's almost as lovely to see them in the vegetable market: an intricate and glossy shade of purple next to the pale green of new peas. . . . Every time one washes spinach and drops it into the wok, there are always one or two broken leaves stuck to the bottom of the bamboo basket. . . . In the light, the fresh emerald leaves displayed against the rectangular weave of the basket call to mind snow pea flowers on a trellis. And why must we call other things to mind at all? Isn't the beauty of the basket itself sufficient? None of this is intended as a display of my fealty to the National Socialist Party and its efforts to coax women back into the kitchen. There is so little point in coaxing, and if one must coax, it would only be right to urge men into the kitchen for a visit as well.[36]

Chang's meditation on the freedom of no longer having a maid makes the best of a social comedown: having grown up in a large, servant-filled home and then dividing her time between that home and the small apartment she and her mother lived in after her parents' divorce, Chang knows how to find the good in a changed circumstance. In her articulation of what is awkward about having servants, Chang claims to leave "the ideal of equality aside," yet she is thoroughly modern in her inability to see a maid as somehow less human than herself. Once you recognize your maid as a person who likely also gets hungry at mealtimes, it becomes difficult to see her otherwise.

She describes the quotidian chores that bring pleasure, beginning with the pleasure of doing the shopping yourself. Her delight in the colors of a market vegetable display resembles her many passages delighting in the colors of textiles, the cut of clothes. She is an aesthete, finding pleasure in the everyday. As she continues her reverie from the market to the kitchen, she compares a broken spinach leaf in a steamer basket to a pea vine on a trellis. The metaphor is lovely, if extraneous, and Chang is quick to check herself: "Why must we call other things to mind at all?" she asks, as if she is composing this essay before our eyes, revising herself. In doing so, she invites us to pause over both images, of fresh green against a geometric pale brown. Then, suddenly, she reintroduces politics: we must not understand her paean to shopping and preparing vegetables as part of an exhortation for women to return to the kitchen, along the lines of the National Socialists—and, in fact, she notes, both sexes should do the cooking.

Later in the essay, in describing those summer days when the privacy of apartment living gives way to opening doors and airing out linens. On those days you can hear "the servant boy . . . as he translates the telephone conversation into German for the benefit of his little master. There is a Russian man downstairs noisily giving Japanese lessons. . . . Someone somewhere is making beef stew, and someone else is simmering a Chinese herbal brew that counters indigestion."[37] The mix of nationalities, languages, activities, and smells emphasizes cosmopolitan Shanghai, favors the Axis powers, and does not demonize the Japanese. Nevertheless, the Russian man giving Japanese lessons troubles any easy sense of who is in league with whom. The combination of the beef stew and the stomach medicine captures her earthy ironies: everyone is mixed up with everyone, and, as she writes, "I utilize equivocal contrast as a means of writing the truth beneath the hypocrisy."[38] In window-shopping, cleaning spinach, or eavesdropping on her neighbors, Chang wanders with all her senses, communicating her unfettered delight in urban wandering.

In these essays and elsewhere, Chang develops an antipolitics. Neither communist nor nationalist, she emphasizes instead the specific things that delight her senses. Her ability to survive and even thrive during this politically tense moment owes a lot to her persistent championing of what it means to be Chinese—an identity that, for her, encompasses and surpasses dynasties, revolutions, and occupations. Chang emphasizes the persistence of the core of Chinese character across overwhelming, rapid change. Her ongoing affection for and loyalty to Chinese culture allows her readers across ideologies to continue in their admiration of her. She writes of wandering the streets of Shanghai with élan. A connoisseur of window displays, she observes the items for sale, the passing crowds, the way a lantern hangs off the back of a passing bicycle untroubled by the worries about being seen that haunt the street-life essays of so many European women writers of the period.

While Chang confidently embraced the identity of an urban wanderer, in her fiction she explored the fate of less certain young women. The novella *Aloeswood Incense* opens ominously. Ge Weilong, the young heroine, is in Hong Kong, but her parents have moved home to Shanghai. With only a year of secondary school left, she wants to stay behind, so she marshals the courage to approach her wealthy aunt and ask for support. As she approaches the gate of her aunt's house, she buzzes with ambition for her education, and a young person's naive hope in a relative's good will. Chang shows us, however, that she has wandered directly into a trap. The rest of the story documents her seduction into the life of a courtesan, precisely the fate she declared it her intent to avoid.

Her aunt is her only relative in Hong Kong, and the only family member with the means to pay her tuition. She is a famous, if fading, courtesan. From the moment Weilong arrives, it is clear that the household operates on principles dedicated to socializing and seduction. Two young maids are fighting. One of their shoes hits Weilong in the head as she walks to the door. Although it is midday, her aunt is still asleep. Still, her request for tuition money is granted, after some negotiation. Shortly after her arrival, she is shown into a large dressing room. There, she finds a closet full of beautiful silk clothes: dresses, robes, tennis costumes, all youthful, fashionable, and in her size. Dazzled by the luxury, it takes her some time to realize they are for her. When she does, she is in awe. But she is much slower to recognize the cost of accepting them. When she, her aunt, and her aunt's former lover are driving home one night in the back of a chauffeured car, he produces a pair of diamond bracelets, one for each woman. She slaps hers away, terrified at the implication, but is called ungrateful for even thinking of refusing. They mock her scruples, but, once the bracelet is on her wrist, her fate is sealed. By the end of the story, she is a young courtesan, married to a playboy, living in her aunt's mansion. As she walks the streets one night with her husband, a group of American sailors mistake her for a prostitute. Rebuffing her husband's outrage, she accepts the label. How is she any different, after all?

Several times in *Aloeswood Incense*, Weilong takes a walk. Once, she gets caught out in the rain on the long walk back up the hill to her aunt's villa. Where, in other writers' hands, such walks represent freedom, for Chang they reveal Weilong's impotence. Without money, isolated on a hill in the wealthy part of town, her walks take her nowhere and reveal her vulnerability to passing cars. Privacy is frequently interrupted in Chang's work. To wander alone in mind or body is not respected. These women are prey to forces that rush them back into obedience.

Weilong is not special. She likes attending college, playing tennis, and singing in the choir with her friends, and she finds pleasure in a modern, relatively carefree world full of amiable peers. She wants to study, but she covets pretty clothes. The moment she is distracted by them, she loses her chance at an unpredicted life. Her aunt Madame Liang wisely, jadedly counsels her on the impossibility of returning home. Weilong tries to imagine leaving: "I know I've changed. I didn't much like myself before, and now I like myself even less. I'm going back because I want to be a new person."[39] But she cannot go back. She acknowledges that she has been living a dream, that the clothes and parties are what any young girl would want; small wonder they come at a price. Her problem at the start of the story is purely financial, or so it seems to her: she needs money for school. And yet, from the outset, Madame Liang warns her that there will be a price to pay. Only when it is too late does Madame Liang spell out the full implications of Weilong's bargain. She wanted to change, and she has changed, but, by changing in the wrong direction, she has lost her way and forfeited her ability to return home.

Weilong's story is a feminist fable. In it, Chang methodically dissects the difficulties faced by an ordinary girl who hungers for something a little more. *Aloeswood Incense* depicts the rapidity with which others will prey on an indecisive young woman who wants something but does not quite know what that something is.

In 1947, Chang wrote the screenplay for *Long Live the Missus* (太太萬歲 Taitai Wan Sui), a Chinese classic, and her second screenplay and second collaboration with director Sang Hu.[40] *Long Live the Missus* combines elements of Chinese culture with the Hollywood comedy of remarriage, in which a husband and wife find their way back to a renegotiated happiness. In *Long Live the Missus*, it is the husband, Zhiyuan, not the wife, whose wandering gets him into trouble. He is saved from ruin by his resourceful, witty, and forgiving spouse, Sizhen. *Long Live the Missus* is a small masterpiece, full of well-drawn women characters. In addition to Sizhen, we have her mother-in-law, a charismatic and demanding force; her mother, the cheerful and long-suffering wife of a playboy-turned-scholar; Mama Zhang, an opinionated maid who demands a raise; Zhiyuan's mistress, Mimi; Mimi's fellow partner in gold-digging; and finally, Sizhen's wholesome sister-in-law, whose romance with Sizhen's brother serves as an innocent foil to her increasingly troubled marriage.

Chang, who, at twenty-seven, was in the process of divorcing Hu Lancheng, her unfaithful first husband, often writes about unhappy marriages, infidelity, and the ways in which couples negotiate major rifts. In an essay, she meditates on the popularity of the Norwegian playwright Henrik Ibsen in China: "Chinese people have learned how to leave home from Nora in *A Doll's House*. There can be no doubt that this stylishly bleak gesture has left an extremely deep impression on a generation of Chinese youth."[41] At the end of *A Doll's House*, after saving her family from financial ruin only to have her husband turn on her in anger for overstepping her wifely role, Nora walks out. Her abrupt and final departure sent an earthquake through world literature.

Its aftershocks continued in 1940s China. Chang contrasts the Chinese admiration for Nora's "stylishly bleak gesture" with the practicality of a constrained environment, where leaving is not only impractical but impossible. She describes a play she is writing and hopes to have produced, entitled "Let's Go! Let's Go Upstairs!" In it, "a destitute man throws himself and his entire family on the mercy of their relatives. When a quarrel erupts, he leaps indignantly up with the exclamation: 'I can't take anymore of this. Let's go! Let's get out of here!' Mournfully, his wife interjects: 'But where are we to go?' He gathers his wife and children around him and says: 'Let's go! Let's go upstairs.' At dinnertime, when it is announced that food is on the table, they come back down again."[42] The empty gesture of the dependent who storms out is pathetically, wonderfully comic. It also emphasizes the revolution of Nora's—and anyone's—total departure from home. Leaving is hard, but the desire to leave is familiar, and even the most pathetic of dependents may occasionally indulge in a diminished version of the gesture, if only to storm upstairs for a bit. I do not know what became of this imagined play; Chang's essays often refer to writing projects imagined, in process, or stalled. However, in *Long Live the Missus*, she revisits a similar scene of domestic frustration and comic attempts at departure and return. This time, her ironic vision focuses on a wife who, in pulling her wandering husband home, achieves a small triumph. Sizhen's husband's failures force her, like Ibsen's Nora, to exercise new skills in negotiation that she did not know herself to possess.

The movie opens with a highly choreographed slapstick scene that sets all the pressures of money, success, and family in motion. It is the morning of her mother-in-law's birthday, and wife and maid are hurrying to set the parlor in order. When the maid breaks a small bowl and cuts her finger, Sizhen hurriedly hides the shard under the newspaper, lying that the noise came from the neighbor children in the courtyard. This makes the mother-in-law cluck that she hopes that soon, she, too, will have children, and that they will be better behaved. Always just barely a step ahead, Sizhen keeps having to move the evidence of the broken bowl—under the newspaper, then a cushion—her fibs mounting all the while. But all her efforts to avoid revealing the bad luck of a broken bowl on a birthday keep bumping up against other, larger challenges of traditional young married life: When will you have a baby? When will my son get a raise?

The son is the hapless Zhiyuan, who is working in a bank, bored and impatient to get ahead. He goes to Sizhen's father for a loan but is rebuffed. As he is leaving, one of his father-in-law's friends stops by, and their easy talk about money just reminds the young husband of how far he has to go to succeed. One openly acknowledged sign of success is a mistress. Everyone in the movie accepts affairs, mistresses, and even concubines (that is, established, publicly acknowledged long-term affairs); most of the other characters talk about a mistress as an everyday indulgence for a prosperous man. When Zhiyuan returns from his first trip to Hong Kong, Sizhen notices the pretty woman who has come home with his business partner, joking that two left, but three have returned. Taking a mistress is an understood symbol of prosperity. It also can be a sign that a wife has limitations: she may be boring, or she may not yet have had a baby. Despite these retrograde values, *Long Live the Missus* feels light, deft, and modern. Its sophistication about sexual desire, its stylish modern settings and costumes—so many boldly patterned qipaos and oversized 1940s Western suits—all contribute to its cosmopolitan air.

Unlike her restlessly ambitious but ill-starred husband, Sizhen is content. She wishes for a radio and a pretty brooch, but these are the ordinary wants of a modern woman. As a *taitai*, she does not work and expresses no desire to do so. She does not hunger for a career, either, and, while she is aware that others want and expect her to have a baby, she expresses no maternal longing. She wishes her husband would take her to the movies occasionally, so when she finds a pair of ticket stubs in his jacket pocket, she feels a pang—both at the fun lost and, more keenly, at the probable affair they indicate. In short, Sizhen is not an especially modern woman, and the ways in which she wins her husband back (lying, weeping, tricking his mistress, and generally plying feminine wiles) are hardly modern or feminist. The technologies of the movie (the radios, airplanes, telephone calls, and movie dates) make it more modern than the plot. We see the plane to Hong Kong take off and land at an airfield in Shanghai, and there are several heroic shots of Sizhen from below, as if she herself is an aviator, off on a heroic mission, not a wife waving her businessman husband goodbye.

Sizhen lies about a broken bowl in the opening scene, but everyone in *Long Live the Missus* lies. The sister-in-law lies about dating Sizhen's brother; the mistress lies to ensnare Zhiyuan; and Zhiyuan lies about the affair. But only Sizhen lies for other people. And she lies and lies. She lies about how her husband will travel to Hong Kong because her mother-in-law fears air travel; she lies about where she is going, helping cover up the young lovers' courtship; she lies to get a loan from her father, claiming that her mother-in-law has dozens of gold bars in a safe. Finally, when the deputy manager runs off with all the money and bankrupts the company, she constructs the most elaborate and dishonest lie of all to trap the mistress and win Zhiyuan back.

When Zhiyuan's mistress reads in the papers that his business has failed, she tries one last con to wring some money out of him: she tells him she is pregnant. Seeing through the ruse, Sizhen sets a trap. She goes to the mistress's apartment and congratulates her on her pregnancy, adding that the bankruptcy means there is no money for her. Instead, she proposes they "eat bitterness together," invoking a Chinese proverb, and that the mistress join their household. She will not mind sharing a bed with Sizhen, will she? But, perhaps (Sizhen looks pointedly around the mistress's fashionable apartment), she and Zhiyuan should move in with her? This is the last straw, and the mistress sends her away. Zhiyuan is the wanderer who is snared in a net of trouble in this film; Sizhen is the reasonable wife who calls him home. Home is now for them a renegotiated space where he understands her support for him, and she sees his weaknesses and vulnerabilities more clearly.

Of all the strategies for approaching modern life, wandering is the riskiest. If Margaret Wise Brown represents the potential of letting someone wander before forcing them into a life pattern, Chang's fiction—and her life—demonstrate the dangers. Her story reminds us of how dependent individual lives are on historical contingencies, and how ready patriarchal forces are to clamp down on women who attempt to wander off the predictable paths. Throughout her writing, Chang is especially subtle at showing how women's desire, once ignited, works at odds with other goals, especially around education and work. Weilong's vulnerability to that closet full of custom clothing is but one of many examples in which desire interrupts one of Chang's character's plans. Layered on all of this are the forces of war, which complicate and intensify Chang's characters' motives and possibilities.

In *Aloeswood Incense* and *Long Live the Missus*, Chang finds gullible youth who wander into the traps set by urban sophisticates. In *Lust, Caution*, she meditates on the vulnerability of a young woman who is less sophisticated than Chang herself, a young woman who, like Chang, must shed any naivete she may have had in college. By the time Chang returned to Shanghai and began her career, she was turning her eye on human folly. And yet another—both aesthetically subtler and more geographically wide-ranging—wandering is at work in her life. Long a lover of movies and Chinese opera, she might have found her way to screenplays in any case. After all, many of her contemporaries did. But Chang needed to write screenplays because, in 1947, she was blacklisted. After Japan's defeat, she was depicted in the press as a fallen woman, tarred by her husband's collaboration with the occupying government. In turning to movies, she could keep writing. And, while she is popular in China today, her work was banned there for decades.

Chang scholars debate her political affiliations, but it seems most relevant to recognize the wisdom she showed in making her opinions difficult to discern. Driven by an intense belief in herself as a writer, Chang brilliantly portrayed the fate of the lost wanderer while, in her life, she cannily wandered to survive, remaining in the open even as she kept some things very much to herself. As Nicole Huang puts it, "Writing and publishing was her way of rising from the ruins and resisting being swept into oblivion."[43] This complex and sophisticated perspective colors all her writing with a delicious, deep, intelligent, ironic voice.

PART 2

Rebels

Rebels show courage, but courage is not a permanent state. Rebels have moments of self-doubt. Courage is a decision made many times. As the wanderer must choose, again and again, to persist in her wandering when others urge her to stick to prescribed paths, rebels, too, must remain steadfast in their opposition to the current. Fiction, with its closely narrated connections between thought and action, is particularly good at depicting mental courage, that internal resistance to convention that helps women retain a sense of self, an awareness of being a private person with private desires, even if their outward actions are not—or not yet—legible as resistant or rebellious. These private moments remind us of the humanity of rebels and may, in turn, inspirit us to more moments of courageous action.

In writing *Mrs. Dalloway*, a novel about a prosperous matron who gives a dinner party, Woolf chose a protagonist deliberately inhospitable to rebellion. Clarissa Dalloway is no rebel, and yet she thinks like one. When she fears that her party may fail, she regrets the risk of gathering people in her home: "She could see Peter out of the tail of her eye, criticising her, there, in that corner. Why, after all, did she do these things? Why seek pinnacles and stand drenched in fire?" Mrs. Dalloway is emphatically not the Joan of Arc of Mayfair, and there is wonderful comic irony in the image.

Clarissa knows she is exaggerating under Peter's gaze: "He made her see herself; exaggerate."[1] The irony is not wholly at Clarissa's expense. When the narrator reveals that Clarissa knows she is exaggerating, she invites us to recognize ourselves in Clarissa's anxiety. That intense feeling of exposure, as if we are being burned at the stake, amuses us out of familiarity.

Earlier in the novel, Clarissa thinks "that it was very, very dangerous to live even one day."[2] What is the tone of that thought? We might be tempted to dismiss her, except that each day is in fact dangerous. Septimus does not survive his, and we leave Rezia, alone, a widow in a strange land. Even Peter faces the ordinary dangers of unemployment and the need to figure out what to do about obtaining a divorce for poor Daisy, the young wife in India who loves him but whom he does not want to marry. Clarissa's thought about danger comes as she watches the taxis on a London street. Standing at the gates of St. James's Park, she looks out at the traffic and feels her solitariness. She imagines herself "far out to sea and alone." In this, Clarissa anticipates Mr. Ramsay in *To the Lighthouse*, who marches about in the novel's final section, reciting snippets from William Cowper's "The Castaway": "We perish'd, each alone." She also anticipates Septimus's hallucination, when he feels himself "macerated, like a veil on a rock."[3] He imagines himself as the shipwrecked Odysseus, having lost his ship and his crew, washed ashore on Nausicaa's rocky island, saved only by the goddess Ino's veil.

Where we sense self-dramatization in Mrs. Dalloway and Mr. Ramsay, the link to Septimus encourages us to look again. We are meant to take his pain seriously, and, in doing so, we are invited to consider taking Mrs. Dalloway and Mr. Ramsay's pain seriously, too. A person need not be suicidally depressed for us to believe their feelings of pain and isolation. Woolf asks us to notice extreme isolation and atomization, and to recognize how ordinary it is to feel at sea, cut off from human connection. This awareness makes the wonder of human connection and communication, when it does occur, all the more precious.

In *To the Lighthouse*, Mrs. Ramsay—a devoted wife, a mother of eight, and an attentive hostess—retains a sense of herself in thoughts she does not share. While Mr. Ramsay reads Sir Walter Scott and mentally composes a rebuttal to Scott's detractors—"Well, let them improve upon that, he thought as he finished the chapter"—Mrs. Ramsay has a less dialectical, more creative reading practice.[4] She reads not to find evidence in her favor, but for beauty and ease, "so reading she was ascending, she felt, on to the top, on to the summit. How satisfying!. . . . And then there it was, suddenly entire; she held it in her hands, beautiful and reasonable, clear and complete, here—the sonnet."[5] Despite Mr. Ramsay liking "to think that she was not clever, not book-learned at all," even wondering "if she understood what she was reading," Woolf's narrator is unambiguous: she understands.[6] She finishes reading the poem, and, in an echo of the final line of *Mrs. Dalloway*, "there it was, suddenly entire." Her husband, by contrast, "could not remember the whole shape of the thing."[7] Hers is a small internal rebellion, but it strengthens her and sows the seeds for other moments of resistance, as when, moments later, she refuses to tell Mr. Ramsay she loves him: "She knew that he was thinking, . . . Will you not tell me just for once that you love me? He was thinking that. . . . But she could not do it; she could not say it. . . . And as she looked at him she began to smile, for though she had not said a word, he knew, of course he knew, that she loved him."[8] It is a tiny act of resistance, and at first it seems hardly worth mentioning. And yet it is essential to her character and our understanding of her power. For all the ways that Mrs. Ramsay outwardly resembles the Victorian ideal of the self-sacrificing angel in the house, Woolf ensures that we witness her holding something in reserve for herself, and that we see the Ramsays' intellects and understandings as different and complementary, one neither inferior nor superior to the other.

Earlier in the day, Mrs. Ramsay is troubled by an unwelcome, automatic thought: "We are in the hands of the Lord."[9] She is quietly knitting, an acceptable activity for a woman, but the narrator is careful to tell us that, in these moments of "sitting and looking," she often "became the thing she looked at—that light, for example." In that meditative state, the phrase intrudes: "Instantly she was annoyed with herself for saying that. Who had said it? Not she; she had been trapped into saying something she did not mean. She looked up over her knitting . . ., searching as she alone could search into her mind and her heart, purifying out of existence that lie, any lie."[10] In the next two paragraphs, Mrs. Ramsay struggles to rid herself of the "lie" of this cliché with the rigor of a philosopher. Mr. Ramsay passes her as she thinks. He is laughing, thinking of Hume, grown fat, and stuck in a bog, but she is the one asking a central philosophical question: "How could any Lord have made this world? . . . There is no reason, order, justice: but suffering, death, the poor."[11] Who is the superior philosopher?

Lily Briscoe, the artist visiting the Ramsays, also practices internal rebellion, but her rebellions occasionally emerge into the world. When Mrs. Ramsay silently pleads with her to make the odious Charles Tansley comfortable at dinner, she resists, remembering her own work. When she finally exclaims, "Oh, Mr. Tansley . . . do take me to the Lighthouse with you. I should so love it," she is repelled by her own insincerity.[12] Her art, too, is a rebellion. Painting in the modernist vein, she insists on remaining faithful to her vision of deep colors and strong shapes, despite the fashion of the region: "The jacmanna was bright violet; the wall staring white. She would not have considered it honest to tamper with the bright violet and the staring white, since she saw them like that, fashionable though it was, since Mr. Paunceforte's visit, to see everything pale, elegant, semitransparent."[13] There is so much integrity in that small phrase: "She would not have considered it honest." Lily is a painter, but she is not a professional; she answers only to herself, and she demands of herself complete honesty. There is no question of her following the fashion: her belief in her vision as an artist, so wary, even fragile, when others are looking at her work, is unwavering when it comes to the painting itself.

If novels introduce us to rebellion in thought, in this novel these are rebellions so mild as to barely make a ripple. Still, this mildness reminds us of how hard it is to act. If Mrs. Ramsay's thoughts interrupt and trouble her, how much effort might it take to speak them? Woolf's nonfiction treats action more directly. In August 1940, more than a year before the United States entered World War II, Woolf wrote "Thoughts on Peace in an Air Raid" for an American women's magazine, *The Forum* (and reprinted in *The New Republic*). In it, Woolf encourages her audience to contribute to the effort to defeat Hitler despite women's lack of defined political power. To an audience divided from the blitzkrieg by an ocean, Woolf describes how air raids make thinking difficult, sometimes impossible. The absence of women's voices from government does feel hopeless, she acknowledges. We might well ask, "Why not bury the head in the pillow, plug the ears, and cease this futile activity of idea making?" Instead, she exhorts us to think. Despite the obstacles, women can use their intellectual power: "'I will not cease from mental fight,' Blake wrote. Mental fight means thinking against the current, not with it."[14]

Woolf urges mental fight, but she finds it difficult, both because she is in immediate danger from bombs and because her opinions put her at odds with some of her contemporaries. Central to the essay is a simple countdown—"One, two, three, four, five, six"—representing the time she waits to see if her house will be bombed: "The bomb did not fall. But during those seconds of suspense all thinking stopped."[15] This physical danger leads Woolf to ask her readers to think on her behalf. There is another, intellectual challenge, too, in thinking against the current. Woolf repeats the image of thinking against the current in her diary, writing: "I'm fundamentally, I think, an outsider. I do my best work and feel most braced with my back to the wall. It's an odd feeling though, writing against the current: difficult entirely to disregard the current. Yet of course I shall."[16] Feeling "braced" is vivid but not comfortable; Woolf, like her character Lily Briscoe, will not be dishonest, but honesty, when the current runs another way, is hard.

Woolf located the legacy of mental fight in the eighteenth-century feminist Mary Wollstonecraft. Her essay on Wollstonecraft is part of a quartet of essays on lesser-known Romantic-era figures, calculated to show "how much influence circumstances have upon opinions." As Woolf wrote, comparing their response to the French Revolution:

> Great wars are strangely intermittent in their effects. The French Revolution took some people and tore them asunder; others it passed over without disturbing a hair of their heads. Jane Austen, it is said, never mentioned it; Charles Lamb ignored it; Beau Brummell never gave the matter a thought. But to Wordsworth and to Godwin it was the dawn; unmistakably they saw France standing on the top of golden hours, And human nature seeming born again.[17]

The dry phrase "strangely intermittent" introduces Woolf's startling contrast. In reminding us of the truism—that historical contemporaries have wildly differing views—Woolf encourages discernment and humility both about the past and the present. Not everyone's blood rang with the glory of the revolution; some, like the dandy Beau Brummell, lived through it without it "disturbing a hair of their heads." (Although, strictly speaking, Brummell was only fifteen at the end of Louis XVI's reign in 1793.) These contrasts form the introduction to Woolf's example of the revolutionary spirit: Mary Wollstonecraft, author of *A Vindication of the Rights of Woman*.

For Woolf, Wollstonecraft embodies an ideal combination of belief and circumstance. Her passion for justice, in Woolf's telling, emerged from her witnessing and trying to prevent her father from beating her mother: "The Revolution thus was not merely an event that had happened outside her; it was an active agent in her own blood."[18] Woolf's essay details Wollstonecraft's passion for justice, her commitment to educational reform, her exciting life, her writings, her participation in the intellectual discourse of her time (including her direct and powerful attacks on Rousseau and Burke), her experimental marriage to William Godwin, and her premature death just days after giving birth to the daughter who would grow up to become Mary Shelley, the author of *Frankenstein*.

Amid all Wollstonecraft's courage, Woolf pauses over a moment of confusion, when she sees Louis XVI being carried off to his execution:

> But when she was in Paris lodging by herself in a great house, and saw with her own eyes the King whom she despised driving past surrounded by National Guards and holding himself with greater dignity than she expected, then, "I can scarcely tell you why," the tears came to her eyes. "I am going to bed," the letter ended, "and, for the first time in my life, I cannot put out the candle." Things were not so simple after all. She could not understand even her own feelings. She saw the most cherished of her convictions put into practice—and her eyes filled with tears. She had won fame and independence and the right to live her own life—and she wanted something different.[19]

This small moment of witness, in which the tyrant is seen to be a man behaving with dignity in his final hours, startles her. Her convictions do not change, but she is brought back into her individuality, her mortality. Wollstonecraft's tears bring us back around to Mrs. Dalloway's isolation. Society does not nurture the spirit of rebellion in girls and women. Nevertheless, many women possess this trait. For some, being a rebel remains confined to thought. Still, even thoughts can help a woman retain her sense of self in a world seeking to erase her desires. For others, open rebellion becomes the best available strategy when so much in the world is so wrong.

We need rebels. They blaze the path for the rest of us. The rebels profiled in this book, Vera Brittain and Muriel Rukeyser, are not the most radical women of their time. Instead, they continue the idea that I have been tracing through Woolf's words, that a rebel spirit exists in many of us, even when it is barely detectable. Both Brittain and Rukeyser are among the most articulate at documenting the mixed feelings behind brave action, the moments of hesitation and despair.

Vera Brittain (1893–1970) grew up in a prosperous provincial home. She loved tennis parties and pretty clothes, but her parents' deep reluctance to send her to university set her at odds with her father. She fought him for several years before he relented. She entered Somerville College, Oxford, in the fall of 1914, just as the war broke out. Brittain fought for an education; she fought to volunteer as a nurse; and she fought harder to get posted to France. The senseless violence she witnessed led her to a lifelong commitment to pacifism.

Growing up in New York City, Muriel Rukeyser (1913–1980) had a rebellious spirit from childhood. Her birth, just before World War I broke out, was central to her personal mythology. As a college student, she traveled to Scottsboro, Alabama, to witness the trial of Black men her age falsely accused of rape, setting her on a path of witnessing and writing that continued through the Vietnam War. In 1936, only twenty-two and already a committed leftist, she traveled to Barcelona for the People's Olympiad, the anti-fascist alternative to Hitler's games. Those games never happened, interrupted by the outbreak of the Spanish Civil War. In Rukeyser's account of her commitment to poetry as a form of resistance, she was remarkably consistent: many times, she tells the story of her flight from war-torn Barcelona, and "the singular image of a boat generates and communicates a vast network of imaginative associations."[20] In her posthumously published novel *Savage Coast*, Rukeyser shares her hesitations about how much good she can do, what the role for a foreign woman in wartime might be. And in her 1968 "Poem (I lived in the first century of world wars)," she documents the cost of living a life bombarded by news: "Most mornings I would be more or less insane, / The newspapers would arrive with their careless stories."[21] Rukeyser is as close to a born rebel as they come, yet some of her best work combines political conviction with a tender recognition of its toll.

Both Rukeyser and Brittain write frequently about the intrusion of the news into their writing lives, and the ways that violence demands to be resisted even as it curtails the imagination. In this, they continue Woolf's message from "Thoughts on Peace in an Air Raid." Both writers' lives were shaped by war, and, of all the women in this book, they witnessed the most violence. They are also the only two who became mothers. In their motherhood, too, they balanced convention with rebellion. Brittain did not change her name upon marriage—to the shock and chagrin of many of her readers and correspondents—and she had a commuter marriage, not following her husband from England to his job at Cornell University. Instead, she stayed in London and continued living with her best friend, the writer Winifred Holtby, who helped her raise the children. Rukeyser, who was queer and whose most important relationships were with women, did not disclose the father of her son for many years. Even so, she insisted on being addressed as "Mrs. Rukeyser." These rebels lived in our midst, mixing rebellion and conformity in unpredictable and fascinating new combinations.

Vera Brittain
1893–1970

FROM PATRIOT TO PACIFIST

Vera Brittain (1893–1970) wanted to be a writer from girlhood; she published poetry during World War I, journalism in college, and several novels thereafter, but her success as a writer came with her memoir of her service in the war and her conversion to pacifism, *Testament of Youth*. Like Brittain, Virginia Woolf was a pacifist; in an essay on peace, she wrote, "We must compensate the man for the loss of his gun."[1] Woolf knew that men have defined their masculinity with warfare and acknowledges the need for peacemakers to offer them alternatives, but she does not consider the possibility of a woman needing similar compensation. For Woolf, as for many women of her generation, the problem of war and violence was a man's problem. As they saw it, the challenge of peace work was to find something to replace a man's gun. The slightly cheap Freudianism of the remark was part of the way Woolf conceived of the problem of turning away from violence: as almost entirely bound up in notions of manhood. Yet, in the first decades of the twentieth century, as opportunities opened for upper-middle-class women, new types of women emerged in public, including women patriots, who, like their brothers, gravitated to what they saw as the patriotic duty, even glamour, of war. One of those women was Vera Brittain. Born in 1893, Brittain was just eleven years Woolf's junior, but that eleven years and a range of other differences—her social class, her provincial upbringing, her character—set them a world apart.

Brittain fought for and won the right to go to college, despite a conventional upbringing in a conservative town. But, when World War I broke out, she left university to become a nurse. First she rebelled against her exclusion from university, then against the idea that women be excluded from war service, taking on some of the most grueling and dangerous work available to women at the time. Only later did Brittain begin to question the purpose of war. But, at just twenty-one in 1914, Brittain was susceptible to propaganda in ways that Woolf, at thirty-two, was not. Woolf was a lifelong pacifist, but Brittain changed her mind: in 1914, she urged her brother to enlist, but her awful losses in the war altered her. She committed her postwar life, from 1918 to 1970—more than fifty years—to peace work. Brittain's story has something to tell us about how an ambitious woman, eager to contribute, unafraid of hard work, attracted to sacrifice, and desirous of fame, navigates public life during and after wartime. Her 1933 war memoir, *Testament of Youth*, remains the best-known account by a woman of World War I service and is a key text for understanding how people come to change their minds. It is also a story of a how a self-described provincial young lady finds the courage to stand up to her family, not once, but again and again. Brittain was a conventional person, not a born rebel, so those moments when she cannot conform stand out.

Brittain was born in December 1893, the elder child of a bourgeois family, in Staffordshire, England. Her father was the wealthy owner of a paper mill, and her mother the pretty and shy daughter of a local church musician. Her younger brother, Edward, was her close companion. Brittain spent several years trying to persuade her father to let her attend university. (His permission was essential, as he controlled the family money.) He finally relented, and she began university in October 1914. She was not quite twenty-one. It was a hard-won but short-lived victory. As she opens her memoir, "When the Great War broke out, it came to me not as a superlative tragedy, but as an interruption of the most exasperating kind."[2]

After first seeing the war as an interruption, she came to see it as an opportunity for her brother and, later, herself. Close to Edward and his Oxford-bound friends, she fell in love with one of them. She and Roland Leighton became engaged during the war. Soon Edward and his friends had all enlisted and were waiting for their postings. Within the year, Brittain, too, decided to take a leave from college and sign up for war service: nursing in a Voluntary Aid Detachment. She became, in the language of the war, a VAD. In December 1915, Brittain was nursing in London and awaiting Roland's return for a Christmas leave when he was killed in action. Blind with grief, Brittain struggled to find meaning in nursing and recommitted to the war by volunteering to go abroad. She served in Malta, then in France. Roland's friends Victor Richardson and Geoffrey Thurlow and, finally, her brother were all killed in the war. As her losses mounted, and as she nursed German soldiers, she continued to see the value of her willing sacrifice, even as she railed against war as the object of that sacrifice.

Much of the rest of Brittain's life was dedicated to coming to terms with the war and her many losses in it. She returned to Somerville College, Oxford, and switched her major to history. She became friends with the writer Winifred Holtby, and they lived together after college, deferring marriage and striving to make it independently as writers. Throughout the 1920s she lectured on behalf of the League of Nations. She published her first novel, *The Dark Tide*, in 1923. Two years later, she married the academic George Catlin, and they had two children, a son, John, and a daughter, Shirley. Catlin took a job teaching at Cornell University. Unable to cope with upstate New York, Brittain returned home and invited Holtby to rejoin her household, and they began what she called their "semi-detached marriage," commuting between London and

Ithaca, New York.[3] In 1933, she published *Testament of Youth*, which remains her best-known work. In 1935, Brittain's father committed suicide, and, a few months later, Holtby died of kidney disease, an affliction she had been battling since 1931. Two years later, in 1937, Brittain joined the Peace Pledge Union, and during World War II she wrote a series of *Letters to Peace Lovers*, preaching pacifism and speaking out against the Allied bombing of German civilian targets. She continued to write for women's rights—especially the rights of working mothers, for peace, against colonialism, and against apartheid, until her death in 1970.

Vera Brittain's 1933 memoir, *Testament of Youth*, documents the gradual transformation of its author from undergraduate to nurse to pacifist. Its opening line, naming the war as simultaneous tragedy and interruption, sets in motion the dual perspective that marks Brittain's account, representing at once her memory and her postwar perspective. In so doing, Brittain contrasts the horrors and heroism of the war with her gradual emergence into a life greater and larger than she could have imagined. Embedded in Brittain's form is an account of the complex interdependence of opportunity, loss, and the chance to change one's mind.

In *Testament of Youth*, Brittain refuses to disparage her younger self; instead, she records the gap between what it was like to be in the war and how she sees it, years later, as a pacifist. Brittain's sincerity and continual pauses over the gap between then and now keep our focus on how much the world and she have changed. An admirer of George Eliot and Olive Schreiner, Brittain, like Eliot's great heroine Dorothea Brooke, suffered from the problem of the ardent woman looking for a cause in a world that is uninterested in providing her with one. It is the problem Eliot, in the opening pages of *Middlemarch*, associates with Saint Theresa: "Many Theresas have been born who found for themselves no epic life wherein there was a constant unfolding of far-resonant action; perhaps only a life of mistakes, the offspring of a certain spiritual grandeur ill-matched with the meanness of opportunity."[4] The problem Eliot identified—how to match ordinary circumstances with an ardent soul in search of an epic life, the central problem of her heroine Dorothea Brooke's life—is one that Brittain shared. Like Dorothea, Brittain was a Theresa: she saw herself as such and could even occasionally laugh at the hubris of the self-conception. In books like *Middlemarch* and Olive Schreiner's *Story of an African Farm*, Brittain found confirmation of her own way of being.

Even before the war, Brittain was casting about for a purpose, but it was not obvious that she would rebel so thoroughly against her upbringing. As an adolescent, Brittain participated enthusiastically in the typical pastimes of girls of her class—tennis, dances, and lectures—but she also developed an increasingly strong determination to pursue her education. By her own accounts, Brittain was an attractive, happy young woman who loved nice clothes, young men, and sport. Her girlhood diary moves equally fluently among delight in tennis, neighborhood flirtations, and self-doubt about her ability to excel on her exams. But running throughout is an enthusiasm for Eliot and Schreiner. When she reads their works, or hears a good sermon from the progressive pastor whom she admired, she rededicates herself to living for something more.

In *Testament of Youth*, looking back fondly at her younger self, Brittain manages to show us her girlish naivete in ways that urge us to condemn not Brittain but the social milieu that cultivated ignorance among its young ladies. She achieves this through retrospect and self-citation, as she explains early on: "The naïve quotations from my youthful diary which I have used, and intend to use, are included in this book in order to give some idea of the effect of the War, with its stark disillusionments, its miseries unmitigated by polite disguise, upon the unsophisticated *ingénue* who 'grew up' (in a purely social sense) just before it broke out."[5]

To her family and those around her, she must have seemed perfectly prepared to assume her expected role as a wealthy provincial wife. However, her intellectual hunger made her long for a university education. She had a good secondary education at St. Monica's School, with university-educated female teachers. The headmistress, Louise Heath-Jones, took her to suffrage meetings and introduced her to the writings of Olive Schreiner. Brittain recalls reading Schreiner's treatise *Women and Labour* as a turning point in her adolescence:

> Miss Heath Jones lent me the book soon after its publication, and I can still tingle with the excitement of the passage which reinforced me . . . in my determination to go to college. . . .
>
> "There is no closed door we do not intend to force open; and there is no fruit in the garden of knowledge it is not our determination to eat."
>
> Thus it was in St. Monica's garden, beside a little overgrown pool where the plump goldfish slid idly in and out of the shadows, and the feathered grasses drooped their heavy heads to the water's edge, that I first visualised in rapt childish ecstasy a world in which women would no longer be the second-rate, unimportant creatures that they were now considered.[6]

Emulating Schreiner and rewriting the book of Genesis in a feminist key, Brittain places herself in a garden, hungrily consuming knowledge and stories of the quest for it. Disavowing any prohibitions, Schreiner asserts her right to eat of all the fruits in the garden, and Brittain is her enthusiastic disciple. It is a powerful conversion narrative: for Brittain, reading had the power, if not to change her mind, then to confirm her in her beliefs, to give words to what she felt, and to strengthen her in her rebellion. The headmistress's partner was Brittain's maternal aunt, Florence Bervon, and both women had gone to university. Brittain writes: "My budding ambition to go to college—which developed as soon as I discovered that such places as women's colleges existed, and learnt what they stood for—met with real sympathy from both Principals and staff."[7] But, despite the headmistress's university education, St. Monica's was not a preparatory school; the education she received there was not nearly enough to prepare her for Oxford entrance examinations. Moreover, her peers had "no particular interest [in] or sympathy" for her ambitions.[8]

Brittain's first rebellion was to fight her family for the right to such an education. *Testament of Youth* describes the strained domestic atmosphere of an angry adolescent at odds with her parents. Vera Brittain fought, and she did not fight quietly: "I never ceased—though often now with a failing heart . . .—to pester my parents to send me to college."[9] With exasperation and impotent rage, Brittain endured her father insisting that "little girls" listen to their elders as she watched him ungrudgingly buy her a piano, the cost of which would have paid for a year's tuition at Oxford: "Each fresh refusal to spend another penny on my education . . . plunged me into further depths of gloom."[10]

While Edward, three years younger, attended Uppingham School, Brittain lived at home, attending extension lectures and fighting with her parents for the right to attend university. In January 1913, she wrote in her diary: "Edward went back to Uppingham today. Now the boring time begins."[11] For students, the academic calendar of Oxford marked the year, but the daughters and sisters of educated men marked their time as interesting or boring, depending on whether their brothers were home. Still, she went to lectures and set herself an ambitious reading program, which she often failed to complete, and then berated herself for her failures in her diaries.

The desire to go to university was Brittain's first rebellion, but the mind she had to change was not her own but her father's: without his financial support, a university education would have been impossible. Vera's father, not university-educated himself, believed such an education was wasted on a girl. The first key person to make significant headway in breaking down Brittain's father's resistance was a family friend, a lawyer whose son had won a scholarship to Oxford. Spending the night with the Brittains, this man boasted about his son, and Vera's father joined in the competition. "Not to be outdone in parental self-congratulation," Brittain writes, her father "not only mentioned his determination to send Edward to Oxford, but threw in my own continual requests to go to college to make up the balance. To his surprise, our visitor took this expression of feminine ambition entirely as a matter of course, and even mentioned one or two of his son's acquaintances among the women students."[12] She continues, "The fact that his highly respected old friend regarded the presence of women at Oxford as in no way remarkable undoubtedly caused him to revise his opinion on the whole subject of the higher education of daughters."[13] The family friend was a trusted connection visiting from an adjoining community, bringing news of slightly different customs. If you are interested in change, it helps to know people from a place where customs are slightly different. Change comes about when an idea crosses into a new community. This man whom Vera's father hoped to impress made it permissible for the family to give in to their daughter without fear of shame.

Once this family friend assured Vera's father that there were nice, normal girls at college, any remaining barriers fell away rapidly. Thus, when Brittain attended some extension lectures over the summer, she got up the courage to ask the professor how to apply to college and found that "the genial matter-of-factness with which he gave it seemed to dispel all doubts, and made the customary objections look so trivial that they were hardly ever mentioned again."[14] So, in the summer of 1913, Brittain interviewed for a place at Somerville College, Oxford, with its principal, Emily Penrose.

That June, she had met her brother's beloved friends Victor Richardson, Geoffrey Thurlow, and Roland Leighton on a visit to Uppingham. Edward was somewhat in awe of his handsome and charismatic friend Roland, whose mother was a writer, and

Roland made an immediate impression on Vera as well. Proud of his friendship, Edward brought Roland home with him for the Easter break in 1914. On that visit, Roland and Vera began to fall in love. Brittain had already read Schreiner's nonfiction, so when Roland gave her Schreiner's 1883 novel, *The Story of an African Farm*, Vera was ready to find a kindred spirit in the heroine. In Lyndall, Schreiner's protagonist, Vera found an image of herself: a woman seeking an education against the odds. Roland and Vera's admiration for Schreiner became a touchstone in their courtship. It also helped keep alive Brittain's determination to get an education even as the obstacles faced by the fictional Lyndall—her poverty, her orphaned status—diverged sharply from Brittain's challenges, which were at first social and then centered primarily around the necessity of overcoming trauma to *return* to university after World War I.

Schreiner's novel traces the fate of three young people on an isolated South African farm: Em, the sweet but ungifted half-Boer daughter of the widowed farm owner; Lyndall, Em's beautiful and headstrong English cousin; and Waldo, the deeply spiritual son of the farm's German caretaker. From the beginning, Lyndall announces her intention to go to school, in spite of the seeming impossibility of that dream. In Schreiner, Brittain found a figure who linked her to both a beloved teacher and her boyfriend. Through the example of Lyndall, she discovered a model for persistence in her determination to seek entrance to Oxford despite her lack of education and the intense cramming that was necessary both before and during her time there.

Brittain attended Speech Day at Uppingham in July 1914—a day of prizes and honors for the graduating students—with Roland, who won most of the awards that year. In her memoir, Brittain writes with tremendous care about that day. Her description goes on and on (her floaty dress with the pink spots, her pretty hat) and then she explains that she spends so much time on recounting these details because that day was "the one perfect summer idyll" of my life. Etched, every moment of it, in memory.[15]

That same month, Brittain studied and took the last of the several tests necessary for admission to university, but, again, her father wavered. In August, war was declared, and Brittain's father briefly withdrew his permission only to relent once more. On October 9, 1914, Vera began her first term at Oxford. But she was alone. Instead of the imagined happy time at university with her brother, her boyfriend, and their friends, the men had all enlisted and were at various training camps. Disappointing as this was, the war suggested itself to Brittain as a purpose. She wanted her brother to join the Army immediately. Edward was always found a little wanting in her family. Vera, like Septimus's boss in Woolf's novel *Mrs. Dalloway*, or the women of the recruiting posters ("Women of Britain Say Go!"), seems to have felt that Edward would gain what he seemed to lack by fighting.

While she encouraged Edward's enlistment, when it came to Roland she hesitated: in him, she felt the pointlessness of a great young man, so full of potential, wasting his time and risking his life in fighting. Once he enlisted, she spent a leave arguing with him "as to why he wanted to go": "He said the vague reason of 'freedom' was hardly strong enough, he had no personal animosity against the enemy, & he certainly did not want to die himself. He has no love for the army at all & admitted that he wished he were at Oxford occupied with Classics & books."[16] Brittain saw the hollowness of these vague, disorganized thoughts, but at the same time, she understood the passion that led him to enlist, writing in the same entry of her diary: "The real reason seems to be the vague moral sense of acting up to his faith in, his highest opinion of, himself—the worship & indefinite pursuit of heroism in the abstract—oh! I know well enough really why he wants to go, why if I were a man *I* should want to go—though I cannot put into words my understanding of my own motives."[17]

This "vague moral sense" that she struggles to describe in 1914 is connected to the feeling Brittain found in characters created by George Eliot and Olive Schreiner. It links Brittain to Dorothea

Brooke and all the "other Theresas," hoping for their epic chance. It is why, in August 1914, she uneasily recalled a passage from George Eliot's novels, *Daniel Deronda*, which she quotes at length in *Testament of Youth*:

> There comes a terrible moment to many souls when the great movements of the world, the larger destinies of mankind, which have lain aloof in newspapers and other neglected reading, enter like an earthquake into their own lives—when the slow urgency of growing generations turns into the tread of an invading army or the dire clash of civil war. . . . Then it is that the submission of soul to the Highest is tested and. . . . life looks out from the scene of human struggle with the awful face of duty.[18]

World War I was such a great movement, and it did enter Brittain's life like an earthquake. The problem of the fictional village of Middlemarch and the suburban Buxton of Brittain's girlhood is that these quiet villages were unlikely to offer the kind of large destiny Brittain wanted. War extended even to the Buxtons of England, and, when it came, Brittain's reading offered her a way to think about facing "the larger destinies of mankind" with "the awful face of duty." For those with a more ironic or pragmatic turn of mind, this could seem self-important. Brittain herself worried that she was a mere "poseuse."[19] To understand Brittain and the changes she lived through, you have to suspend that ironic turn of mind and imagine what it feels like to take seriously the call to serve.

It cost Brittain a lot to fight for the right to attend university. She spoiled the domestic peace of her little family in ways that upset both her and her parents; she wore herself out studying for exams that measured skills beyond what had been taught at St. Monica's. When she took the entrance exam for literature in March 1914, she was initially frozen by the recognition that she had studied all wrong and then considered abandoning the test altogether.

After all the domestic turmoil and personal sacrifice, she gave up university after only a year to volunteer for war service.

Why did she change her mind again? In part, it was because she was lonely at Oxford without her brother and her boyfriend. With Roland in France in late March, she spent April not studying but scanning casualty lists. It is possible to understand her decision to ask for a year away from Oxford in May 1915 not so much as a rebellion but as a reversion to feminine norms. A university education is a risk, both financial and social; it is a new ambition for women. By contrast, dropping out of college to volunteer as a nurse while your boyfriend fights in a war may be brave, but it also satisfies gender norms. Her mother, for one, found voluntary nursing much easier to understand than attending university. Still, Brittain took seriously the idea of "the larger destinies of mankind" and was determined to follow her life's path where it led her. On June 15, 1915, Brittain was granted leave from Oxford. She passed her first-year exams two days later, and, by June 27, 1915, she was a VAD. Although civil service may have made more sense for her education and her talents, she wanted the hard physical labor of nursing. She was also drawn to the romance of the work: she speaks in *Testament of Youth* of how her work with wounded soldiers in the London hospital in 1915 was a way of nursing Roland by proxy.

On August 20, 1915, Roland came back to England on leave. He proposed marriage, but she hesitated. Her fierce independence and deep loyalty to her own convictions kept her from behaving precisely as expected. She wanted to be a writer and earn her own money and had not planned to marry before achieving financial independence. Her hesitation enraged her mother: "'She can't make up her mind, the little fool,' Mrs. Brittain was overheard to exclaim angrily the next morning."[20] After all the family tension over the college issue, how frustrating and predictable it must have been to have her mother angry at her for delaying a young woman's most conventional decision: accepting the proposal of a suitable man. Brittain longed for a connection with her mother, continually sought it, and recorded good outings and conversations with her with delighted surprise, but they were not sympathetic to each other. These stumbling blocks occurred intermittently in Brittain's life; her determination to think for herself, combined with her largely conventional nature, meant that she remained connected to her thoroughly conventional family but was often painfully just a bit out of step with their hopes and expectations for her. An unappreciated aspect of rebellion is the way that one decision to go against your family leads to dozens of little decisions and moments that remind you and your family of your distance from each other.

While *The Story of an African Farm* became a touchstone, uniting Vera and Roland, the poetry of Rupert Brooke nearly tore them apart. Their differing reactions to his poetry and Brittain's continued unalloyed admiration for it as late as 1933 offer another index of how far her mind did—and did not—change. Brooke was a gifted poet and a much-photographed, very handsome young man, most remembered today for his sonnet "The Soldier," which begins by imagining a heroic, English death: "If I should die, think only this of me: / That there's some corner of a foreign field / That is for ever England." The patriotism of this wish still has the power to divide readers. During the War, it proved valuable for recruiting soldiers, something that angered pacifists. Already a promising writer before the war, Brooke had been a friend of Virginia Woolf and an early part of what would become the Bloomsbury group, though he distanced himself from that set. In 1914, Brooke enlisted in the Navy and served as an officer but died early in the war, in April 1915, when it was still possible to believe that this would be a brief, heroic fight. Brooke's death, however, was not heroic; he contracted a blood infection from an insect bite en route to Gallipoli. He was twenty-seven. Dying on a ship in the Aegean Sea linked Brooke's demise to Lord Byron's, another poet-hero who died of blood poisoning on his way to war, and Brooke's posthumous reputation was secured. Since then, Rupert Brooke's poetry has stood for the last gasp of a heroic-sentimental mode killed by the machine gun as surely as Brooke himself died on the eve of the Dardanelles. He became a symbol, with those who opposed the war opposing what they saw as the exploitation of his memory, and others celebrating the clear, traditional beauty of his verse and mourning him as a martyr. Most famously, perhaps, Woolf opposed the exploitation of Brooke's good looks, his patriotic poetry, and his death as war propaganda. Woolf called his *Collected Poems* (1918) "a disgraceful sloppy sentimental rhapsody."[21]

Brooke's *1914 and Other Poems* came out a month after his death. In *Testament of Youth*, Brittain recalls a tutorial at Oxford, her tutor with the book fresh in its wrapping from Blackwell's bookshop. She asked her tutor to read some of the poems aloud and found herself moved beyond words. Remembering that moment in 1933, Brittain has only praise for Brooke and his legacy, privileging the memory of that first encounter as but the beginning of his posthumous fame: "For the young to whom Rupert Brooke's poems are now familiar as classics, it must be impossible to imagine how it felt to hear them for the first time."[22] Enthusiastic about his poems, she sent the book to Roland, who, like Vera, was an aspiring poet. Only after she sent them did she have second thoughts about the wisdom and sensitivity of such a gift: "Would he ever write any more such poems, I wondered, a little uncertain whether it had not been cruel of me to send him the volume of Rupert Brooke on which he now commented with so bitter a sense of achievement postponed."[23]

Even once Brittain had begun nursing, she clung to Brooke's heroic rhetoric. This only increased the rift with Roland, who had no time for Vera's need to make meaning of the war. In a letter to Brittain in September 1915, he defied anyone's ability to persist in thinking "that War is a glorious golden thing" in the face of "a pile of sodden grey rags that cover half a skull and a shin bone and what might have been its ribs."[24] His words, echoing the language of Wilfred Owen among many other war writers, did not penetrate Brittain's consciousness. Even long after the war, Brittain never adopted the angry tone of Roland's letter. This consistency makes her rebellions—the fight to go to college, the hesitation at George Catlin's proposal of marriage—stronger and stranger.

Brittain writes about "a more cynical post-war generation" throughout *Testament of Youth*, but she herself does not become cynical—numb, traumatized, disillusioned, but not cynical.[25] This consistency means that her look back on the war rarely has the bite of irony. Instead, it offers something different that is also of value in resisting war. She remembers how hard she and the other VADs worked, seeing the hard labor not with resentment but as having "a sacred glamour which redeemed it equally from tedium and disgust."[26] As 1915 progressed, Roland distanced himself from her and her concerns: her work in London as a nurse with convalescing patients permitted her to continue believing in the glamour of war while his experience in the trenches seems to have shattered him. Through letters, the distance strained their relationship. Brittain writes how "after weeks of waiting for some sign of interested sympathy, this evidence of war's dividing influence moved me to irrational fury against what I thought a too-easy capitulation to the spiritually destructive preoccupations of military service. I had not yet realised—as I was later to realise through my own mental surrender—that only a process of complete adaptation . . . made life sufferable."[27] We can hear, at one and the same time, her loneliness ("weeks of waiting"); her youth and passion ("irrational fury"); her righteousness, even self-righteousness ("spiritually destructive preoccupations of military service"); her compassion for Roland; and her compassion for her younger selves—both the Vera who lost her temper and the Vera who found that she, too, had to surrender and adapt to life in wartime.

The dispute with Roland was never resolved. He was killed on December 23, 1915, a day before his planned leave. In the wake of his death, Brittain requested an overseas posting and was sent to a hospital in Malta. Upon arriving there, she realized how close she was to Brooke's "foreign field"—long before she had ever been to

Roland's grave. Even after Roland's death, she continued to be inspired by Brooke. And her awareness of the power of that desire to be inspired remains an asset and a distinctive feature in her rhetoric of pacifism. Unlike other pacifists, Brittain, having come from a conventional patriotic background and persistent in her admiration for Brooke, understood the appeal of the fight. "It is, I think, this glamour, this magic, this incomparable keying up of the spirit in a time of mortal conflict," she writes, "which constitute the pacifists' real problem—a problem still incompletely imagined, and still quite unsolved."[28] As Woolf said, "We must compensate the man for the loss of his gun"; we must recognize the ways ordinary soldiers find meaning, deep bonds of friendship, and heroism in war and find ways to create those feelings in peacetime.[29] Brittain understands the ways people bond in moments of intensity and trauma; she knows the pride participants take in their contribution to a cause, even after the cause feels hollow or unjust.

Roland's death was shattering, but Brittain was a writer and knew, immediately, what a powerful story she had. In her diary from 1915, she included a folded sheet of paper: the final page of a play, about a love triangle between a nurse, a doctor, and the nurse's mortally wounded soldier-boyfriend. The doctor tells the nurse not to grieve excessively; his admonitions are at once romantic and menacing. She shuns him definitively and kisses the dead hand of the dead soldier (called, tellingly, "Rupert"), her beloved. Just months after Roland's death, we see Brittain trying to make art of her loss, associating him with Rupert Brooke and insisting on the exalted meaning of her nursing.

The early part of Brittain's life was marked by her big fight to attend university and then the slight return to tradition in her decision to leave university and become a VAD. During the war, too, Brittain went through a rebellion and a return. First, she accomplished a gradual but ultimately revolutionary revision of her understanding of Germany and German soldiers, no longer seeing them as "the enemy," but as brothers. This transformation paved the way for her pacifism. In the midst of this revolution, she submitted, again, to the yoke of family, returning from the fields of France to tend to her nervous mother in 1917. Brittain was a compulsive diarist, but there are only very sparse diary entries for the years 1918–21: an index of the cumulative effect of the grief and trauma of those years.

Volume 2 of *Testament of Youth* opens with a shocked Brittain trying to decide how to proceed with her life in Roland's absence: "Whenever I think of the weeks that followed the news of Roland's death, a series of pictures, disconnected but crystal clear, unroll themselves like a kaleidoscope through my mind."[30] In her diary, on January 1, 1916, she wrote: "This day last year was the first New Year's Day I had had with Him in my life. To-day is the first New Year's Day I have had with my life empty through the loss of Him."[31] The disagreements over Brooke's poetry that shadowed the autumn of 1915 faded as Brittain deeply grieved Roland's death. Finding his mother, a writer, more sympathetic than her own, Brittain spent time with the Leightons. She recalls with disbelief and horror helping the family sort through his final effects, including the bloody uniform in which he died:

> I had arrived at the cottage that morning to find his mother and sister standing in helpless distress in the midst of his returned kit, which was lying, just opened, all over the floor. The garments sent back included the outfit that he had been wearing when he was hit. I wondered, and I wonder still, why it was thought necessary to return such relics—a tunic torn back and front by the bullet, a khaki vest dark and stiff with blood, and a pair of blood-stained breeches slit open at the top by someone obviously in a violent hurry. Those gruesome rags made me realise, as I had never realised before, all that France meant. Eighteen months afterwards the smell of Étaples village, though fainter and more

> diffused, brought back to me the memory of those poor remnants of patriotism.[32]

It is a grim memory, and it requires an unflinching character to record it in diary form at the time and then return to it, nearly twenty years later, and make it part of a memoir. Writing up this memory in 1933, Brittain still refers to Roland's volunteering as "patriotism." Her astonishment at the thinking behind sending bloody clothes home to a grieving family—"I wondered and I wonder still"—captures the wrongheadedness of the British Army's decision. In a memoir so committed to contrasting the young Vera with the older Vera, this moment emphasizes a consistency in her hope for humane institutions.

With Roland dead, Brittain decided to throw herself deeper into service. She volunteered to go abroad and was posted to the Mediterranean island of Malta, where convalescing soldiers, too sick to return to combat or be transported home, recuperated. It was more challenging than her London work, but she was not in immediate danger, and the quiet island setting gave her a chance to begin healing. In May 1916, Geoffrey was killed in action, and Victor was badly injured; Brittain broke her contract and returned to England, intending to offer herself to the blinded Victor in marriage. In so doing, she recalled a letter in the newspaper's agony column that she and Roland had wondered over years before: "Lady, *fiancé* killed, will gladly marry officer totally blinded or otherwise incapacitated by the War."[33] In her diary she recalls—and quotes—her reaction to it at the time, which she had recorded in a letter to Roland two years earlier: "The lady (probably more than a girl or she would have called herself 'young lady'"; they always do) doubtless has no particular gift or qualification, and does not want to face the dreariness of an unoccupied and unattached old-maidenhood. But the only person she loved is dead; all men are alike to her and it is a matter of indifference whom she marries, so she thinks she may as well marry someone who really needs her."[34] What was pathetic and incredible fodder for correspondence in 1914 had by 1916 transformed into a possibility. In any event, Victor died before they could marry, and Vera requested another overseas posting, this time to France. We hear in her recollection, as we observe in her actions, what a remarkable and ordinary person she was: braver than most but channeling that bravery into paths still legible as feminine service and sacrifice.

In France, grieving the deaths of Roland, Geoffrey, and Victor and worrying over her brother, Vera underwent another transformation. She was asked to nurse wounded German soldiers, and this experience became "one of the things I like best to remember about the War."[35] It was the germ of her pacifism, and although it only makes up a few pages of her memoir, it shaped the rest of her life. She remembers, with pride, the privations and the hard work, and how she found some glamour and even exultation in the muddy gray tents. She was proud of the way that her fellow nurses and VADs "took for granted that it was they who must be overworked, rather than the prisoners neglected."[36] And she writes candidly about her experience being in close contact with Germans for the first time in her life:

> Before the War I had never been in Germany and had hardly met any Germans apart from the succession of German mistresses at St. Monica's, every one of whom I had hated with a provincial schoolgirl's pitiless distaste for foreigners. So it was somewhat disconcerting to be pitch-forked, all alone—since V.A.D.S went on duty half an hour before Sisters—into the midst of thirty representatives of the nation which, as I had repeatedly been told, had crucified Canadians, cut off the hands of babies, and subjected pure and stainless females to unmentionable "atrocities." I didn't think I had really believed all those stories, but I wasn't quite sure.[37]

Brittain admits her awareness of anti-German war propaganda and wonders at the degree to which she believed it, which her retrospective account does not fully clarify. "I didn't think I had really believed," she says, suggesting, that, in spite of herself, she partly did. That much seems to admit some recognition, perhaps even shame, at finding herself susceptible to propaganda. Then she adds, "But I wasn't quite sure," and it is not clear what she's unsure of: the stories, the degree of her credulity, or the degree to which she ought to countenance them, now, in the wards. Brittain is specific and unflinching about what she once believed about Germans. She takes a strong interest here and throughout the memoir in what a person can be expected to know, based on their information environment. She remembers the propaganda she read and absorbed. She tries to read it with a skeptical eye, but the prospect of being alone as the only worker in a tent full of wounded German soldiers frightens her. Knowing where she came from underscores the vastness of the personal change that she underwent nursing these soldiers. These admissions matter, as does the self-sacrificing professionalism of her colleagues, for, despite all that she had heard about German war atrocities, she joins her fellow nurses and VADs in working to save the lives of the patients in her care.

Edward wrote to marvel at how "strange" it was "that you should be nursing Hun prisoners," a fact that, in spite of the racial slur, proved to Edward, too, "how absurd the whole thing is."[38] When Brittain began nursing, she harbored a fantasy that she might one day nurse a wounded Roland. After only a few weeks of seeing the real agonies of war injuries, she regretted that wish and begged him only to return safe. But, in the muddy tents of France, she was able to return to some of that sacrificial sense she had in 1914 and 1915 when she imagined "it was always Roland whom I was nursing by proxy."[39] Instead of a romantic, individual notion, however, she came to a recognition both religious and political: of the folly of war and the dignity of all life. Pitchforked into a ward full of wounded Germans, Brittain's mind began to change again.

Recollecting it in 1933, Brittain remained proud of her war work, even despite her knowledge of the waste and carnage of the war.

She recollects the intensity of the work, and the strange way that life must carry on, even in the grimmest environments, marveling at "how we were able to drink tea and eat cake" in a ward that "might justly have been described as a regular baptism of blood and pus."[40] The combination of her nursing experience, her ongoing belief in heroism, and her dawning conviction of the wrongness of war make her an unusual and valuable spokesperson for pacifism. This interjection, in the middle of *Testament of Youth*, could well be Brittain's credo:

> Since those years it has often been said by pacifists—as in a brave, lop-sided pamphlet which I read only the other day—that war creates more criminals than heroes; that, far from developing noble qualities in those who take part in it, it brings out only the worst. If this were altogether true, the pacifist's aim would be, I think, much nearer of attainment than it is. Looking back upon the psychological processes of us who were very young sixteen years ago, it seems to me that his task—our task—is infinitely complicated by the fact that war, while it lasts, does produce heroism to a far greater extent than it brutalises.[41]

She recognizes her own naivete, but she also sees the strength of her determination to work because she believed her work had purpose. In this same passage, she describes her continual rededication of herself to the cause, noting that the more she doubted the war, "the more ardent and frequent was the periodic rededication." Brittain lived an experience that few peace advocates have articulated as clearly: There is an excitement and a sense of purpose and honor in fighting that is hard to replicate. We overlook the power of the idea of service to a cause at our peril. Brittain persists in a common definition of heroism—she is not doing anything fancy with the word or trying to trick people into an insincere alternative along the lines of "the real heroes are the ones who stayed home." She retains the familiar idea of the hero and admits that the kinds of bravery, the acts of persistence, these things that happen in wartime—they create heroes. She takes seriously the fact that many people care about having a cause to believe in and to fight for, and that, once that cause is found, they will sacrifice in its name. Her experience of war as producing heroism means that, in her work for peace, she had a deeper understanding than most of how necessary it would be to compensate the soldier for the loss of the gun. Her compassion for German soldiers would have even more profound and far-reaching effects. Witnessing their deaths, being called "Schwester" (sister) by men her brother's age, brought the absurd waste of war vividly home to her. She came to see German soldiers as fellow humans, fellow Europeans, and fellow victims of the cruelties of war.

With all this loss, Brittain still had to face her parents. They expected her to be a good daughter on the most conventional terms. During an especially busy push in France in 1917, with many wounded soldiers to attend to, Brittain's father wrote to say that her mom has "cocked up"; can she come home? Frantic with worry and indecision, she woke in the night with the phrase "The strain all along . . . is very great . . . very great," running through her head and tried to identify its source:

> What exactly did those words describe? The enemy within shelling distance—refugee Sisters crowding in with nerves all awry—bright moonlight, and aeroplanes carrying machine-guns—ambulance trains jolting noisily into the siding, all day, all night, gassed men on stretchers, clawing the air—dying men, reeking with mud and foul green-stained bandages, shrieking and writhing in a grotesque travesty of manhood—dead men with fixed, empty eyes and shiny, yellow faces. . . .
>
> Then I remembered; the phrase came out of my father's letter, and it described . . . the troubles at home.[42]

The extent of Brittain's indignation was vast. For her parents to appropriate the idea of "war strain" and apply it to themselves must have enraged her. The strain at home was indeed great as compared to life in peacetime, but it was still nothing compared to what Brittain was enduring. In a 1923 essay for the feminist journal *Time and Tide*, she reflected on the unfair expectations put on daughters: "The idea that the duty of man concerns Things, but the duty of woman concerns Persons, is not the monopoly of reactionaries. We are living still under the shadow of an age which made a woman the first servant of her parents, with the usual alternative of standing in the same relation to her husband, and later to her children."[43] By this time, she was able to see her family's opposition as part of a larger cultural pressure. "Our mothers were brought up to believe in this supreme duty of individual service," she wrote. "They have bound the consciences of their daughters to the same iron tradition."[44] Even so, when she returned to this episode for her memoirs, she kept her personal animus against her parents at the center of the story.

Toward the end of volume 2, we learn of her brother Edward's death in Italy. Of the four men whom she loved, none were left. She records her frantic efforts to learn more about the circumstances of his death, lamenting how the massive volume of war casualties meant that few men knew her brother well enough to write a proper tribute, like the ones Roland had received two years earlier. In *Testament of Youth*, she speculates on Edward's final heroic moments and desperately appeals for an eyewitness account. After publication one of Edward's fellow soldiers wrote to her with the truth that she must have, in her frantic and failed efforts, begun to suspect: Edward did not have the kind of heroic death she wished for. Instead, his death was a cruel byproduct of the Army's homophobia. He had been discovered in a relationship with an enlisted man and was shot—or, perhaps, put himself in a position where he was almost certain to die—for violating the military's code of conduct, which prohibited homosexual relationships.[45] Even so, Vera was slow to accept her brother's sexual orientation, and "in 1939 she was nonetheless shocked to learn from her mother that Edward had been implicated at Uppingham in acts of what in public school jargon was known as 'beastliness.'"[46] Still, at some level, she knew. Her 1936 novel, *Honourable Estate*, features a character whose brother dies in World War I, leaving behind a letter confessing that his death was connected to his homosexuality. In that, Brittain grants her character a clarity that she only belatedly received.

After the war, Brittain returned to Oxford. Interested to understand the causes of war, she changed her major to history. She witnessed the very first women awarded university degrees in the Sheldonian Theater. She joined the debating society, where she met the writer Winifred Holtby. After a disastrous start, the two became lifelong friends, bonding over their war work (Holtby had been a WAAC), feminism, and political activism. They toured Europe together several times, to visit Roland's and Edward's graves, as journalists, and to attend the Annual Conference of the League of Nations Union.

When Holtby and Brittain graduated, they moved in together, striving to make their living by writing and to avoid the intrusive demands of family. They collaborated, and they each depicted each other—and their friendship—in early novels. But Holtby had more success than Brittain early on, and only Holtby was taken up as a protégé of the charismatic feminist Lady Rhondda, the patron of *Time and Tide*. Brittain married in 1925, and by 1930 she had two young children and a husband who spent part of the year teaching at Cornell University in the United States. During this time, Holtby remained single; she continued living with Brittain and her family, helping with the children, lecturing and traveling with Brittain, and publishing journalism, reviews, and fiction. In the ten years between the publication of *The Dark Tide* and *Testament of Youth*, Brittain was juggling small children and facing rejection from publishers. In those same years, Holtby wrote six novels, a study of Virginia Woolf's life, and more. Unsurprisingly, Brittain felt discouraged, jealous, and frustrated. Nevertheless, she stuck to her ambitions. When her husband was unhappy alone at Cornell, and people criticized her for keeping her birth name, everything pointed to an easy retreat into family life: Brittain could move to the United States and blend into the role of faculty wife. Instead, she kept writing and remained loyal to Holtby, despite her jealousy, of her closest friend and professional prop.

Brittain was not a lesbian, although her intimacy with Holtby often gave rise to speculation that she might be. Some base that on the chastity of her relationship with Roland. At the time of his death, her knowledge of male bodies came entirely from her work as a VAD. Although she and Roland had been engaged, they never slept together—something that surprised even her mother. Human sexuality is notoriously complicated, and no single word can describe Brittain's most intimate relationships. She loved Roland; she married George Catlin, the father of her children; she had an affair in the late 1930s with the American publisher George Brett; and yet she was happiest when living, working, and traveling with Holtby. There is no evidence of a sexual affair between them, but their intimacy seems to have been the most important relationship of her life. She fights her deeply internalized homophobia, insists on Holtby's straightness, when it seems likely that Holtby, who never married, was bisexual. In *To the Lighthouse*, Lily Briscoe reflects on how her love for Mrs. Ramsay is both a crush on a woman and a feeling of being in love with the whole family, the summer home, and all of it. After all, she thinks, "love had a thousand shapes," and no one label suffices to capture the ties of a heart.[47] In Brittain, there is a restraint and propriety, a buttoned-up quality and a love of romance over sex that makes it narratively convenient to shape the story of her love for Roland as she does, despite evidence that pulls the story in a slightly different direction.

At the end of *Testament of Youth*, Brittain writes about her struggle to decide to marry—a struggle because marriage might get in the way of her writing and would certainly mean looking toward the future and leaving behind the life that she had been leading, memorializing the past and the dead. She considers how marriage promised the possibility of motherhood, a dream she had given up. In recounting her thinking from 1925, she expresses her gratitude for peace and the passage of time in language that deliberately echoes war propaganda: "I might, perhaps, even have the children that years ago I had longed for—children who would know and care nothing of the life that had been mine before I met their father, and who would certainly never ask me: 'Mother, what did you do in the Great War?' because the War itself would be to them less than a memory."[48] The structure of the sentence seems to marvel at the distance of the war, but like Clarissa Dalloway's "The war was over, thank god, over," the very articulation of that thought brings the war back into being. There is a more sinister meaning, too. Brittain was bitter at those who found her war work embarrassing. Even as she announces, with apparent thankfulness, the closing of the war chapter of her life, she alludes to a famous propaganda poster, aimed at shaming men into war service, and insists that, unlike the shirker, she has nothing to be embarrassed about and everything to be proud of.

Testament of Youth covers Brittain's life to 1925. When she wrote it, in the early 1930s, her best friend and constant companion Winifred Holtby was dying of kidney disease, and Brittain's children were very little (John was born in 1927; Shirley, in 1930). From 1925 until her death in 1970, Brittain made a life for herself that was shaped by the two main rebellions of her youth: her decision to go to university and make herself into a self-supporting writer, and the recognition of the humanity of German soldiers that made her a pacifist.

In shaping her memoir, Brittain borrowed the triple-decker form of the Victorian novel, using it to emphasize how far her life seemed to be from an expected one while being sure to conclude with her own marriage. Three-volume novels dominated the English fiction market in the nineteenth century. Publishers encouraged novelists to write long books, divided into thirds, to boost sales. Many novels were initially serialized in magazines and then bound into so-called triple-deckers for lending libraries. These market conditions led novelists to craft complex plots with chapters and volumes ending with cliffhangers. In Oscar Wilde's *The Importance of Being Earnest*, Miss Prism scolds us not to "speak slightingly of the three-volume novel. . . . I wrote one myself in earlier days." Pressed for details about the plot, she simply says, "The good ended happily, and the bad unhappily. That is what Fiction means."[49] In Woolf's *To the Lighthouse*, pretty and dimwitted Minta Doyle gets nervous during a dinner conversation about George Eliot because "she had left the third volume of *Middlemarch* in the train and she never knew what happened in the end."[50] Anyone can guess that stopping a novel partway through may leave one with an imperfect understanding of its message. Readers who know *Middlemarch* will know that, by losing volume 3, Minta Doyle never learns that two of the three marriages in the book end disastrously. Given this, we are not surprised when Minta, too, hurtles into marriage and finds herself unhappily matched.

Brittain, an enthusiastic admirer of George Eliot, absorbed this structure and applied it to her life in *Testament of Youth*. Volume 1 ends with her fiancé's death, a cliffhanger that is also the end of narrative. Where can the bereaved heroine go? Volume 2 relates her grieving during a post in Malta, her return to London, and her work in France nursing wounded German soldiers. It ends with the end of the war: her brother and two best friends now dead. It's a bleak narrative; it's also her life. And it is hard to imagine where narrative will go. But volume 3 takes the grieving and numbed Brittain back to Oxford, where, traumatized, she strives to reintegrate herself into a world of cocoa parties with a group of classmates who find her war work embarrassing and worse. *Testament of Youth* ends, tentatively, with the author married with children, living with her husband (who begged not to be included in the book and who, consequently, remains shadowy, referred to only as "G.") and—wonderfully, but even more out of sync with tradition—her best friend, the novelist Winifred Holtby. In absorbing the form of the Victorian novel and applying it to her life, Brittain achieved the success that her novels never did. *Testament of Youth* is her best work; it was an immediate success and remains popular to this day in print, with film, television, and theatrical adaptations.

In *Testament of Experience*, her memoir of the years 1925–1950, she shares that "to both G. and Winifred I now confessed the desire for a Christmas baby," without seeming to recognize the unusual nature of her putting her best friend and husband on equal footing.[51] It is indeed common for women to discuss with both husbands and close friends their hopes of getting pregnant, but Brittain's rhetoric makes ambiguous the intimacy that, in other moments, she was keen to explain away. Even the phantom-like "G." she uses to refer to George Catlin emphasizes the intimacy of Brittain's bond with Holtby. So, when she goes to the trouble to insist, as she often does, that she was not a lesbian, and that Holtby's continued residence with her after her marriage was a simple matter of professional convenience for both writing and childcare support (despite the fact that both children were at boarding school for much of the year from an early age), there is a quality of protesting too much to her explanations.

Whatever the reason, Brittain and Holtby loved and supported each other personally and professionally. Starting in 1931, Holtby's health began to fail, and she was intermittently seriously ill during the years that Brittain was writing *Testament of Youth*. That book's publication brought Brittain closer to the great liberal publisher Victor Gollancz, who became a great friend, and led to speaking engagements and invitations that continued for the remaining decades of her life, including multiple trips to the United States, which she came to know and like better. It also, as we have seen, definitively answered the family's lingering questions about the circumstances surrounding Edward's death.

As Brittain and Holtby worked on their books, they also dedicated considerable time to activist journalism for internationalist and feminist causes. They joined the League of Nations Union and traveled frequently, both to give speeches and gather information, making a tour of Europe in 1922 to investigate postwar conditions on the Continent. Holtby's trip to South Africa in 1926 transformed her outlook on race and racism, earning her the respect of many Pan-Africanists, including Una Marson, who wrote a poem in her honor. As part of that work, Brittain petitioned on behalf of Paula Wallisch (née Pinter), the wife of Koloman Wallisch, a socialist party leader in Austria who was executed for taking up arms against the right-wing government in 1934. Brittain's advocacy on Wallisch's behalf led her to write to Virginia Woolf, who signed a petition and, in a cover note, congratulated Brittain on *Testament of Youth.*

Brittain's father committed suicide in 1935. Several months later, Holtby died, a loss that prompted a second, tender condolence letter from Woolf. In the years following Holtby's death, Brittain dedicated herself to a memoir of their friendship, *Testament of Friendship*, which also serves as a tribute to Holtby's talent, promise, and achievement as a writer. It was after these two deaths that Brittain joined the Peace Pledge Union (PPU) and openly affiliated herself with the pacifist movement, an affiliation that had long been implicit, but an official designation that would change the course of the remainder of her life. When Dick Sheppard, the charismatic leader of the PPU, died unexpectedly in 1937, Brittain became a leader of his movement, speaking sometimes as often as thirty times a month.

This powerful association with pacifism made Brittain's sense of futility at the outbreak of World War II especially acute. She felt as if she were seeing the end of everything to which she had dedicated herself since her transformation in the tents of France in 1917. She recorded her exact feeling of listening to the declaration on the radio, flanked by her children:

> September 3 [1939]
>
> First thing this morning the news was still indefinite + I half decided to go up to London to the P.P.U. Hyde Park gathering as promised for to-night. Then at 10–0 the B.B.C. made the "important announcement" that our ultimatum asking Germany to leave Poland would expire at 11. a.m.—And if no answer had been received Mr. Chamberlain would speak at 11.15. At that time we turned on the wireless again + heard his statement that from 11.0 this morning a state of war existed between England + Germany. His voice sounded old and trembled—and suddenly as I sat on the camp bed in the study listening between the two children, I found that the tears were running down my cheeks—I suppose from some subconscious realisation of the failure of my efforts for peace over 20 years, for I had expected the announcement.[52]

At the end of *Testament of Youth*, Brittain recalled that she had her own proud answer to the propaganda poster "Daddy, What Did You Do in the War?," in which a shamefaced man sits in an upholstered chair, his young son and daughter playing at his feet. Just six years later, the scene repeats itself, but not as a scene of humiliation or pride, but of shock, fear, and defeat. The return of war is an undeniable defeat for the pacifist project.

In the face of this cataclysm, both global and personal, Brittain deliberately chose to continue her work, despite the cost. She reflected: "So long as one has dear human beings to live for one is a potential coward, and courage is the more costly."[53] If her rebellion in youth was driven by passion, her rebellion in middle age was fueled by a steely determination. Never a flexible thinker, Brittain decided that the best way to survive the war was to persist: "Surely the path which I had trodden for two decades now summoned me to struggle against that catastrophic process? Though I still underrated the cost of such a stand, I knew that the routine performance of dangerous duties would be stimulating and congenial compared with the exhausting demands of independent thought and the task of maintaining, against the deceptive surge of popular currents, a conscious realisation of what was actually happening."[54]

She could not have anticipated the cost of this decision. It was difficult to witness her daughter at school, "a fair-haired child with limpid blue eyes, hugging our parting gift a toy brown horse, against her red check frock, and swinging her gas-mask in the other hand as she ran uphill to school."[55] After some agonizing months, she and George decided to make the heart-rending decision that more than three million British parents made to evacuate their children to a safer place. Because of their ties to the US, they were able, with some difficulty and thanks to the invitation of friends, to send the children there. However, the distance, and Brittain's work as a pacifist, meant that her correspondence to her children, aged just thirteen and ten, was censored and delayed, sometimes by months. A letter from their host family dated August 10, 1941, requesting help with back-to-school clothing, did not arrive in England until January of the following year.

As Roosevelt announced the US war budget that same month, Brittain decided she wanted the children back home, but they could not secure John and Shirley's safe return until late 1943. This long separation haunted her. A carnation from their farewell bouquet remains taped to a page of her June 1940 diary. She reflects, in 1957, "In two books, *England's Hour* and a novel, *Born 1925*, I have described our parting with the children, and I do not propose to repeat it here. In those chapters I never succeeded, as I have so often succeeded elsewhere, in 'writing out' a bitter experience from my recollection. The carnation pressed in my diary from the parting bouquet which John and Shirley gave me remains a poignant relic, for the lost years of their childhood are lost to me still."[56]

At the end of Brittain's first novel, *The Dark Tide* (1923), the Brittain character counsels her college rival—an unkind caricature of Holtby—to recommit herself to writing. Rather cruelly, if realistically, she predicts that this woman will not be a great writer but that her work will, nevertheless, have value if she makes a commitment to "write the same thing that's always being written and always being forgotten—the thing that people need to be told again and again and again."[57] She goes on to explain in greater detail:

> Write that the apparently truest love is not always worthy of trust, that the grandest human life is often the most mortal, and that amidst all these transitory things success is the most worthless, most transitory of all. Tell them that one's plans may crash, and one's love fail and one's idols be shattered, but that this is only the beginning of the things that are worth while.[58]

Although in the novel, this is a Brittain-character speaking to a Holtby-stand-in, this speech is as much a note to self as an exhortation. We see it in the structure of her 1933 memoir: at the end of the first and second volumes, we seem to be in the ashes, but Brittain keeps showing us how she found the strength to keep living.

Muriel Rukeyser
1913–1980

VIOLENCE AND CREATION

Muriel Rukeyser was primarily a poet, but the publication of her forgotten novel of the Spanish Civil War, *Savage Coast*, in 2013, brought her work to a new group of readers who might hesitate to read poetry. *Savage Coast* is an extraordinary account of the war through the eyes of a young woman. When I first taught it, one of my students raved about the line "She would always have this street before her for a birthday," confident that I, too, had singled it out for its beauty.[1] Alas, I had missed it, but her admiration made me look again. What might it mean to have a street for a birthday? The main character Helen's thought is a very American one. The audacity to believe you can claim and choose your birth is typical of an American faith in the possibility of self.

Birth, including birthdays, mattered to Rukeyser. She wrote poems about maternal longing, and, when she chose single motherhood as a queer woman in 1947, she wrote poems about pregnancy, birth, and her rebirth as a mother. When she was pregnant, she wrote to a friend, "The small object is kicking now, and that is marvelous. There are times of being scared, but they are growing fewer. I feel, as September approaches, that I am going to die or be born—and/or be born, I suppose it is."[2] In Rukeyser's letter, these maternal joys and fears transform into something abstract, fully engaged in the enormity of the experience. As *Savage Coast* shows,

Rukeyser is interested in the full significance of birth: physical, metaphysical, and personal and symbolic.

Decades later, after her own difficult experience of giving birth, Rukeyser recounts witnessing a woman torn apart. This occurred as part of a ceremony she attended while visiting the indigenous Kwakwaka'wakw people (once called the Kwakiutl) on Vancouver Island. In that ceremony, a woman appears to be split open, with the shaman holding up bloody entrails for all to see:

> I thought of the story the Indian woman told me on Vancouver Island—Did you ever see a woman split down the middle? . . . She was standing in what we call the community house, and everyone came in and she stood there and said in the strong voice Won't somebody come and kill me? A shudder of shock and release went through me. . . . Then, said the Indian woman, the shaman came into the house, he walked forward with the obsidian knife gleaming black in his hand and he said I will—and drew his sharp knife hard down her front til the blood spilled on the ground. He held the entrails up. We all saw them. Then we left the house.
>
> Next day we came back. We stood in our places around the big room. There was the woman who was killed. She was wearing the evergreen leaves at her temples; she danced the dance of rebirth.[3]

Rukeyser tells the story so that we can share her shock. Only later does she explain that the woman had a dead seal under her robe: it was the seal's blood that spilled on the ground, the seal's entrails that he displayed. Brought up from childhood "not to talk about three things: sex and money and death," the wet, sticky, messy ritual thrills her and teaches her profound lessons about the possibility of birth-in-life.[4]

This ritual gives rise to one of Rukeyser's most celebrated lines: "What would happen if one woman told the truth about her life? / The world would split open."[5] The assertion indicates how far she believes men are from understanding women's truths as truths. This line revises one of Virginia Woolf's most quoted observations about the challenges faced by women writers: of "telling the truth about my own experience as a body."[6] But, where Woolf focused on what she called inward obstacles, Rukeyser emphasizes others' unpreparedness for the truth. Rukeyser had a traumatic childbirth: after a long labor, she was anesthetized for a cesarean section and learned later that she had had an unplanned hysterectomy.[7] This experience and the Kwakwaka'wakw ceremony influence the understanding behind her writing. The lines quoted above appear in her poem in honor of the great artist Käthe Kollwitz, celebrated for her drawings of motherhood, and again in her play *Houdini*, spoken by Houdini's wife, Bess, who grieves her inability to have children even as she delights in her partnership with the escape artist.

For Rukeyser, to be split is not to be broken. Something that is split can be opened, revealed. A splitting may be part of birth—as a woman's body literally splits in childbirth—and rebirth, as in the Kwakwaka'wakw ceremony. So, when my student found that line in Rukeyser's early novel, she had zeroed in on one of Rukeyser's core beliefs: that we can be reborn back into ourselves. Central to her rebellion against convention is this belief in the human ability to harness violence into creativity and the moral imperative to do so. Even during World War II, when Jewish people across Europe were forced into hiding, Rukeyser declared the imperative to accept the gift of Judaism and for American Jews not to hide but to reject the false cloak of invisibility:

> To be a Jew in the twentieth century
> Is to be offered a gift. If you refuse,
> Wishing to be invisible, you choose
> Death of the spirit, the stone insanity.
> Accepting, take full life. Full agonies:[8]

These unflinching lines have been quoted often and have even made their way into some reformed Jewish prayer services.

Muriel Rukeyser was in her early twenties when she wrote *Savage Coast* in a matter of weeks, but the novel was not published until 2013, long after her death. Rowena Kennedy-Epstein rescued it from the archives, where prior scholars had either ignored it or, more damningly, assented to the negative judgments of publishers in the 1930s; seeing its value, she edited and published the novel. It may seem strange to focus on a work that was unpublished in the author's lifetime. Ordinarily, we do not place as high a value on archival or unpublished work as on the published. But, when it comes to women writing on radical topics, ignoring what was rejected or neglected risks ignoring them altogether. Limiting ourselves to published work equates to limiting ourselves to the gatekeeping judgments of a previous time, less interested in and less willing to listen to voices at variance with the mainstream.

It is not hard to understand why publishers were unready for the novel in the 1930s. Early on, the heroine begins a guilt-free love affair with an anti-fascist German athlete whom she meets on a train, only learning his name in a moment of postcoital glow. That, combined with her modernist experimentation and anti-fascist politics, proved too much for the delicacy of male publishers at the time. Rukeyser's physical courage in Spain exceeds that of most, and it was matched by the intellectual courage displayed in the novel—a courage that publishers could not match.

As soon as her career began, Rukeyser expressed a clear, committed leftist point of view. So fundamental was her rebellion that it can feel as though she knew no other way to be. And, in some ways, that seems to have been true. In an autobiographical essay, she writes of railing against her mother's turn to Judaism when Rukeyser was little, how suddenly the trips to the museum on weekend afternoons were replaced by visits to temple, and how anemic and dull she found the sermons of her Reform rabbi. Passionate about justice and ravenous for experience, Rukeyser was willing to put herself in the way of danger in order to bear witness. When Helen in *Savage Coast* declares the street in Barcelona as her birthday, she is marking how time and space intersect for her, moving her out of a tourist's perspective toward commitment and a surer sense of purpose. Despite this confidence, Rukeyser's poems, novel, and essays also narrate the moments of envy, doubt, and hesitation that visited even this strongest of rebels: these moments and her love of Woolf connect Rukeyser to the other women in this book.

"Breathe-in experience, breathe-out poetry": the first line of *Theory of Flight*, Muriel Rukeyser's first book of poems, stands as a fitting credo for her life.[9] Rukeyser approached life with passion and transformed into words her many experiences as a poet, activist, lover, mother, educator, and friend. Muriel Helen Rukeyser was the first-born child of Lawrence and Myra Rukeyser, both American-born Jews. Her father was in the construction business, her mother a housewife who hoped that Muriel, too, would become a mother and saw education as primarily in the service of becoming a better mother. In a 1944 autobiographical statement for the *Contemporary Jewish Record*, Rukeyser notes that "most of the younger Jewish writers in America are the children of immigrants, and I am not representative of that generation."[10] Her father's family had immigrated to Wisconsin in 1848, and her mother grew up in Yonkers when it was still a farming village. Although Rukeyser downplays the place of religion in her childhood, her connection to Judaism is strong and a source of great pride. She notes the "legend that my mother's family was directly descended from Akiba," the second-century BCE scholar and rabbi executed by the Romans, and wrote several poems dedicated to him.[11]

Rukeyser was educated at the Society for Ethical Culture School and at the Fieldston School, both renowned for their liberal bent and strong college preparatory curriculum. After graduating at sixteen, she went to Vassar, where Mary McCarthy and Elizabeth Bishop were among her classmates. With them, she worked on literary and political journals. In the summers, she took classes at Columbia, where she met the author Zora Neale Hurston, the anthropologist Franz Boas, and the sculptor Augusta Savage, among other intellectuals, artists, and civil rights activists. In the summer of 1933, she traveled with two white men to Alabama to report on the retrial of the "Scottsboro boys," nine Black men falsely accused of raping two white women. She was arrested for what was then the crime of talking to a Black person and contracted typhoid fever in jail.

Her father's business failed during the Depression, and Rukeyser took a leave from Vassar, enrolling in the Roosevelt School for Aviation on Long Island, which offered classes in piloting and aviation mechanics. Her first collection, *Theory of Flight*, borrows its title from the school's textbook. That collection won the Yale Younger Poets Prize in 1935. The prize, started in 1918, made careers: James Agee won it the year before Rukeyser, and subsequent winners include Margaret Walker (1941), Adrienne Rich (1950), John Hollander (1957), and Carolyn Forché (1975).

The next year, 1936, was a momentous year for Rukeyser, as it was for Europe. That year, she traveled to West Virginia, England, and Spain. In West Virginia with her friend the photographer Nancy Naumburg, she attended hearings regarding the Gauley Bridge mining disaster. Construction on the Hawk's Nest Tunnel had begun in 1930. The three-mile tunnel, under Gauley Mountain, was needed to divert water to a new hydroelectric plant. The mountain was composed of rock with a high silica content, and the dry-drilling technique was speedy but created large amounts of silica dust, which coated the miners' skin and entered their lungs. Although the dangers of silica dust were well known, the mining company persisted in dry-drilling and denied even the most basic safety equipment to the miners, even prohibiting them from wearing their own safety gear. More than half of the 5,000 men who worked on the project worked inside the tunnel. Of these, at least 764 died of silicosis. Most of the miners were African American, as were a majority of those who died. Black workers were segregated in life and in death—living in shacks without electricity and sleeping two men to a bunk and then buried in an open grave at a nearby farm, excluded from the whites-only cemetery. The hydroelectric plant that they helped to build still operates. The Hawk's Nest Tunnel disaster remains one of the worst industrial catastrophes in US history. Rukeyser documented the disaster and the government response in *The Book of the Dead*, which combines expert testimony, poems in the voice of the miners, newspaper quotations, and even chemical formulae to create a passionate, richly textured indictment of greed and racism.

Later that year, Rukeyser traveled to England and then on to Spain, encouraged to witness and document the People's Olympics. She met and had an affair with the German anti-fascist athlete Otto Boch. When the games were canceled and fighting broke out, Boch joined the Republicans and was ultimately killed in Spain. A fictionalized Otto appears as Hans in *Savage Coast*; Rukeyser appears under her middle name, Helen. These youthful experiences, particularly in Spain, set in place the major themes of her poetry: a passionate commitment to social justice, a willingness to travel to see things for herself, the desire to make her poetry and her life into something of use for the causes that mattered to her—racial justice and socialism above all. These experiences in Spain remained a touchstone for the rest of her life.

During World War II, Rukeyser had a peripatetic existence, dividing her time between New York, California, and Mexico, where Rukeyser spent six months in 1939. On her return, she collaborated with the German anti-fascist artist Rudolph von Ripper on a poem cycle about the white abolitionist John Brown. She lectured at Sarah Lawrence (and got her collaborator and sometime lover Berenice Abbott a job teaching photography there) and Vassar and worked as associate editor at *Decision* magazine, a short-lived project by Klaus Mann, son of Thomas Mann, to highlight the writing of anti-fascist wartime refugees. Among the writers she worked with there was May Sarton, who also became one of her lovers.

She also worked for a US government agency in the Office of War Information (OWI), helping develop wartime propaganda. She left the OWI in 1943 because so few of her suggestions were taken. Even so, her ideas about the potential for a richer relationship between image and caption remain pathbreaking for collaborative and multimedia artists. Rukeyser believed that captions might not simply describe the image's contents but might in themselves be art. The caption, considered alongside the photograph, might produce something in combination greater than either could accomplish alone. All this time, and for years after, the FBI followed her, suspicious of her leftist politics and her teaching at California's Labor School. During her time in California, she met the Mexican poet and diplomat Octavio Paz, who had also been in Spain, and whose work she was the first to translate into English.

The 1940s also marked the beginning of a decline in her reputation. Rukeyser's opposition to fascism and Nazism made her an early supporter of US involvement in World War II, but her government work rankled some fellow leftists. In 1942, she published the long poem *Wake Island*, celebrating the bravery of the US Navy soldiers who were defeated by the Japanese surprise attack on the remote Pacific atoll on December 8, 1941. Rukeyser's poem was perceived as a lame, patriotic celebration and, as such, a betrayal of her earlier position. The *Partisan Review*, already frustrated with her in a more local way for turning down the job of poetry editor, published a one-sentence review by Weldon Kees. It read, in its entirety: "There's one thing you can say about Muriel: she's not lazy."[12] The extreme brevity, the jokey tone, the reference to the poet by her first name (and thereby insisting on her sex), and then the judgment that it was the result of quick work, not of care and genius—all conspire to damn the poem from the moment of publication. The review is at once funny and breathtakingly mean. It was followed up by a longer attack on her, signed with the editors' initials. This was perceived as so cruel that the review followed up with two defenses of Rukeyser, from Rebecca Pitts, a writer in

Indianapolis, and another from the critic F. O. Matthiessen, who became a friend. When Matthiessen committed suicide in 1950, leaving behind a note expressing his distress at the political tensions of the Cold War, Rukeyser wrote a poem in his honor.

In California, away from her disapproving parents, she briefly married, had the marriage annulled, and then, in 1947, gave birth to her only child, a son. She kept the father's identity secret for many years and insisted on the title "Mrs. Rukeyser." (Although she told her intimates it was David Woolff, a teacher, the biological father was Donnan Jeffers, son of the poet Robinson Jeffers.)[13] She revised and published her wartime lectures as *The Life of Poetry* in 1949. Around this time, she began the love affair with her literary agent, Monica McCall, that would last until her death. She returned east and began teaching at Vassar, writing and publishing poems all along. She continued her political involvement as well, traveling to Hanoi with poet Denise Levertov and Jane Hart, the wife of Senator Gary Hart, in 1972, and served as president of PEN in 1975. In that capacity, she traveled to South Korea to bear witness to the political imprisonment of poet Kim Chi-Ha. Kim and the failure of her mission to secure his release became the subject of her last collection of poems, *The Gates* (1976). Rukeyser suffered her first stroke in 1964 and had another serious stroke in 1977. She seemed to be on the verge of publicly coming out as lesbian or bisexual and acknowledging her thirty-year relationship with McCall, having accepted an invitation to speak on a panel on lesbian/feminist literature at the 1978 MLA Convention, but had to cancel due to illness.[14] She died in 1980 at age sixty-seven. Rukeyser's life is the life of a strong and passionate rebel. But, in her novel, she offers glimpses of the inner uncertainty behind brave public action.

Savage Coast, Rukeyser's only novel, follows Helen, a young American journalist who, like Rukeyser, travels to Spain to cover what was to have been the People's Olympics, an anti-fascist alternative to Hitler's Olympic Games. Instead, her train is held up for days outside Barcelona, where she witnesses the opening days of the Spanish Civil War. Eventually, Helen and the leftist friends she has made on the train reach Barcelona and their rooms at the Hotel Olimpiada, where the athletes and their supporters all stay. When Helen thinks that "she would always have the street for a birthday," baptizing herself, she is looking out the hotel window with her friends Peter and Olive.[15] It is early in the morning; after some frightening moments the night before, she woke up, refreshed, confident, and unafraid. "One morning, and the fear of death is replaced," she thinks in wonder.[16]

Savage Coast is a beautifully constructed war novel. With scenes on a train and on the streets, in restaurants and a hotel, and, finally, aboard a ship fleeing a war zone, Rukeyser focuses our attention on the sites of urban warfare and, through them, a range of responses to the outbreak of war. For all the ways it resembles other war stories in setting, it is an experimental and highly literary novel. Each chapter begins with an epigraph, and the sources become more urgent as the novel progresses, drawing from C. Day-Lewis (whom she had just met in London), W. H. Auden, Karl Marx, Sylvia Townsend Warner, Hart Crane, André Malraux, the program for the People's Olympiad, French and Spanish newspapers, and popular song. At the center of it all is Helen, the stand-in for Rukeyser.

Toward the end of the novel, Helen tells her lover Hans, "I came in as a tourist, with tourist eyes and wishes."[17] Helen's transformation from a tourist into something else—Rukeyser does not give it a definitive name—drives the novel. The exploration of a woman's experience of becoming useful, of coming into her purpose, echoes the trajectory of some suffrage novels of the 1910s and 1920s (e.g., Constance Maud's *No Surrender* and Rebecca West's *The Judge*) and sets it apart from the typical bildungsroman, which tends to focus on male achievement and female preparedness for marriage. The love affair in *Savage Coast*, between an American Jew and a

German anti-fascist athlete, is sexy and exciting; it is also to the side of Helen's development. Hans is a love interest for Helen—he is not strictly necessary to her.

The novel opens on a train bound for Barcelona. The opening shots of the war and the announcement of a general strike stop the train in the town of Montcada i Reixac, less than ten miles from the center of Barcelona. When the train comes to a halt, a cacophony of mixed reactions from the international passengers erupts, and Rukesyer shows her gift for rendering, in English, the confusion of a multilingual conversation among speakers with wildly varying fluency. The great minor character of the novel's first half is a ninny of a woman from New Jersey who knows nothing of politics and frets excessively. Like many from New Jersey, she is eager to claim her affiliation with Helen as a New Yorker, and, like many a native New Yorker, Helen scorns the association. Peapack, New Jersey (then an exurb of fewer than 1,500 people), is nothing like New York City, and Helen refers to her simply as "Peapack" throughout.

The comedy of Peapack's fear; her narrow concern for only herself, her luggage, and her husband (whom she was to meet); and her utter confusion about the purpose of the People's Olympiad—"Why should there be games *against* games?"—make her the naive tourist foil to Helen's inquisitive and engaged observer.[18] Helen says she began as a tourist, but Rukeyser makes sure we see there are several kinds of tourists, and Helen is far from the worst. Even so, she has a lot to learn. While the train is stopped, she finds her new friends Peter and Olive making plans in a first-class carriage and expresses surprise that they are there. Peter snaps, "Don't be class conscious when it's irrelevant."[19] Helen is still following the old rules and needs Peter to explain the rules of revolution.

The travelers walk through the stopped train, collecting signatures in support of the general strike and against the fascist coup. Helen immediately grasps the need to do something, and her idea of something is focused not on her personal safety but expressing solidarity with the Spanish Republicans. As they gather signatures,

Rukeyser shows us a wide range of reactions, including her own enthusiastic assent, Olive's ironic "It's manifesto time," the Hollywood executives who put money in the hat as insurance against violence, and the New Yorker who pretends to be French so as not to have to take a side: "'Kesker say?' . . . with a strong New York thickness in his words."[20] Meanwhile, an Englishman whistles in admiration at the bravery of a fleeing fascist before reassuring Helen, not entirely persuasively, that he is "on the right side."[21] Rukeyser encourages us to see how the train's passengers have split, not so much by nationality as "between the ones who are for the town and the ones who feel this is spoiling their trip."[22] The idea of "spoiling the trip" connects to Helen's pride in emerging from her tourist mentality. She remembers, with embarrassment, her "tourist spasm" of impatience as she watches the anxious Swiss, still focused only on how to leave.[23] Quickly, she adjusts.

More sympathetic than "the pudding solicitude" of Peapack is the South American matron who worries about getting word of her delay to her twenty-two-year-old son.[24] She seizes on Helen, who is her son's age, and makes an appeal: "I might be your mother."[25] This connection and her fear touch Helen to the core: "The words came, shaking the blood inordinately, filled with a compassion that was unlooked-for, indeed undesirable, filled with every softness, an echo of the need of the other world which had just ended. . . . The softness reached her, the unhappy older woman reaching with a phrase, taking her hands, stroking her with the words, recalling an old unhappy softness. And through the window of the café, the break came."[26]

In response, Helen offers the woman her papers, so that she might make a safe passage to Barcelona and cable her son in Geneva: "Helen hurried ahead to the lady from South America. She had not answered the lady's phrase; she hoped she had shown how closely it had touched, how it had canceled the wish for softness. She spoke hurriedly and impersonally."[27] In this moment, Helen changes. She feels the woman's emotional appeal and finds the strength to respond in tune with the larger political purpose of the moment. She might be a daughter, but she came for the games, to modify a phrase of Rukeyser's. She has a commitment larger than personal emotion.

Even so, Helen knows the risk of giving up her papers: "The lady moved the beautiful russet mouth. 'You are extravagantly kind,' she was saying. A shot came like terror out of the hills."[28] In this moment, the stakes are high, as the violence in the background reminds us. Helen is trying to figure out what kind of person she wants to be. The South American lady appeals to her with softness, which Helen recognizes and does not spurn. At the same time, however, her softness cancels "the wish for softness." The words are filled with "a compassion that was unlooked for," but they also kindle in Helen a new determination to turn from the world that has just passed toward the wish to be part of the revolution. Her disciplined response echoes the author's note at the beginning of the manuscript: "This tale of foreigners depends least of all on character."[29] In her response to the lady, Helen acknowledges the appeal but answers impersonally; Rukeyser shows us a young woman who knows how to respond as a daughter and is training herself to respond as the kind of adult she wants to become. When the woman admits, moments later, that she has not been able to "go" since the train stopped, Helen is appalled by the intimate detail, even though she admits that the toilets of the stalled train are disgusting.

Helen is wholly "for the town," but what that means remains murky. At times it resembles the political correctness of early communism. More than once, a character—Helen included—labels an action as "correct," deploying the habit of ideological assessment that emerged in early communism and, not long after, made the notion of political correctness more an accusation or even a bitter punch line than an aspiration. As confident as Helen is, she finds it hard to participate in the political talk. In one conversation, she listens, observing her hesitation even as she thrills to the potential of the moment. Rukeyser conveys the range and rapidity of Helen's thoughts in a burst of short paragraphs:

> Helen thought how weak she was to let everyone talk on so, and to enjoy hearing them, to think always that if she had the poetic genius that produced the clue, she could find them, hear the real sound that could be spoken only at a moment like this, during such a night.
>
> There were hidden causes.
>
> The armies covered the world.
>
> Let them win, let them only win, and we can bother about this later, she thought, helplessly.
>
> All the moments flew, colored and clear. Now is my life, she thought. It comes to this night.
>
> Only wait.[30]

Helen listens, aware of the tremendous potential of the moment, hopeful that she might be one who could rise to meet it, but anxious, too. She feels at once vulnerable and full of awe for what she might be able to be and do.

Urgently, she thinks, "The dedication. . . . Give me something to do for this."[31] The desire to be of use persists: in a 1939 poem, she writes, "But I remember I am hands and whole, / head, breasts, and white, and to be used."[32] It consumes her when she looks down at the street and imagines the streets of Barcelona as her birthday: "She was proud in herself for a moment: this is how I come of age!"[33] She is keyed up, alert, in an ecstasy of purpose: her youth and her powerful determination both shine out. Rukeyser gives Helen a few more hesitations before the novel's end. She contrasts her emerging sense of purpose with Hans's, which, to her, seems stronger and earlier arrived at. At one point, she is literally stuck behind a stack of suitcases belonging to other women travelers, the accoutrements of bourgeois femininity separating her from her lover and revolution.

But, as *Savage Coast* acknowledges, and as Rukeyser writes about often elsewhere, the transformation of a young man from athlete to soldier is easier and far more familiar than that of a young woman from tourist to poet for the revolution. It is a change that still has no single clear name. Nevertheless, Rukeyser shows us how Helen makes her way, and her friend Olive recognizes it: "You really were clear all the way through."[34] Helen gives Hans credit for the change in her ("You began anew—you set in motion—"), but the novel invites us to see the seeds of her change as both connected to and separate from him.[35] As they board a ship to sail away, the novel ends in exaltation: *"Now you are about to return to your own countries. The boats are ready: the English will leave on their own boat, the Belgians will take all others on a ship they have chartered. If you have felt inactivity, that is all over now. Your work begins. It is your work now to go back, to tell your countries what you have seen in Spain."*[36]

Those last words of *Savage Coast*, set apart and italicized, make for a rousing conclusion to the novel, and it is tempting to linger in that moment of inspiration. But Rukeyser demands that we remain awake and alert to our lives, to face the fears as well as the defeats. Our last sight of Helen is on board the ship leaving Spain. Helen's creator did indeed return to the United States to tell people about what she learned, but, as she wrote several years later, at the top of the first page of her manuscript: "Everybody knows how that war ended."[37] The fight against fascism in Spain was unsuccessful, and World War II ravaged Europe. The Allies won, but only after the devastation of the Holocaust and the nuclear bombing of Hiroshima and Nagasaki. History has a way of troubling our hopes for a clear narrative of progress.

For all the bravery of her social actions in the 1930s, Rukeyser was protesting in a community of activists. When she drove to

Alabama and West Virginia, she was with friends. During and after World War II, she was often alone. Rukeyser faced setbacks in the 1940s and 1950s, as the wartime and postwar cultural climate grew increasingly hostile to leftists and independent women. Rowena Kennedy-Epstein explains that Rukeyser was working in an environment in which "her own life—as a radical, queer single mother—was often used to justify the dismissal of her work. She was called a 'threadbare' Sybil, a lesbian Helen, and a 'gloomy humanitarian'" in a period where women's lyricism was encouraged to eschew the philosophical and historical in favor of "minute particulars."[38] As another critic notes, "A woman Whitman, a woman whose work recalls the boldness and scope of Whitman's, was offensive to critics of the forties and fifties."[39] These changing tides of literary taste affected her. They continue to affect how we view her and her work.

While it can seem churlish to complain about the prizes one did not win, Rowena Kennedy-Epstein and Eric Keenaghan conduct a thought experiment about Rukeyser's failure to win the Bollingen Prize in 1948. She was one of four finalists, and the only woman finalist, but the jury ultimately awarded the prize to Ezra Pound. In the face of Pound's fascist radio broadcasts and his incarceration in a mental hospital, the judges congratulated themselves that, by overlooking his politics, their decision represented a triumph of art over politics. In retrospect, however, celebrating Pound had the added benefit of denying a woman attention. In not choosing Rukeyser, the committee, which included T. S. Eliot, chose a fascist poet over another one whose work, inconveniently, opposed fascism. How would the story we tell of twentieth-century poetry differ, Kennedy-Epstein and Keenaghan ask, if we saw it not as the "Pound era," as an influential book of that title had it, but as the "Rukeyser era"? The question is a worthy one, and a sobering reminder of the professional costs of rebellion. Rukeyser lacked allies and was called names by others, but, when asked to define herself, she was remarkably straightforward: "To live as a poet, woman,

American, and Jew—this chalks in my position. If the four come together in one person, each strengthens the others."[40]

As early as 1939, Rukeyser braced herself against the backlash. The prophetically named collection *A Turning Wind* begins with a poem poking fun at those who claim not to have time for poetry: "Reading Time: 1 Minute 26 Seconds." The title makes the point: the rejection of poetry is not about a lack of time. "The fear of poetry is the / fear," she writes. She goes on to describe fear as "that climax when the brain acknowledges the world."[41]

In her 1949 book *The Life of Poetry*, she recounts a conversation with a psychologist who greeted the mention of poetry "with extreme violence," insisting that "he had cut poetry out of his life." He was so angry that he "began to raise his voice and cut the air with his hand flat."[42] The violence of his reaction against poetry testifies to poetry's power. Throughout *The Life of Poetry*, Rukeyser acknowledges, considers, and then dismisses what she calls "The Resistances," the reasons that adults give for not making time for poetry. However, just as important as the resistances to poetry are the ways in which poetry resists the culture of war. By "the culture of war" Rukeyser means not only battles but everything that contributes to war and violence and detracts from working for peace and justice. In defending poetry in a time of violence, Rukeyser writes in a way that resists war and the culture that leads to and sustains it. At the same time, she acknowledges the fact of violence.

Violence must be acknowledged because, natural as it is, we need to work to overcome it. In that struggle, Rukeyser was not always successful. Her granddaughter, Rebecca Rukeyser, tells the story of a party in 1969 when Rukeyser grabbed a hatchet and wielded it at her friend Ella Winter for mentioning the man who fathered Rukeyser's child and from whom she was estranged.[43] She did not strike a blow, but she was angry enough that others had to hold her back. In a late poem, she wrote of her personal struggle not to be violent:

I say across the waves of the air to you:
today once more
I will try to be non-violent
one more day
this morning, waking the world away
in the violent day.[44]

Several times in recorded readings, she half-joked: "I think of myself as a violent woman who tries like the members of AA; I try not to be violent one more day."[45]

For Rukeyser, more dangerous than violence are the mental shortcuts that lead people to set poetry aside. Only through poetry can we imagine and then work toward living in a different, more just way, and thus of breaking the cycle of violence. She is particularly appalled by wartime propaganda, where government policy "was to win the war first, and work out the meanings afterward. The result was, of course, that the meanings were lost. You cannot put these things off."[46] Rukeyser's extensive work in documentary, as a film editor and with documentary photographers, taught her to see the potential of new media both for art and for cheap manipulation.

In her work with photography, both in the War Office and with her friend, collaborator, and lover Berenice Abbott, Rukeyser tried to rethink what captions could be. She contrasts the thrilling photography then being printed in *Life* magazine with the accompanying boring captions, which were "like labels on cans of soup."[47] Captions were too close to advertising, which she saw as corrupt, a dead and crass use of language. On the opposite end of the spectrum is poetry, but poetry faces resistance at every corner. Even so, what Rukeyser calls the life of poetry continues: in song, in dance, in the blues and the way that Southern African Americans found ways to make art even when denied the rudiments of literacy. Rukeyser finds inspiration in the dreams of immigrants, dreams that resist the harsh realities of America's failure to live up to its promise: "In many families, we were parented by the wish to move differently, to believe differently—that is, more intensely—from the past and the past place. . . . Their awakening is sharp, and we can tell their dreams. They do not long for home; they long for America."[48] In these lines, Rukeyser expands the vision of America to be wholly inclusive, considering the specific struggles of immigrants and former slaves and their descendants, but envisioning us all as participating in an American dream that is larger than even the idea of home itself. Dreams retain their power for Rukeyser because she sees America as partly a dream: one built by people who broke rules. Acknowledging the gap between the dream and the sharp awakening to ongoing injustice, Rukeyser keeps the idea of dreaming alive. Instead, she suggests that others follow her and bring the two art forms together in a way that would create a new third meaning, separate from words or images alone, entailing "the two in combination."[49] This combination has the potential, Rukeyser believed, to touch people in the deep way propaganda does, but without manipulating them.

The moment of belief for Rukeyser, when she "began to say what I believe," was also a moment in which she confirmed with her lover that fighting and writing had equal value in the battle to end fascism.[50] That justification in the face of resistance motivates and animates *The Life of Poetry*, which begins with a rousing call to writing as action, to writing as a form of resistance, to writing as a source of strength: "In time of crisis, we summon up our strength. Then, if we are lucky, we are able to call every resource, every forgotten image that can leap to our quickening, every memory that can make us know our power. And this luck is more than it seems to be: it depends on the long preparation of the self to be used."[51] Here, again, is the feeling of how crisis threatens violence but can lead to creativity, the feeling Helen had that morning in Spain when she saw the war-riven street before her like a birthday. Throughout *The Life of Poetry*, Rukeyser articulates how to stand against war and for life through a recommitment to poetry itself. As she writes in the book's final pages: "To be against war is not enough, it is hardly a beginning."[52]

As a teacher, Rukeyser was charismatic, demanding, unpredictable, and intimidating: "Students who had more sophisticated fronts came running from the house in tears, in fright, in anger."[53] Those who appreciated her found her charismatic and direct. She structured her poetry workshop at Vassar around one of her favorite novels, Virginia Woolf's *Orlando*. The novel, published in 1928, is a fantastical mock-biography based on the life and ancestry of Woolf's lover and friend, Vita Sackville-West, that follows Orlando, an Elizabethan aristocrat and poet, across four hundred years of English history. Over the course of Woolf's novel, the titular character meets many of the great poets of the English tradition, so one can imagine Woolf's novel, with its satiric depiction of the canon, as the spine of a college syllabus. Orlando barely ages but transforms, midway through, from a man to a woman. *Orlando* explores what Woolf called "androgyny": the idea that we each contain male and female, in varying mixtures, inside us, and that how we act and dress may have an enormous impact on how we are treated but scant impact on our fundamental selves. For Woolf, the greatest writers have what she called an "androgynous mind": they are able to imagine the experience of both men and women.[54] Such ideas appealed greatly to Rukeyser, who, since her first book, set store in the power of the imagination and recognized the complex mixture of male and female in herself. Orlando is also a poet, and in a key early scene he struggles to describe a shade of green. He looks out the window "in order to match the shade of green precisely he looked (and here he showed more audacity than most) at the thing itself. . . . After that, of course, he could write no more."[55] Orlando's efforts to get his description right earn him praise from Woolf's narrator, not only here, but later in the book. In her critique of Edwardian fiction, Woolf herself asks, "Is life like this? Must novels be like this?"[56] For Woolf, good writers keep looking at life to see if their words capture it justly. This is a lesson Rukeyser took to heart.

However, when she forced this lesson—of the importance of looking at the thing being described—on her students in 1959, it had an unexpected result. As one of them remembered it, she bullied a hapless undergraduate. Elaine Edelman, a student in that class who later became a friend of Rukeyser's, recalled the awful moment of confrontation:

> In the session I'm remembering here, we were getting into a poem in a new way. . . . But something wasn't working, and Muriel soon stopped whoever was reading, asking another student to go to the window, describe this living day. I can't remember who the girl was who slouched out of her hard-backed chair to the window side of the room, only the look on her face—vague and terrified. She stood looking out. "I see dead trees," she started, hopelessly. Abruptly, Muriel scraped her own chair back from the table and walked heavily toward the windows. . . . "The trees are not dead," she announced.[57]

Edelman recorded the relief, then shame, she felt that another girl and not she had not been put on the spot. That recognition brought one of Rukeyser's lines to mind: "Were we all brave, but at different times?"[58]

Not knowing what else to do, Edelman wrote a letter to her professor. It took her two days. She slipped it under Rukeyser's office door: "I told Muriel any one of us could have answered as badly as that girl, including me, and I felt she'd been unfair and harsh."[59] Rukeyser summoned Edelman to her office. Terrified, she went: "She didn't seem angry at me (as I'd expected). She talked. . . . She handed back my letter—refolded in thirds—saying, 'Yes.' Then her head and shoulders drooped forward slightly, but when she stood up to let me leave, her smile was clear again. She laid her hand on my arm and thanked me."[60] Edelman is too elegant an essayist to offer up an interpretation of that gesture—the droop—but it merits our attention. It is the beginning of their friendship, one in which she never stopped being Rukeyser's pupil. The gesture is at once vulnerable and strong: Through it, Rukeyser reveals the energy it takes her to gather herself into the person with the clear smile, the one who can take criticism from a student with gratitude. We might connect it to feelings of defeat she occasionally expresses elsewhere, as in the line "Thirty years, and my full strength, and all I touch has failed."[61] The flash of defeat is cousin to the flash of anger that she admits more readily elsewhere. The acceptance of criticism is linked to her commitment to living with integrity.

Kenneth Rexroth called Muriel Rukeyser "the best poet of her exact generation"—an arresting and somewhat patronizing moniker.[62] It is quoted often in part because of its wit, and because it is true: Rukeyser focused on her exact generation from the beginning. In "Poem Out of Childhood," the opening poem of her first collection, she writes, "Prinzip's year bore us," identifying her birth with Gavril Prinzip, Archduke Franz Ferdinand's assassin, and thus the beginning of World War I.[63] (Rukeyser was born in 1913: close enough.) Throughout that poem, she describes a childhood shadowed by war, tangled up in it, so that bike rides are connected to battles, and even the girlhood desire to grow up to be Joan of Arc is tinged with a precocious knowledge of war.

When Elaine Edelman put her note under Muriel Rukeyser's door, criticizing her teacher for being too harsh, she thought about the line "Were we all brave, but at different times?" It bolstered her courage. Rebels need to be brave, but not all the time and not all at the same time. Furthermore, bravery takes stamina. Rukeyser narrated that challenge as a young woman in *Savage Coast*, and we can see its ongoing evolution in her poetry, especially her well-known short lyric "Poem (I lived during the first century of world wars)." The poem is her 1968 response to the times. She writes as a middle-aged woman, born in 1913, just before the outbreak of World War I, and who came of age in that hopeful moment in Spain, when it seemed that it might be possible to stop the fascist threat. It continues her preoccupation with what it means to be a writer in uncertain times. The arresting first line, "I lived in the first century of world wars," seems to assume a posthumous voice and a heartbreaking confidence in the ongoingness of these conflicts: a total reversal from 1919's hopeful avowal that theirs had been a war to end all wars. The second line, "Most mornings I would be more or less insane," admits the damage of news of war. Her account of the distractions of the news invites us in. The way the "various devices" pull her attention away from her writing rejects the notion of the poet as insulated from daily anxieties and instead encourages the reader to understand her connection, too, to forces that pull us away from our focus and purpose:

> I lived in the first century of world wars.
> Most mornings I would be more or less insane,
> The newspapers would arrive with their careless stories,
> The news would pour out of various devices
> Interrupted by attempts to sell products to the unseen.
> I would call my friends on other devices;
> They would be more or less mad for similar reasons.
> Slowly I would get to pen and paper,
> Make my poems for others unseen and unborn.
> In the day I would be reminded of those men and women,
> Brave, setting up signals across vast distances,
> Considering a nameless way of living, of almost unimagined values.
> As the lights darkened, as the lights of night brightened,
> We would try to imagine them, try to find each other,
> To construct peace, to make love, to reconcile
> Waking with sleeping, ourselves with each other,
> Ourselves with ourselves. We would try by any means
> To reach the limits of ourselves, to reach beyond ourselves,
> To let go the means, to wake.
> I lived in the first century of these wars.[64]

"Poem" catalogs the distractions that stand between the poet and the page as it makes a plea for the connections across time and space that poetry can create. Rukeyser refuses to name the various devices that bring her the news. By refusing that cute gesture of much twentieth-century poetry, reveling in naming brands and technological specifics, Rukeyser avoids some of the pitfalls of locking her poem into too specific a context. I was born in a time of violence, Rukeyser's speaker begins, but this is not a soldier's poem; nor does she offer battlefield scenes. What she shares is the harm that comes even to those of us who experience war secondhand, and how the daily updates of that violence threaten her sanity and keep her from her work. That work, as a poet, is to use language not for the news but to help create connections—between states of being, among people, and within our divided selves.

"As the lights darkened," Rukeyser writes, "we would try . . . to imagine them." This "them," while not entirely clear, seems to be the "men and women, / Brave, setting up signals across vast distances," from a few lines earlier. The act of setting up signals recalls war work, and, specifically, the terrifying disaster of Wake Island, the subject of Rukeyser's controversial 1942 chapbook of the same name. In that December 1941 battle, which began nearly simultaneously with the attack on Pearl Harbor, American soldiers on a remote Pacific atoll were surprised by a Japanese air attack. It is a more general line, too, recalling the predicament of so many communications officers in wartime, of revolutionaries in hiding, of poets and visionaries. In short, she introduces the idea of bravery as an idea broadly applicable. As the poem moves from day to night, the context shifts from war to poetry.

War frames the poem, but it is not only about war. The line "To construct peace, to make love, to reconcile" is enjambed, meaning that its meaning carries over into the next line. We read "to reconcile" both as an end and as an introduction to the three necessary reconciliations that follow. First comes waking with sleeping, a reconciliation that asks us, perhaps in Jungian fashion, not only to take our dreams seriously but also to awaken into reality, to be present for the news and the world. Second, we must reconcile ourselves to each other, a reconciliation that exemplifies the best of the now-familiar idea of the personal as political. Finally, we have to reconcile ourselves to ourselves. That split self is important to Rukeyser. She is well acquainted with the feeling of being complex, variable, a surprise to oneself; she is intimate with contradictory impulse. In "No More Masks," she describes the way childbirth simultaneously split her in two—making two bodies where there once was one, while tearing her apart with labor itself—and reconciled her to herself.

Near the end of the poem, she offers an intention or a hope with two infinitive phrases: "To let go of the means, to wake." It is surprising for a poet to advocate letting go of means. Poetry is, after all, a craft of language that cares for means—the choice and order of words—more often than most of us ordinarily do. But Rukeyser gestures toward something larger than craft.

To split, to wake, to be born. In her novel, she celebrated her ability to be born into an adult self, fully participating in the world, no longer a tourist. That full participation, however, was curtailed by a culture that had no place for a woman with a strong, prophetic voice, passionate in her fight against fascism and for the life of poetry. In the era of the war in Vietnam, "Poem (I was born in the first century of world wars)," she, once again, offers us both solace and challenge. The chaos of our world makes us more or less insane: write anyway.

PART 3

Explorers

While a wanderer may have a desire to move without any fixed goal, explorers have an aim: to find a new trade route to Asia from Europe, a novel way of measuring the movement of the stars, a clearer understanding of a coastline or mountain range, or perhaps a more metaphorical exploration of an inner landscape or idea, combing the library for information on the origins of a language or experimenting with methods of composing a symphony or painting a landscape. Explorers may go alone, with a trusted partner or guide, or even an entire expedition. Although they often fail, they seem endowed with an almost unquenchable desire to persist. They are brilliant improvisers, strategizing their way out of tricky spots and changing plans as circumstances shift.

Virginia Woolf's very first preserved letter, written when she was just six years old, offers a glimpse into her lifelong avidity for exploration. When her godfather, the American poet James Russell Lowell, returned to the United States, the young Virginia wrote: "MY DEAR GODPAPA HAVE YOU BEEN TO THE ADIRONDACKS AND HAVE YOU SEEN LOTS OF WILD BEASTS AND A LOT OF BIRDS IN THEIR NESTS YOU ARE A NAUGHTY MAN NOT TO COME HERE GOOD BYE YOUR AFFECTE VIRGINIA."[1] This exuberance was not just the mood of a moment. When she borrowed books from her father's library, one of her favorites was Richard Hakluyt's *Voyages and Discoveries* (1589), an anthology that compiled the stories of British explorers, especially maritime explorers in search of a northwest passage across the Atlantic to India. Famous explorations by the likes of Francis Drake and Walter Raleigh are represented, but so are many forgotten voyages, some more fanciful than others.

Voyages and Discoveries was collected to serve Queen Elizabeth I and the rise of what would become the British Empire, but the impression one gets reading the collection centuries later is not so much of glorious conquest but of stumbling misadventure, unrealistic ambitions, random success, and petty crime. (Often, frustrated explorers would give up and simply ransack the first Spanish ship they could find rather than return empty-handed.) These stories fueled young Virginia's imagination, kindling a lifelong fascination with the discoveries of travel and a rich and ironic appreciation for the voyage that, while not reaching its official goal, yields a great story and unexpected, miscellaneous delights.

Given the eloquence with which Woolf wrote about how hard it is to be a woman wanderer, one might expect her to be even more emphatic on the difficulty of exploration for women. Instead, she celebrates exploration and adventure. She knew a number of Victorian and modern explorers, many of them women. Her mother, Julia Prinsep Duckworth Stephen, was born in India, and her father's family, the Stephens, had a long-standing tradition of work as Anglo-Indian colonial administrators. Perhaps most famous among these was her maternal great-aunt, the pioneering Victorian photographer Julia Margaret Cameron, who is depicted in Woolf's comic play *Freshwater* packing coffins for herself and her husband in case they die on their journey. And her husband, Leonard, had been a colonial administrator in Sri Lanka (then still Ceylon) when she and he began courting; he would bring many Indian intellectuals to their Bloomsbury home, where Woolf eagerly quizzed them about their lives. In homage to this lineage, one of Mrs. Dalloway's party guests is an elderly aunt who has written a book on the orchids of Burma.

Woolf's father, Leslie Stephen, was a prominent alpinist who made his first climbing trip to the Alps in 1857, the year the Alpine Club was founded. He joined the club the following year "and was soon reckoned to be among the first rank of English alpinists. He had many first ascents to his credit, accomplished without excessive difficulty, indeed in an almost casual manner. He was described as having 'walked from peak to peak like a pair of one-inch compasses over a large-sized map.'"[2] When Woolf's new friend and soon-to-be lover Vita Sackville-West told her about a hiking trip in the Dolomites, Woolf teased away the romance of such an adventure: "How could I think mountains and climbing romantic? Wasn't I brought up with alpenstocks in my nursery, and a raised map of the Alps showing every peak my father had climbed? Of course, London and the marshes are the places I like best."[3] Woolf claims exploration for herself, expanding the idea of exploring beyond physical feats.

Sackville-West was an explorer who accompanied her husband, the diplomat Harold Nicholson, to his post in Tehran and wrote a book about it, *Passenger to Teheran*, published by the Woolfs' Hogarth Press in 1926. Woolf's lover knew and spent time with the archaeologist and diplomat Gertrude Bell, one of the most famous British explorers of the Arab world in the period. Sackville-West's trip to Iran came as her and Woolf's affair was at its height, and Woolf's letters to her are full of imaginative exploration. Thus, not only did Woolf have an affair with a woman explorer, but she also practiced wide-ranging and playful imaginative exploration in her letters. Teasing Sackville-West that her letters are "dumb," she seizes on the vivid detail: "How my mouth watered over the casual paragraph about a park of dromedaries and racehorses in the Ukraine before the war."[4]

Hungry for more, she describes what she thinks Sackville-West must be doing: "You were sitting on the floor this time last week, where Grizzle [the dog] is now. Somehow, as you get further away,

I become less able to visualize you; and think of you with backgrounds of camels and pyramids which make me a little shy"; "I cannot think what it will interest you to be told of, now you are embedded in Persia. I see you always picking little bright red flowers high up on stony mountains"; "No letter since you were careering through the snow in Westphalia—that is nothing since Monday. I hope this doesn't mean you have been eaten by brigands, wrecked, torn to pieces."[5] Upon Sackville-West's return, she promises, "Grizzle and Virginia will rush down to meet you—they will lick you all over. So then, when you are tempted to folly, tremble on the brink of a precipice, sleep out on the Steppes, and so on. . . . Remember how desolated we shall both be should you lose a hair of your head, or a scratch one scratch on those lovely pillar like legs."[6] So invested was she that she teased she "could write a book about not being a Passenger to Teheran."[7]

More practically, their correspondence during Sackville-West's travels fueled *Orlando*, Woolf's mock-biography of her lover, which opens in the Elizabethan age and continues to the present day, including a crucial trip to Istanbul: "Orlando will be a little book, with pictures and a map or two. I make it up in bed at night, as I walk the streets, everywhere. I want to see you in the lamplight, in your emeralds."[8] Scattered throughout this playful correspondence are letters putting Sackville-West off due to Woolf's own illness, and letters dreaming of travel and then moderating or canceling plans to go to America or the East or France, perhaps just for a week after all. Although Woolf was not much of a traveler in middle age, in her writing she was an adventurous explorer.

The imaginative flights of Woolf's letters to Sackville-West were not the first time that Woolf put herself in the shoes of an explorer. In her first novel, *The Voyage Out* (1915), Woolf imagines a journey that she herself never took: a transatlantic sea voyage to a South American colony. In that novel, the characters draw on Elizabethan accounts of South America to describe what they see. Catching sight of the coast for the first time after weeks at sea, Mr.

Pepper recognizes the sight from his reading of Elizabethan travel narratives:

> As they drew nearer and could distinguish details, the effect of the earth with its minute objects and colours and different forms of life was overwhelming after four weeks of the sea, and kept them silent.
>
> "Three hundred years odd," said Mr. Pepper meditatively at length.
>
> As nobody said "What?" he merely extracted a bottle and swallowed a pill. The piece of information that died within him was to the effect that three hundred years ago five Elizabethan barques had anchored where the *Euphrosyne* now floated. Half-drawn up upon the beach lay an equal number of Spanish galleons, unmanned, for the country was still a virgin land behind a veil. Slipping across the water, the English sailors bore away bars of silver, bales of linen, timbers of cedar wood, golden crucifixes knobbed with emeralds.[9]

Woolf describes how chatter on a ship falls to a hush at the sight of the coast. Everyone senses the gravity of the change, but only one traveler has the context for it. Heretofore mainly an armchair traveler, Mr. Pepper's view of South America comes through the filter of his reading about exploration, and Woolf's details can be traced to Francis Drake's account of his circumnavigation of the globe.[10] While readers are treated to a vision of English pirates overlaid on the contemporary view, Mr. Pepper's fellow travelers lack curiosity, and his vision of "bales of linen" and "golden crucifixes" dies "within him" as he turns aside and takes his medicine. The details that enrich our reading are often unsuitable for conversation.

Woolf's awareness of the richness of inner exploration informs her depiction of the novel's young protagonist, Rachel Vinrace. Rachel is a pianist, and for all her awkwardness elsewhere, she knows herself to be "the best musician in South America."[11] Her piano playing is at once admired—as on the night when she takes over at a hotel dance—and seen as a threat, as when her aunt sees her practicing piano concertos and understands that this is a young woman who needs to be taken in hand. Even so, when Helen takes charge of Rachel's education, she knows that she must provide her with a room of her own. And she understands that, for a young woman, a room can become a world:

> When she shut the door Rachel entered an enchanted place, where the poets sang and things fell into their right proportions. Some days after . . . she was sitting alone, reading a brightly-covered red volume lettered on the back *Works of Henrik Ibsen*. Music was open on the piano, and books of music rose in two jagged pillars on the floor; but for the moment music was deserted.
>
> Far from looking bored or absent-minded, her eyes were concentrated almost sternly upon the page.[12]

This space, at once ordinary and "enchanted" is essential for Rachel's self-exploration. She can build towers with her music books, but she is not wandering; she is exploring. Her attention is focused; her purpose, although obscure to us, is fixed. That single-minded focus is the problem with her musicianship, too. Her father counsels that "a little less of *that* would do no harm," and, later, the man to whom she becomes engaged interrupts the intensity of her practicing, insisting that he "has no objection to nice simple tunes."[13] But there is no exploration in a "tune." Rachel becomes a great musician because she pursues difficulty with focus and determination, a focus and determination that is off-putting to those around her who want her to be a "reasonable person."[14]

Meeting the two young men who change her life, Terence Hewet and St. John Hirst, gives her new grounds for exploration. St. John takes the matter of her incomplete literary education into his hands and loans her Edward Gibbon's *History of the Decline and Fall of the Roman Empire*. Rachel's initial encounter with Gibbon's prose has the force of a discovery: "Never had any words been so vivid and so beautiful—Arabia Felix—Aethiopia. But those were not more noble than the others, hardy barbarians, forests, and morasses. They seemed to drive roads back to the very beginning of the world."[15] Gibbon's language enchants, but the men around Rachel use books to insist on their superiority, and her ignorance: she is pressured not just to read Gibbon, but Burke, Plato, Balzac, Sophocles, and more. One hot afternoon, she listens as Hewet, now her fiancé, reads Milton to her. Despite Hewet's insistence that Milton had "substance and shape," Rachel finds that she "could not keep her attention fixed on them."[16] Soon after, she retreats to bed. She and Hewet are ill-suited to make this expedition together.

Ultimately, Rachel's voyage out has no return. Engaged to a man insistent on interrupting her music and reading Milton to her even as she suffers from a headache, she develops a fever, sickens, and dies. It's a shocking ending. And it is surprising to recognize that, at the start of her career, even Virginia Woolf could not resolve how to offer a woman a chance to explore within the boundaries of the structure of the British novel.

Hewet objects to Rachel practicing her piano with intensity; while other men in the novel suggest books for Rachel, he reads to her aloud. In both instances, Hewet makes demands on her attention that prevent her from exploring her interests. He experiences her independence of mind as a threat. Her intense interest in music, rather than being a mark of distinction, is an oddity to wear away. Exploration can be both physical and imaginative, external and internal. More significantly, explorers possess contradictory impulses: the focus to pursue something wholeheartedly until its limit, and the willingness to abandon it. Rachel's rooms, strewn with books and music, indicate a passionate mind that works with tremendous concentration and then moves on. Her explorations are intense and varied.

The intensity required of an explorer is less apparent on a physical journey. We expect travelers to be intense; we are unsurprised to find them distracted or lost; we offer grace for a traveler who is unfamiliar with local customs. All of this allows women to take liberties (entering traditionally male spaces, wearing trousers, being physically vigorous) that would be difficult, if not impossible, at home. Often, this physical exploration takes on an imperialist cast: exploration is a common precursor to conquest and acquisition. However, the two explorers discussed in this chapter offer an important counternarrative of exploration for its own sake, especially Una Marson. As a Black Jamaican woman moving between a colonized nation and London, the center of empire, Marson offers a critique of the unthinking explorations of an imperial tourist.

Under patriarchy, physical exploration may be more available to women than the imaginative variety. Exploration as an imaginative pursuit faces more gendered obstacles, precisely because women are supposed to be interruptible, not passionate or single-minded. While traveling, a singularity of focus may not be so noticeable, but, at home, a woman occupied in a singular pursuit with intensity is likely to be perceived as a problem.

Both Sylvia Townsend Warner (1893–1978) and Una Marson (1905–1965) were well-traveled, but their most important explorations came in the ways they consistently reinvented themselves. Warner began her career as a composer, musician, and musicologist; continued as a novelist and poet; spent decades working part time as a communist organizer; and ended by writing fantasy stories, inventing a kingdom of elfin, with lore all its own. All along the way, she wrote essays and journalism. Warner's vast range makes her hard to summarize, but she is consistent in her interest in characters who pursue ideas to their logical conclusion, who reflect over long stretches of time before making what appears from the outside to be a sudden change.

Marson, too, was a writer and activist of great versatility. Her exploration of what it might mean for Jamaica to develop a national literature took her to London. Ironically, it was in London where she learned to understand Pan-African solidarity, finally moving away from the very, very traditional education that she had received in Jamaica to embrace a richer African- and African American–inflected literary heritage brought to London from the United States. Her curiosity, her willingness to explore, and her openness to new forms of expression, not to mention her ability to overcome the snobbery in which she was raised as a girl, made her a champion of the Jamaican language and Rastafarianism when many other educated Jamaicans scorned these developments as low class. Despite not having a college education, Marson rose to become the first Black producer at the BBC, and at the end of her career was invited to Israel for an international women's summit.

Explorers fill in the map; they show us new possibilities in both physical and imaginative realms. Explorers cross the border, refusing to stop there. Even when they are sent back, or their experiments falter, their journeys expand the horizons of the possible. Their willingness to regroup and move in a new direction after a setback helps fend off those other voices telling them to quit. Explorers may lead the way, but they bring others along with them.

Sylvia Townsend Warner
1893–1978

SHE HAD CHANGED HER MIND

Sylvia Townsend Warner's first novel, *Lolly Willowes* (1926), was the first-ever selection of the Book-of-the-Month Club, and it remains her best known work. As it opens, Lolly Willowes's father has died. She leaves her beloved country home to go to London as the unpaid caretaker for her brother's children. Twenty years pass, and her nieces have children of their own. They think it wonderful that Aunt Lolly, as they call her, is still around to care for them and their children. Restless with a desire she cannot name, Lolly (whose given name is Laura, but who is known by the babyish nickname her nieces give her) begins exploring London on her own, taking long walks and buying extravagant bouquets of flowers. One day, she happens upon an enchanting shop full of beautiful chrysanthemums and, on impulse, buys them all. It's a small gesture that leads to a complete life transformation. The passage describing her purchase lays out a cascade of events, one thing leading to another:

> When he brought her the change from her pound-note and the chrysanthemums pinned up in sheets of white paper, he brought also several sprays of beech leaves. These, he explained, were thrown in with her purchase. Laura took them into her arms. The great fans of orange tracery seemed to her even more beautiful than the chrysanthemums, for they had been given to her, they

> were a surprise. She sniffed. They smelt of woods, of dark rustling woods like the wood to whose edge she came so often in the country of her autumn imagination. She stood very still to make quite sure of her sensations. Then:
>
> "Where do they come from?" she asked.
>
> "From near Chenies, ma'am, in Buckinghamshire. I have a sister living there, and every Sunday I go out to see her, and bring back a load of foliage with me."
>
> There was no need to ask now who made the jams and tied on the bladders. Laura knew all that she wanted to know. Her course lay clear before her. Holding the sprays of beech as though she were marching on Dunsinane, she went to a bookseller's. There she bought a small guide-book to the Chilterns and inquired for a map of that district. It must, she explained, be very detailed, and give as many names and footpaths as possible. Her eyes were so bright and her demands so earnest that the bookseller, though he had not that kind of map, was sympathetic, and directed her to another shop where she could find what she wanted. It was only a little way off, but closing-time was at hand, so she took a taxi. Having bought the map she took another taxi home. But at the top of Apsley Terrace she had one of her impulses of secrecy and told the driver that she would walk the rest of the way.[1]

Her extravagant purchase—"He did not expect such a good customer at this late hour"—leads the shopkeeper to give her some beech sprays. The sprays spark a conversation. The conversation opens a portal: suddenly, the adventure of buying the flowers herself suggests another adventure altogether: Lolly can buy a map—a complicated errand in itself—and go to the countryside, where the flowers grow.

She leaves her stunned family and moves to Great Mop. She studies her map and goes exploring, "and in the evening . . . she looked at the map and marked where she had been with little bleeding footsteps of red ink."[2] This continues for some time, with

Lolly marking up her map with the seriousness of a land surveyor. Then, unexpectedly, she comes to realize that the map, so essential in the beginning, has become an obstacle to her starting her new life in the country, not as an explorer but as a resident. Just as she is settling into the realization that there are things about her new home that she will never understand, "she [does] an odd thing":

> In her wanderings she had found a disused well. It was sunk at the side of a green lane, and grass and bushes had grown up around its low rim, almost to conceal it; the wooden frame was broken and mouldered, ropes and pulleys had long ago been taken away, and the water was sunk far down, only distinguishable as an uncertain reflection of the sky. Here, one evening, she brought her guide-book and her map. . . . Looking into the well she watched the reflected sky grow dimmer; and when she raised her eyes the gathering darkness of the landscape surprised her. The time had come. She took the guide-book and the map and threw them in.[3]

This second leap frees Lolly. All that has been mysterious about Great Mop begins to reveal itself. Trusting herself, she plunges into a new life, recognizing that "wherever she strayed the hills folded themselves round her like the fingers of a hand."[4]

Exploration is often figured as traveling great distances, but the explorations at the heart of Warner's work often involve withdrawals into the details of village life. For Lolly, life in Great Mop offers a return to the love of nature, of botany, and of animals that had made her hope, as a girl, that she might stay in her childhood home and take charge of the family brewery. In Great Mop, she finds a surprising affinity with her landlady, who helps her fend off unwanted visits from a nephew. That affinity grows into something strange and wholly unexpected: Great Mop is a village of witches, and, as a series of strange incidents begin to confirm, Lolly, too, is a witch, something she would never have discovered about herself had she not moved to Great Mop. At her first witches' Sabbath, she finds herself dancing with a red-haired woman whom she recognizes from the village: "The pasty-faced and anemic young slattern whom she had seen dawdling about the village danced with a fervor that annihilated every misgiving. They whirled faster and faster, fused together like two suns that whirl and blaze in a single destruction. A strand of the red hair came undone and brushed across Laura's face. The contact made her tingle from head to foot."[5] Enchanted by the companionship, and finally free of the last of her nieces and nephews, Laura (she is Lolly no more), is stirred by this beautiful witch. Not long after, she has a conference with Satan. She promises him her soul and, in exchange, secures her earthly freedom.

Three years before Virginia Woolf argued for privacy and financial freedom in *A Room of One's Own*, Warner articulated the necessity and delight of such a room and independence for women. Turning the Faust myth on its head, she irreverently proposes the devil as a protector against convention and revives the fantasy of village witchcraft as a haven for middle-aged women. *Lolly Willowes* offers a joyful story, not of distant lands but of the ways that a forgotten village, explored without a map, offers freedom.

Sylvia Townsend Warner was born in 1893, the only child of her father, George Warner, a popular and gifted history master at the famous Harrow School outside of London, and her mother, charismatic and beautiful Nora Hudleston Warner. Although Warner had almost no formal schooling and no university education, she was known, sometimes mockingly, as the "best boy at Harrow," and, in her twenties, she became "that odd thing—a musicologist."[6] Warner's long and productive career, as a musicologist, composer, poet, novelist, biographer, translator, and communist, is so various that it is difficult to summarize. Her nine novels are set in rural England of the fourteenth, nineteenth, and twentieth centuries;

the contemporary South Seas; France during the 1848 revolution, and eighteenth-century Spain. Her short stories range from realist tales of wartime England to the late fantasy stories of *Kingdoms of Elfin*. She wrote a biography of her friend T. H. White and was the first to translate Marcel Proust's volume of essays, *Contre Sainte-Beuve*, into English. True to her origins as the intellectual daughter of a historian, Warner's fictional explorations travel across space and time.

At nineteen, Warner began an affair with Percy Buck, the music master at Harrow, who was forty-one and married. She was composing music and intended to travel to Austria to study with Arnold Schoenberg, a plan that was interrupted by World War I. In 1915, she answered a notice to become a munitions worker—a daring choice for a young woman of her social class, when most women would have served as ambulance drivers, VAD nurses (as Vera Brittain did), domestic aid workers, or not volunteered at all. Her father encouraged her to write up her experiences, and the pay she received for her first publication—an essay in *Blackwood's*, "Behind the Firing Line" by "a Lady Worker"—was substantial: "sixteen guineas, as compared with the six shillings, including bonus, she earned per shift in the munitions factory."[7] Sadly, it was the only publication of hers that her father ever saw. He died suddenly that September, leaving a twenty-two-year-old Warner bereft and her mother bereft and angry, often lashing out at her only child.

Her talent for music saved her in these sad years. As part of a national musical revival in England, a grant from the Carnegie UK Trust funded a project to collect and print for the first time church music from Tudor England. Partly through Buck, but also by dint of her own musicianship, she was hired to be one of the editors—the only woman and the only so-called amateur—of the massive ten-volume *Tudor Church Music*, a project that "took five people twelve years to complete."[8] Warner moved to London, escaping the strained atmosphere of home. There, she began singing with the Bach choir and studying the notation of Tudor music. As part of her research, she visited "university towns to rummage through archives, or arrived at remote rural churches where she was met by a warden, or the woman who cleaned. . . . Occasionally, she played the organ."[9]

Starting in 1921, Warner began spending less time in London and more time in a Dorset village, visiting a friend, the writer Theodore Powys. In 1930, she bought a cottage in East Chaldon, planning to visit on weekends. Soon after, she offered it to Valentine Ackland, a young poet who had fallen on hard times and been kicked out of her flat nearby. Ackland stayed in the cottage during the week, and Warner visited on weekends. They corresponded as Warner set up house but did not often cross paths. Then, one October weekend in 1930, when both women were home, they heard about a servant girl who ran away from an abusive employer, was caught and sent to an insane asylum, and tried to escape. While the employer's abuses were common knowledge in the village, this incident enraged Warner and Ackland. They ate a hurried supper and went to confront the employer, who denied wrongdoing. That night, against their custom, they talked to each other through the thin walls of their adjoining bedrooms. After some time, Ackland said, "I sometimes think I am utterly unloved."[10] Moved, Warner went to her. Ackland embraced her, and they became lovers, not parting until Ackland's death.

Five years later, in 1935, both women joined the Communist Party, largely due to Ackland's influence. The following year, Warner's fourth novel, *Summer Will Show*, was published. She and Ackland went to Spain in support of the Republican side in the Spanish Civil War; they returned less than a year later as delegates to the International Congress of Writers. This is a big change. One does not necessarily expect a bookish thirty-seven-year-old woman, even one whose novels are magical and delightfully queer, to suddenly fall in love with a woman, make a new life with her, and become a communist. In fact, at an age when many women of her generation would have been preoccupied with family obligations—unmarried and childless women were often expected to contribute as much or even more than wives—Warner shook herself free of all custom. She changed her life, and, as a result of her love for and relationship with Ackland, she also changed her mind.

Life together was not simple. Ackland was an alcoholic and unfaithful. Her decade-long affair with Elizabeth Wade-White strained their partnership almost to breaking. But she and Warner stayed together, and they remained in Dorset. Warner kept writing novels and, increasingly, short stories. Her novel *After the Death of Don Juan* (1938) continues her response to the Spanish Civil War, and *The Corner That Held Them* (1948) is a minor masterpiece, considering the complexities of communal (and communist) life through a historical novel set in a remote convent during the Black Death. Her contributions to the *New Yorker* were a mainstay of the magazine through the 1940s and 1950s and sustained Warner financially—she referred to the magazine as "her gentleman friend"—and, through her close friendship with William Maxwell, her editor, they sustained her emotionally, too.[11] Her and Maxwell's letters, collected as *The Element of Lavishness*, show a professional relationship that blossomed into a deep and long-standing friendship, punctuated by visits to England and New York, a shared interest in leftist politics, and admiration and support for each other's writing. At the end of her life, Warner appointed him her literary executor. She died on May 1, 1978.

Summer Will Show came out of the exciting period in Warner's life when she was falling in love with Ackland, and, through her, becoming more committed to leftist politics. It is a political novel about changing your life and your mind. It combines an exploration of the 1848 Revolution, what Karl Marx and Friedrich Engels called the "spectre haunting Europe," with the story of one woman's life.[12] When the novel opens, Sophia Willoughby has little interest in politics, but she transforms into the woman, who, on the final page, renounces her aunt's offer of reconciliation, stating, "I have changed my ideas. I do not think as I did," and returning to her deceased lover's apartment to pore over a draft of *The Communist Manifesto*.[13] The novel shows how love and politics can inform and enhance each other.

Sophia is a wealthy Englishwoman, estranged from her husband, Frederick. She has two sickly children and custody of her uncle's half-Black, out-of-wedlock son, Caspar. Taking an instant dislike to her charismatic ward and the burden he represents, Sophia sends Caspar to boarding school. When he departs, her children sicken and die. Childless and separated, she goes to Paris with the intention of confronting Frederick and persuading him to give her another child. Against her strongest intentions, she is drawn to her husband's lover's salon. Frederick's lover, a charismatic Jewish storyteller named Minna Lemuel, casts a spell on the assembled guests, a mix of bohemians and aristocrats, as she tells the story of her family's murder by an anti-Semitic mob, and of her escape from Lithuania. Her story is cut short by the beginning of the failed 1848 revolution. Spellbound, exhausted, and overwhelmed, Sophia falls asleep in Minna's apartment, thus beginning *her* love affair with Minna. After several half-hearted attempts at reconciliation with Frederick, Sophia casts her lot with Minna and revolution.

As the revolution continues, Sophia and Minna fall in love and grow poorer and poorer, and Sophia gradually becomes a revolutionary of a sort. She sings English hymns on the street, pretending to be an Englishwoman kidnapped into a convent, while a colleague gives revolutionary speeches against the church. Her ward, Caspar, arrives unexpectedly in Paris, thin and miserable, having run away from a school where he was badly treated. His presence threatens to spoil the women's happiness, so Sophia enlists Frederick to enroll him in a school in Paris. (Her callous treatment of children primarily as an annoyance to be overcome remains consistent.) Frederick secretly enrolls Caspar in the antirevolutionary Gardes Mobiles. Meanwhile, Sophia works for the revolution by distributing copies of an important contraband manuscript, posing as a woman running errands. While wandering Paris with her envelopes of contraband revolutionary literature, the fighting begins. Sophia joins Minna on the barricades only to witness Minna being bayoneted by none other than Caspar. In retaliation, Sophia shoots him in the mouth. Both Caspar and Minna die, and Sophia is imprisoned with the other revolutionaries. But the mass execution is paused at the sight of a woman, and Sophia is freed on account of her sex. Grief-stricken, she returns to Minna's apartment, opens the final envelope of revolutionary literature, and begins to read. It's *The Communist Manifesto*.

For Sophia to become someone who assuages her grief by reading Marx and Engels, she has to overcome her rigid sense of class hierarchy. As she reflects, she recognizes that she "had been brought up in a world policed by oughts."[14] She is a strong woman, and perhaps even a protofeminist, but of a very distinct, aristocratic type. She is trivial, imperious, self-important, overconfident, and she knows it. At one point, she thinks, accurately, that her jealousy of Minna is "prim, disapproving, schoolmistressly."[15] When the fighting first breaks out in the streets, and the concierge announces that carriages are needed to buttress the barricades, Sophia fusses to her estranged husband, "I wish you would get me a cab."[16] With the streets of the Left Bank still full of revolutionaries, Sophia thinks to celebrate her first night with Minna by going out to a restaurant. With some trouble, they pick through the barricades and at last find a place that is open. Still utterly unconcerned about the revolution in these early days, Sophia is preoccupied by the challenges of ordering from a menu, reassuring herself: "It had been an axiom of Papa's that under doubtful circumstances it was best to order Beaujolais."[17] She even deludes herself that she remains in Paris neither because she seeks reconciliation with Frederick nor to pursue Minna, but because "I must certainly improve upon my bonnet."[18]

Still, early on, there is a sign that Sophia might be open to change. When her children die, as she fumbles blindly for what to do next with her life, she briefly considers going to the limekiln man and asking him to help her get pregnant. She marches off to the kiln in the middle of the night, but, before she can proposition him, he makes the bitter and, to her ears, disrespectful observation: "Rich and poor can breed alike, I suppose."[19] His comments outrage her, but they also do her good. "She found herself tautened and stimulated," and she pauses to reflect on her assumptions: "All her life long Sophia heard it said that the labouring classes were insolent, mutinous and violent. She had agreed to this as to a matter of course. . . . Yet until this evening she had never heard a speech that was not respectful. Even the Labourers' Rising of 1830 had shown itself to her as a procession of men wearing their best clothes, men with washed smocks and oily church-going heads."[20]

Warner depicts how Sophia's sex and class have sheltered her from ever hearing a disrespectful word. From Mary Wollstonecraft to Virginia Woolf, feminists have described the negative consequences of denying women the responsibilities of citizenship. Among these consequences is the way that wealthy women do not have to think but are raised simply to agree, to dwell within the world of "oughts," the world that ensures that the mistress of an estate in Dorset will never hear a disrespectful word.

Sophia's memory of the Labourers' Rising of 1830 is the middle term in a series of processions in the novel. *Summer Will Show* opens on the thirteenth of July, the day before Bastille Day, and thus a date that loudly signals the imminence of revolution within the narrative—and that suggests the sense of foreboding in Europe during the early 1930s, when Warner was writing this book. On that July 13 of the book's opening, Sophia thinks back to another year on that same date when, as a little girl, "she had been taken to see the Duke of Wellington. At ten o'clock precisely the open barouche came to the door, and Sophia . . . ran down the steps to admire the turn-out."[21]

For the young Sophia, there is no difference between the Duke of Wellington's carriage and the Labourers' Rising: both are spectacles for a girl to observe from afar. We know, then, that she has truly changed when she moves from being a spectator to a participant. In one of the book's final scenes, Sophia is among a group of prisoners, "being shouted to their feet, ranged closely together, as though they were inferior exhibits on the back-staging of a flower-show."[22] No longer an observer, Sophia is part of the spectacle, and her focus is not on how the guards view her but on the words of a fellow prisoner. Her transformation is complete.

Sophia must also overcome the subtle sabotage of those who, in seeming to support her independence, are diminishing her agency. She feels exasperated by how, as a woman, any action, however irrational, can be dismissed because she is expected to be irrational:

> It was boring to be a woman, nothing that one did had any meat in it. . . . Free as she might be to do as she pleased, all her doings were barrened. Should she have her horse saddled in the middle of the night, ride through the dark and the rough weather till morning, she rode to no end. Should she enforce her will over convention, go out into the woods and cut down another tree, the deed would only be granted to her on the terms that it was a woman's whim, a nonsense to be tidied up as soon as possible by the responsible part of the world. If she were to shoot a poacher, the Justices of the Peace would huddle it away as an accident. Yes, they would say that she was frightened, a timid female acting in fear of her life. . . . Yet there, what could she do to appease her desire to leave a mark?[23]

Not only has she been protected from politics, but her actions have been stripped of significance. Sophia knows that any rebellion of hers, personal or political, will be understood as fear or petulance.

The strongest symbol of this conservative power is Sophia's French aunt, Léocadie. When Sophia lashes out at her estranged husband over tea, spoiling the reconciliation that her aunt is trying to broker, Léocadie treats the outburst as a tantrum: "My child, say no more of that. At my age, when one has outlived for so long one's own impetuosity, one is touched to see an act of impulse."[24] And, at the end of the book, with Minna dead and Sophia out of prison, Léocadie is once again ready to bring her back into the fold, with a warm but trivializing "Ah, Sophie, what a pleasure to hear you laugh again!"[25]

Sophia can well imagine how the story will be told, should she permit herself to return to her aunt's accepting embrace, imagining how one day the people will say: "'Do you know, in the year '48 old Mrs. Willoughby murdered her uncle's illegitimate son—a boy of fifteen, a poor stupid blackamoor who worshipped the ground she trod on?' 'No, really? One would never think it.'"[26] Imagining the gossip, Sophia recognizes the impossibility of a return to her old life. Her explorations have changed her completely. It is then that she turns to her aunt and says, "I have changed my ideas. I do not think as I did."[27]

Minna's charisma, both intellectual and sexual, is the force that drives Sophia to change. Moreover, with Minna, Sophia is happy: "Their words, light and taunting, rose up like bubbles delicately exploding from a wine they were to drink together. People whom they encountered turned round to stare after them. It was not common, in those lean days, to see two faces so carelessly joyful."[28] This joy has a powerful autobiographical corollary: Warner and Ackland traveled to Paris together in 1932 and found, to their delight, that Parisians not only accepted them as a couple but openly admired Ackland and greeted Warner with looks of congratulations. The joy of being out together is profound, especially for same-sex couples.

Warner's biographer writes: "Outside a grocer's shop in the Rue Mouffetard, Sylvia was suddenly aware that she wanted to write a novel about the 1848 revolutions."[29] As the political tensions mount, and Minna's friends spend more and more time with Minna and Sophia, Sophia finds herself missing "those habits of the two sprigged coffee-cups on the table by the window, the clock set by the compline bell, the paired plates and glasses that her hand could with certainty take down from the shelf and replace there."[30]

Decades later, Warner herself remarked on her own tendency to fall into habit: "'The truth is,' she wrote to William Maxwell [in 1972], 'I was growing rather alarmed by the way I was acceding to routine; compliance with it felt increasingly like madness. "Now I hang up the tea-cup on the 3rd hook. Now I put the blue plates in the rack."'"[31] With Minna, Sophia finds both revolution and domestic bliss, as Warner had found with Ackland. When Sophia has finally shed her ties to her husband and her fortune, Minna remarks with approbation: "To give up a thing or a person, that is of no significance. It is when you put out your hand for something else, something better, that you declare yourself. And though you may think that you have chosen me . . . or chosen happiness, it is the Revolution you have chosen."[32]

To choose revolution is both an act of hope and a serious matter. In the opening of an essay on Rosa Luxemburg, Warner contrasts our childhood "dark-lantern, 'let's play at conspirators'" notion that "it is pretty good fun to be a revolutionary" with the reality of a woman who "lived hard and uncomfortably, was several times in prison, and in the end was murdered."[33] Warner hoped *Summer Will Show* would encourage others to work for revolution, but it does not shrink from revolution's toll. Heather Love emphasizes the novel's fascinating "combination of intense joy and total devastation."[34] The book invites us to see the analogy between the failed revolutions of 1848 and the politics of 1936. In that, Warner was more prophetic than she could know. The Spanish Civil War broke out in July, with fascist generals fighting the Republican government. Warner attended an International Peace Conference in Brussels in September, and she and Ackland were on a ship to Barcelona later that month. They spent a month there and then returned to be part of the Second Congress of International Writers in June 1937. Democracy fell in Spain while Hitler and Mussolini rose to power in Germany and Italy.

For her gravity and hard work, she was mocked by the young British radicals of the 1930s; Stephen Spender caricatured her as a

"Communist lady writer [who] looked like, and behaved like, a vicar's wife presiding over a tea party given on a vicarage lawn as large as the whole of Republican Spain. Her extensory smiling mouth and her secretly superior eyes under her shovel hat made her graciously forbidding. She insisted—rather cruelly, I thought—on calling everyone 'comrade.'"[35] For decades, Spender's dismissal affected how critics viewed Warner, with the literary world taking as gospel a young man's impressions of a middle-aged woman and either diminishing or ignoring entirely her activism and her literary contributions to the literature of anti-fascist Spain. Only recently has the story begun to change. Back home in Chaldon, Warner and Ackland were known for their willing and efficient assistance with the bureaucratic business of political work for the Communist Party: they wrote poems, organized meetings, and became well acquainted with the challenges of local politics. In her first grief, Sophia Willoughby thinks she might get pregnant, make jam, or go foxhunting. Freed from husband and children, Sophia chooses love and change. To use Minna's phrase, she puts out her hand for something.

In ordinary usage, to explore is to move outward and far away, but Warner's explorations tend to go inward and back in time. Even so, these movements against the grain of expectations are neither small nor safe. As the move from London to the village of Chaldon lead her deeper into village culture and closer contact with people of all classes, so, in her fiction, does she explore the intricacies of a small community. This reaches its zenith in her 1948 masterpiece, *The Corner That Held Them*, a novel written "on the purest Marxian principles" about a group of nuns in a struggling convent in a marshy part of Norfolk in the fourteenth century.[36] Where *Lolly Willowes* follows a woman's quest for freedom, and *Summer Will Show* portrays how a couple can live as revolutionaries, *The Corner That Held Them* observes the challenge of living experimentally after the first fervor of commitment has worn off. The plot stretches over four decades, and, while there are remarkable figures, the novel does not have characters in the traditional sense. The long duration means that some of the most important personages at the novel's opening die midway through the book, while those who matter to the resolution have only just entered the story.

Over the course of the book, Warner offers a wide range of reasons why a woman might choose to become a nun. Rarely is it because of a vocation—and, in fact, one of her only comments about visions is "Of all the menaces to peace and quiet, a visionary nun is the worst, and when that nun is the novice-mistress the worst is ten times worsened."[37] In fourteenth-century England, a woman could marry or become a nun. Becoming a nun, she was stuck in a small convent—a narrow life, perhaps, but not likely much more limiting than the scullery of a family home. Moreover, within the world of her convent, the roles she could fill offered variety: she might design a spire for the chapel, learn to read, admit that she would like to be the prioress, or focus on making really fine marzipan. None of this has much to do with religion, but it does suggest that there are ways to have a life more in tune with your desires and abilities than marriage and motherhood alone can provide. In this, Warner affords herself the chance to explore Marxist principles in a different key.

Warner had learned the nuances of communal life starting with her work in the munitions factory during World War I, lessons that were reinforced through her participation in village politics. In her very first publication in 1916, she describes making conversation with other munitions factory workers on a break: "Introductions were prefaced, as among all primitive peoples, with gifts. . . . 'The girl-with-the-dirty-face has got an egg,' said some one. 'She says it's a country egg, too.' We looked admiringly at the damsel thus designated, and registered, each one of us, a silent vow to write home as soon as possible."[38] Unafraid of work and fascinated by the ways that ordinary things, like hunger after a hard day's work, unite us, Warner values common speech and common ground.

In her 1959 lecture "Women as Writers," she identifies the ways that women learn how to talk to each other across class partly from the necessity of communicating about children and dinner. "Another pantry window trait is the kind of workaday democracy, an ease and appreciativeness in low company," an acquaintance "with human passions and what they can lead to," and "a willing ear for the native tongue, for turns of phrase used by carpenters, gardeners, sailors, milliners, tinkers, old nurses, and that oldest nurse of all, ballad and folklore."[39] An essay about an operatic fight between her mother and another Red Cross volunteer during World War I about whether pajamas for wounded soldiers should have a button on the fly is characteristic of Warner's interest in the combination of competence, hard work, competition, and spite of a workplace:

> Mrs. Moss-Henry entered the room.
>
> "Not still talking about buttons, surely?"
>
> Her tone was sarcastic. My mother replied with firmness, "I am."
>
> Mrs. Moss-Henry feigned a yawn.
>
> "I really don't think we want to hear any more about them."
>
> "You will!" riposted my mother. "This afternoon I am going to Devonshire House."
>
> Such words struck awe into every hearer. Devonshire House was the Ark of the Covenant.[40]

The women head off to Red Cross headquarters in London in a snit, demanding a hearing. Their rivalry has banished the larger shared goal of winning the war from their horizon, and Warner's mother's ultimate victory in the fight becomes, in Warner's comic essay, the moment that she won the war for England.

Critics who wanted more piety in a book set in a convent forgot how seldom ordinary people talk about shared values. Warner's mother and Mrs. Moss-Henry were united in their support for England; their vehement disagreement was about whether pajamas should have buttons. The nuns are all Catholic, so there may be little reason to argue about faith. By contrast, whether to make up a shortfall in the convent budget through opening a school or selling marzipan may be a matter with great variance of opinion. When everyone agrees to a life dedicated to Christ, the rightness of one side in a war, Marxist principles, or the rules of the commune or kibbutz, the shared values no longer need debating; instead, other issues rise to the fore, including, especially, the budget and internal politics.

So, in *The Corner That Held Them*, a momentary error in judgment throws the succession of the convent into disarray: "Dame Lovisa, long accepted as inevitable, was out of the question, since it was she who had let the enemy in among them, and Dame Eleanor, her natural rival, was now felt to be out of the question also; for if you choose the lesser of two rivals you create a schism, and though under some circumstances a schism can be enlivening, it is a fair-weather luxury; one cannot afford it in times of misfortune."[41] This specific calamity occasions a more general observation about political infighting. Schisms are "a fair-weather luxury"; it matters to try to get along. As amusing as her mother's fight with Mrs. Moss-Henry may be in retrospect, Warner sides with those who recognize that there are times when such rivalries need to be set aside. (And, indeed, the hard feelings caused by the pajama button fight caused Mrs. Moss-Henry to leave the Red Cross, with Warner's mother resigning soon after.)

Warner's observations about village politics are as astute as anything in *Middlemarch* or the novels of Anthony Trollope. The difference in Warner's case is that every actor, every rival, every ally, every foe, is a woman: the bullies, the brilliant administrators, the dogged fools who rise, the ambitious ones thwarted in their aims, the shy ones with a gift—every single one, a woman. If women are to enter public life on their own terms, if women are to be independent and free, if women are to take advantage of the new opportunities afforded by access to professions and the vote, women need to figure out ways to be in community, ways to fill *every* role, including roles long almost exclusively occupied by men. Imagining a convent, Warner offers women an imaginative history of leadership, warts and all. She unlocks a common thread of female community, depicting women enacting the full range of human emotions and impulses, possessing the full range of human talents and foibles.

One tender quest at the heart of these books often revolves around loneliness and the need to find a friend. She captures extreme intellectual isolation in a moment when Dame Matilda wonders whom to consult for advice: "That is the drawback of being so very sensible: one cannot take counsel because it is against common sense to seek it."[42] Another nun "was subject to the usual calamity of the bedridden, to be visited only by bores."[43] Several times in *The Corner That Held Them*, a character recognizes him- or herself to be in the presence of a fellow intelligent person, and all else ceases to matter. Philosophical differences melt away, as in this moment between two men: "It took him aback to hear Henry Yellowlees chuckle. They turned to face each other. Intelligence flashed from one to the other, and then they began to look rather sheepish, embarrassed at the sudden discovery of a common bond."[44]

A hallmark of Warner's explorations is her interest in people who, after gradually considering their unease—sometimes for years, even decades—make a sudden change. At the end of *The Corner That Held Them*, the convent has, once again, hit a financial crisis, and two nuns are sent to the city to beg for alms. Both are restless spirits; both have come to feel miserable at the convent. One wants to become an anchoress (i.e., a nun living in extreme seclusion), but the other watches the pilgrims on their way to Jerusalem and suddenly decides to join them. As Warner is suspicious of visionaries, she suspects the motives of the aspiring anchoress. To her, there is something immoral in desiring total retreat from the world. The pilgrim, by contrast, is celebrated. All at once, she makes a way where there seemed to be no way. She is not particularly special—none of the nuns are, but she seizes her chance.

Dame Sibilla, the nun who becomes a pilgrim, claims a headache and sends her companion out to beg alone among the pilgrims streaming through town. Overwhelmed by the crowd, the aspiring anchoress looks up from her alms bowl at a pilgrim, and "in that same moment she saw that the pilgrim was Dame Sibilla. Their eyes met. Dame Sibilla gave a little nod, as much as to say, *I told you so.* Dropping an alms into the dish, she leaned forward and said rapidly, 'Do not betray me. Do not say that you have seen me here among the pilgrims.'"[45] When the companion objects that she will be missed at the convent, Sibilla counters, "I assure you, it is all God's will. I am a pilgrim, I am inexpressibly happy. I shall pray for you in Jerusalem."[46] And, with that, the novel ends.

All her life, Warner's commitment to revolution was bound up with her love of Ackland. When Stalin's murderous excesses emerged, and it became clear how far the Soviet Union was from a dream of communist peace and harmony, Ackland left the Communist Party. Warner never did. As late as 1977, she speculated on the unlikelihood of anyone producing the opera based on her novel *Mr. Fortune's Maggot*. Columbia University had already canceled a planned performance "in a fit of McCarthy-mindedness," as both she and Paul Nordoff, the composer, were "badged with unsound political views."[47] Stating the fact with neither anger nor pride, Warner holds on to her commitments, regardless of the consequences. Tenacious to the end, her integrity is unmatched. She explored and changed, she tried new things and continued to enjoy them, but, when she found an object worthy of her love and loyalty, she stayed true.

Una Marson
1905–1965

A COSMOPOLITAN FROM JAMAICA

Una Maud Victoria Marson was a parson's daughter, the youngest of the Marson children. Her biographer notes that, in her early forties, when she returned to her village in Jamaica, "old women from her father's former church hugged her, calling out 'Parson's Baby.'"[1] If you have heard of Marson at all, it is likely as a poet or as the first Black producer at the BBC, but she was also a journalist, activist, and playwright. Her third play, *Pocomania* (1938), draws on the autobiographical experience of being a parson's daughter to explore the spiritual conflict of Stella Manners, the daughter of a deacon in rural Jamaica, stuck at home but curious about the wider world.

While Stella's sister Dawn awaits her marriage to Pastor Craig and settles into mending lace for the altar, Stella herself is restless. *Pocomania* opens with a prologue of the sisters as little girls, and we see that Stella, from childhood, has been drawn to the rhythm and the passion of the drums that are used in the Pocomania ceremonies presided over by Sister Kate next door. In the prologue, we see her luring her sister and her foster brothers to the window to listen. Overcome, she dances herself into a trance and collapses, an action that repeats, with grave consequences, at the play's climax. Drawn to the forbidden, Stella never forgets the drums. When *Pocomania* begins in earnest, years have passed; Stella is still in the same village, still living with her father and sister, still hearing Sister Kate's drums at night.

Stella, named for the stars, is set in opposition to her more sensible daylight sister, Dawn. As a little girl, after recovering from her first trance, she enlists her nurse's help to experience the drums again, in person: "Take me one night, just for a little."[2] Despite the danger, she wants more, and she goes exploring. Although she is only six, she is already in charge of an expedition, recruiting her nurse as a native guide through the bush to the next yard, which might as well be another world. Years later, the Deacon revives his campaign against Sister Kate, threatening to remove her from the church membership. At this, Sister Kate spills the secret of those expeditions: "You used to send you servant and all you pickney, you two daughters and you two godsons to de meeting. Dem stan in a bush onside, but de spirit tol' me dem was dere."[3] The Deacon denies it; he never did know about Stella's expeditions. But Sister Kate backtracks. Maybe the Deacon did not *send* his children to hear the drums, but she is firm in the main thing: "I have witness to prove dem was here."[4]

For Stella, a naive, motherless girl, her stern father's rejection of Pocomania only increases its attraction. The warm and welcoming Sister Kate practices a version of indigenous religion, brought to the Caribbean via the slave trade, passed down over generations. Marson based Pocomania on the Afro-Jamaican religion "Pukkumina . . . [which] fused the Afro-folk spiritual elements of Myal with the Christian aspects of the Great Revival in 1860s Jamaica."[5] When Stella asks Sister Kate how the lead drummer, Josiah, learned to drum, she says his father who was taught by "him puppa, dat is Josiah granfader, come here a little boy pon slave ship from Africa."[6] The lineage is unmistakable. Through Pocomania, Stella gains both a mother figure and a connection to her African heritage. Moreover, Sister Kate's ecumenical attitude to religion offers Stella religious and intellectual freedoms unknown in her father's home: Sister Kate both leads the Pocomania cult and also attends the Deacon's church, and she encourages her followers to attend both, as well. Sister Kate offers Stella (and, by extension, Marson's Black Jamaican audience) a way to reconcile multiple strands of their heritage—African, European, and Caribbean.

When the play begins in earnest, we see the sisters, bored and waiting: Dawn for her wedding, and Stella for the return from London of her fiancé, John. But John dies of pneumonia in London, and a shocked and grieving Stella seeks solace from Sister Kate. After a visit, Sister Kate says to herself, "What a sweet pickney Deacon Manners hab. She tek after her moder dough. She don't have a dying ting fe de miserable puppa."[7] Stella does not hear this, but we do, and in Sister Kate's comments we understand more deeply the bond between the two women. Soon, Stella does more than visit during the day. She takes to disguising herself in a wrap and turban and participating in the rituals at night.

David, her fiancé's brother, who has come to love Stella himself, discovers the ruse and seeks the Pastor's advice on how to help Stella extricate herself from the "obviously obnoxious cult" that has "too much that is base and erotic" in it.[8] Pastor Craig, who is set to marry Dawn, condemns the cult almost as fulsomely as her father had. By contrast, David understands that Stella "needs love," that "your churches are cold and strict and severe," not answering the needs of people "made of sun and fire. Take from them the joy of life and you take everything."[9]

Understanding Stella's need to explore, David asks, "What is there in this district to interest anyone with a grain of imagination?"[10] While the men worry about her, Stella continues attending the ceremonies until, once again, overwhelmed, she collapses during a particularly ecstatic ceremony. Act 3 opens a full year later, with a convalescing Stella taking a sip of brandy from an attentive David. As the act unfolds, David declares his love, and Stella accepts him, and her acceptance is sweetened by a mutual promise: "No more Pocomania" but "something better": "a little madness." She says, "We all need a little madness in our lives perhaps."[11]

Stella collapsing twice at Pocomania rituals, first in the prologue at age six and again years later, as an adult mourning the death of her first fiancé, speaks to the dangers of exploration and the difficulty of integrating seemingly contradictory parts of oneself into a coherent whole. All of this is made more painful with the recognition that what is most familiar to her, the "Nordic" Protestantism of her father, has alienated her from what ought to be her birthright: an Afro-Caribbean faith. Marson wrote *Pocomania* in Jamaica after her first extended stay in England, at a time when she was reassessing her education and heritage. It bears the marks of her reconsideration of her relation to traditional white English culture and the African heritage that she had never learned about or been encouraged to value. The end of *Pocomania* is conventional, but its insistence on a bit of passion, of madness, allows Marson to endorse the value and importance of allowing people to embrace their full complexity. In later years, when Jamaicans expressed shame and embarrassment about Louise Bennett's dialect poems or mocked the Rastafarian faith, Marson defended both.[12]

Stella's spiritual exploration captures just one aspect of the many explorations Marson herself undertook. In addition to being a playwright, she was a journalist, the founder of several magazines and a publishing house, a poet, and a pioneering broadcaster for the BBC. Her career was mainly spent between London and Jamaica, but she traveled widely, with extended visits to Turkey, Sicily, and, at the end of her life, Israel.

Marson knew well the straitened, morally upright atmosphere of a pastor's home depicted in *Pocomania*. Unlike the characters in the play, however, she and her father were close, while her mother was loving but conventional, unable to understand her daughter's longing for more. In 1915, at age ten, Marson left her village to attend the Hampton School for Girls in Malvern, Jamaica. Her schooling there was traditional, but she had the experience of learning a traditional, entirely white, Anglocentric, imperial education in multiracial classrooms, more integrated than usual because World War I prevented some wealthier white Jamaicans from sending their daughters to England for school. On scholarship and one of the darker-skinned students, Marson faced double discrimination. This was worsened by her studying in the shadow of her more academically gifted older sisters. Adding to her isolation, her beloved father died. Not only did the family lose him, but they also lost their tenancy at the parsonage where Marson had grown up. Her mother, Ada, moved the family to Kingston, where Marson returned for school holidays throughout her time at Hampton.

Hampton was the extent of Marson's formal education. She left school in 1922, at seventeen, and sought work as a stenographer, working first at the Salvation Army and later, at the YMCA, where she found a sympathetic and supportive white boss in Edgar Hallett. In 1928, Marson embarked on her first public literary venture, founding *The Cosmopolitan Magazine*, which ran from 1928 to 1931. From the start, this magazine had a distinctly anticolonial and feminist vision, although it was not strictly or primarily a "women's magazine," nor did it bear any relation to the better-known American fashion magazine *Cosmopolitan*. In fact, it was subtitled "A Monthly Magazine for the Business Youth of Jamaica and the Official Organ of the Stenographer's Association." Marson contributed the editorial each month, and her opening letter outlines her large ambitions, in a wonderfully confident voice studded with cliché. The charm is all the greater knowing that the author was twenty-three:

> It can well be said . . . that a country may be unmistakably judged by the standard of the literature she produces. Our chief aim is to develop literary and other artistic talents in our Island home. The Editor of our esteemed "Daily" thinks that if Claude McKay had remained in Jamaica he never would have won such well deserved

> recognition, and we cannot but agree with him. It is a fact that local talent and ability in any field of art is not encouraged nor sufficiently appreciated in Jamaica by our people and our papers. Our ambition is to do all we can to encourage talented young people to express themselves freely. We know there are good writers in our island and we want to place them in the limelight. The pen is certainly mightier than the sword and there is no limit to the amount of influence that can be brought to bear upon the public by the writings of men and women of vision who are artists at heart: men and women who have the sunshine of hope ever shedding its radiance in their hearts and perpetuating its light in their faces thus adding brightness to this work-a-day world. We desire to be used as a medium to broadcast to thousands of people the sentiments, convictions, and suggestions of all our talented Jamaicans.[13]

From the outset, Marson champions Jamaican culture and expects her advocacy to reach "thousands." She is not playing small; long before she worked for the BBC, she imagined herself "broadcasting." Her rhetoric is soaring, and her ambitions are vast. Educated on Wordsworth, Keats, and Shelley, she believes in the poet-legislator. With an eye on Claude McKay, Marson announces her allegiance with home-grown talent; she will explore the possibilities of her island home first. McKay's success in New York was a complicated model for Marson. Within a few years, she would realize that, to achieve the kind of success she desired, she, too, would have to leave, but she avoided New York, because she knew that Jamaican women there ended up as maids and factory workers—her worst nightmare.[14]

The Cosmopolitan was a lively, general interest magazine, each black-and-white issue a little over thirty pages, including poetry, ladies' pages (which Marson also wrote), fiction, a crossword puzzle, and photography. Many of Marson's contributors were, like her, part of the Jamaica Poetry League. The league's leader was Clare McFarlane, an anti-feminist whose *Case for Polygamy* (1932) was far from Marson's own view of marriage. *The Cosmopolitan* allowed Marson the editorial control to express her feminist views without censorship. Early issues featured profiles of Violet Mills, Blanche Thompson, and other Black Jamaican musicians. However, by 1931, *The Cosmopolitan*, which lost money in the face of the Depression, had failed. Marson had taken on Aimee Webster, a college-educated Creole journalist, as an editorial and financial partner. Marson, never careful with finances, used some of the money Webster offered as backing to settle some personal debts. Decades later, Webster still felt the breach, but Marson was off to her next adventure: London.

She had published her first collection of poems, *Tropic Reveries*, in 1930 and debuted her play *At What a Price* the following year. The play was a success, and, with her earnings, Marson booked a passage to England, arriving in Plymouth on July 9, 1932. Housing discrimination in London was extreme, and, after struggling to find lodgings, Marson, like many other West Indians, found a room with Harold and Christine Moody, with whom she would lodge for three years. Moody was the founder of the League of Coloured Peoples, and his home was a social and political hub for Black West Indians in London. Soon, Marson became the league's assistant secretary. It was not what she had wanted, but no other office would hire her (racial discrimination was rampant, and there were no legal protections at that time). Through this work and her connection to the more conservative Moody, she expanded her horizons. She rallied league members to perform *At What a Price* in London, and it was such a success that she applied to move it to the West End. Once the censors passed it, with few revisions (and they clearly thought that Ruth, the educated protagonist, was white), it had a well-received three-night run in January 1934, making Marson the author of the first play written and performed by people of color from the British colonies in London.[15]

In her role as assistant secretary to the League of Coloured Peoples, Marson organized an evening's entertainment, a musical variety show, at the Indian Students Hostel.[16] She also became editor of *The Keys*, that organization's quarterly magazine. Focused on Black Britain, with coverage of the challenges faced by colonial seamen in Cardiff, for example, *The Keys* took interest in matters across the African diaspora, including the Scottsboro case, in which two young white women falsely accused a group of Black men of sexual assault. The group (the youngest was just twelve) had hopped a freight train in search of work in a nearby town. (Muriel Rukeyser traveled to Alabama to cover the case as a college student.) With over two thousand subscribers by 1934, it was likely the widest audience Marson had yet reached. She published her poem "Nigger," about the feeling of having that epithet hurled at you in the streets of London, in the magazine's first issue.

Moody's focus was on Black *men*, and, in *The Keys*, Marson did not have the same editorial control as she had had with *The Cosmopolitan*. To feed her feminist ideas, she turned to the British Commonwealth League (BCL).[17] The BCL was one of many international feminist organizations that sprung up between the wars. Although, like the others, the BCL was overwhelmingly white and middle class, Marson found a place there, where she met Winifred Holtby, the novelist, activist, and best friend of Vera Brittain. They bonded immediately, speaking together on a panel about equal pay for women. During the last year of Holtby's life, Marson and Holtby saw each other several times and developed a strong friendship, spending an evening together discussing writing that Marson remembered as "one of the most beautiful memories of my life."[18]

When Sir Nana Ofori Atta and his delegation arrived in London in July 1934 from what is now Northern Ghana, Una Marson was the official representative of the league, sent to greet him. For much of the summer, Marson "escorted him to meetings, prepared his farewell speech for the BBC Talks Department and shared his private thoughts."[19] It appears, as Marson's biographer says, "that they became, briefly, lovers." An unsigned letter in Ofori Atta's papers is consistent with Una's voice, which breathlessly hopes for more:

"Will you write to cheer me up since I shall not see you until Sunday evening."[20] Love affair or no, Marson's intimacy with Ofori Atta introduced her to African politics and history, and she began to read widely. He came to London to advocate for a stronger African role in the Gold Coast government, and his failure to secure that aim, too, was instructive, if profoundly discouraging. After that summer, Marson became a more confident and informed commentator on African issues and global issues around the African diaspora.

In just a short time, Marson had become "the leading black feminist activist in London."[21] In April 1935, the Women's Social Service Club of Jamaica asked Marson to be their representative at the 12th Annual Congress of the International Alliance of Women for Suffrage and Equal Citizenship. Thirty nations were represented by 280 delegates, mostly from Europe, but also from Brazil, Palestine, India, and Australia. Marson was the first and only Black delegate to attend.[22] She gave an emotional speech on the history and status of Jamaican women that brought some delegates to tears and was widely reported in the international press. As a result, she was invited to work, on a temporary basis, at the League of Nations headquarters in Geneva, where she arrived in August.

Marson's reading in African history and politics while working with Ofori Atta, along with her experiences in Turkey, prepared her to recognize immediately the gravity of Mussolini's invasion of Ethiopia in early October 1935. As the only African nation never to be colonized, with a seven-thousand-year history, a strong presence in the Bible, and an ongoing Christian tradition, Ethiopia stood as a beacon for pan-Africanists everywhere.[23] When the invasion happened, Marson immediately offered her help to the Ethiopian representative at the League of Nations and soon became an English-speaking secretary to the Ethiopian delegation, intensely studying Ethiopian history, culture, and politics, while managing the delegation's correspondence.[24] She was among those who met a defeated Haile Selassie when he arrived in London in May 1936, and she followed him back to Geneva a month later. There, as Selassie's secretary, she witnessed him address the League of Nations in Amharic while the Italian delegation jeered. Europe's condemnation of Italy was mild; the covenant of the League of Nations did not, it was clear, extend to Africa. The sense of betrayal, for Selassie, Ethiopia, all who cared about Pan-Africanism and the African diaspora, and Marson herself was profound. The young woman who had arrived in London eager to be in the nation of Wordsworth and Shelley increasingly saw England as a site of barbarity and looked to Africa for solidarity. Disheartened, exhausted, and close to a nervous breakdown, she returned to Jamaica, arriving in Kingston in September 1936.

She lived with her sister Etty and, after getting some rest, began to work again, continuing this most productive period of her career, and, as in London, pursuing literary, journalistic, and activist projects at once. She published *The Moth and the Star*, her best poetry collection including poems written in London and upon her return, and whose Shelleyan title spoke to her continued faith in his idea of the poet as "the unacknowledged legislator of the world." She wrote and produced two plays, *London Calling* and *Pocomania*. She joined other writers and journalists in contributing to the weekly *Public Opinion*, a new alternative to the more traditional *Daily Gleaner*. And, in 1938, she started JamSave, the Jamaican branch of the Save the Children Fund.

JamSave was a characteristic Marson innovation, born out of her frustration at the usual charities purporting to alleviate poverty and unemployment. JamSave was to be a charity led by Black Jamaicans working together to help the poorest children, not the pastime of a white woman, offering, as one particularly self-satisfied woman did, embroidery classes for twenty-five women, as if that might alleviate poverty on an island with a million inhabitants.[25] Marson was a passionate advocate, and, on the strength of her pleas, she received financial support to return to England and speak to the Moyne Commission about the causes of unrest in Jamaica and raise money for JamSave there.

The motives for Marson's return were mixed. She was still struggling financially—money was a lifelong challenge—even appealing to JamSave for a personal loan (which they refused) and hoped that she might make more money in London. Moreover, with two new plays and a book of poems, she was eager to find literary success outside Jamaica, corresponding with African American poet and civil rights activist James Weldon Johnson (1871–1938) and others about the possibility of US publication. Nothing could have prepared her for how a visit to a radio exposition with Winnie Casserley, a white Jamaican beauty pageant winner, altered and expanded her career. Marson was accompanying Casserley in her role as a correspondent for the *Jamaica Standard.* That year, RadiOlympia was almost exclusively about television, and both Casserley and Marson were interviewed for a television program. Afterward, Cecil Madden of the BBC offered her freelance work, interviewing visiting West Indians for *Picture Page* magazine. Marson's work with the network had begun.

At the BBC, Marson was a freelancer, then a probationary employee for quite some time. Eventually, an ally appealed for her promotion.[26] And, while the development of television was paused for the duration of World War II, Marson transferred to the radio division and worked steadily at the BBC until 1946. There, as their first Black producer, she was an on- and off-microphone presence, coordinating broadcasts of *Calling the West Indies* and, starting in 1943, *Caribbean Voices,* a weekly half-hour show modeled on "a six-part poetry programme titled *Voice*, edited by George Orwell over at the Indian Section of the Eastern Service, in which Una had taken part."[27]

With a wartime paper shortage and travel restrictions, radio broadcasts were a crucial part of helping West Indians abroad keep in touch with family at home. Marson interviewed West Indians of all stripes from across England, using her show to promote their culture and contributions and broadcasting poetry, music, and news. She also created a beloved and important segment that allowed service members to greet their families over the radio. Outside of her work during the war, Marson's home became a hub for West Indians, much as the Moodys' home had been a decade earlier. She and her roommate cooked and entertained soldiers and war workers. One such serviceman, Flight Lieutenant Dudley Thompson, a twenty-four-year-old Rhodes Scholar from Jamaica, became her lover.

Marson's tenure at the BBC was marked by challenges. She faced resistance and pressure from all sides, mistrusted by many and criticized for being bossy (when, in fact, she was the producer of the program and, thus, the boss). Then her affair with Thompson ended. The stress of war work at a BBC that was often hostile to her leadership compounded with heartache precipitated a serious depression. She attempted suicide in 1944 but made a partial recovery after some rest. Marson returned to work, hoping that a trip home to the West Indies would offer some respite alongside the chance to gather additional material for her radio show. As the only program covering the West Indies, she faced much criticism, with many listeners quick to perceive favoritism toward Jamaica over other islands.[28] Eager to answer her critics, at the end of the war Marson traveled to the United States for the first time and then made a tour of the Caribbean. Huge crowds greeted her at every stop across the West Indies, and, as Marson met old friends and new, her ambitions to promote Caribbean culture from the BBC grew.

However, when she returned to London, she was again exhausted, unwell, and unable to work. Her old friend Clare McFarlane accompanied her back to Jamaica in April 1946. She remained unwell for several years, recuperating from the strain of working at a racist and resistant BBC in London during the war years. When Langston Hughes visited Jamaica in 1947, Marson was not well enough to see him, though she wrote thanking him for including her poetry in his anthology.

By 1949, Marson was sufficiently recovered to rejoin the literary world, starting Gleaner Press, a local press devoted to publishing local authors, out of the offices of the *Daily Gleaner*, but that venture, too, faced financial and political difficulties. She moved to the United States for eight years, living mostly in Washington, DC, and even briefly married Peter Staples, a dentist. The marriage was not a success, and they soon separated. In 1961, back in Jamaica, she rejoined JamSave. In 1964, Israeli Foreign Minister Golda Meir invited Marson to attend an international seminar on women's leadership in Haifa, Israel. At fifty-eight, Marson was in fine form, impressing the Israelis and other delegates and taking great pleasure in a return to international travel and feminist leadership. Afterward, she stopped in London for several months and resumed her old activities, including work on a memoir. (The manuscript has not been found.) The old depression returned in force, however, and she went back to Jamaica, gravely ill. She died of a heart attack on May 9, 1965.

Marson's plays have largely disappeared from criticism, and her activism and journalism, a central part of her career, is seldom commented on.[29] Over the course of her career, Marson wrote for many periodicals based in both Kingston and London: *The Cosmopolitan*, *The Keys*, the *Jamaica Standard*, *Picture Page*, and more. These writings have yet to be collected and can be difficult to track down. Her contributions covered every imaginable topic, from worker exploitation at banana plantations to the state of poetry in Jamaica. From the publication of her first editorial in *The Cosmopolitan* until her death in 1965, Marson worked and wrote on behalf of Jamaican women, understood in the broadest possible terms. In one early contribution, she took up the question of marriage in a parody of Hamlet's soliloquy:

> To wed, or not to wed: that is the question:
> Whether 'tis nobler in the mind to suffer

The fret and loneliness of spinsterhood
Or to take arms against the single state
And by marrying end it?
. . . .
To wed, to match;
To match, perchance mismatch: aye, there's the rub.[30]

This delightful, lighthearted parody typifies the young Marson: strongly feminist but still fully engaged in a traditional British education.

More typical of Marson's voice in her political maturity is the July 17, 1937, editorial "Racial Feelings?" from *Public Opinion*, a then-new weekly magazine out of Kingston. In this piece, we see Marson at the height of her powers, going after mainstream Jamaican opinion with confidence and authority. She opens already spoiling for a fight, noting that her title "must be quoted otherwise I might be accused of plagiarism." Marson is responding to an editorial in *The Gleaner* about a strike in Trinidad. Like many work actions across the globe that year, workers were striking in part out of sympathy for the plight of the Ethiopian people. The editor of *The Gleaner*, joining the white governor of Jamaica, boasted that the average Jamaican worker had a harmonious relationship with his employer and was not in danger of striking out of mere "racial feelings." Opening with a concession, Marson disarms her interlocutor: "I could not defeat him in an argument—I am not clever enough," and then, with the precision of an assassin, she establishes her authority: "I served at the Abyssinian Legation in London from the outset of the war to the final defeat of Haile Selassie at Geneva in June of 1936 and until August. . . . The entire correspondence of the Legation passed through the Minister's hands to me. . . . I dealt with thousands and thousands of letters—and when the Emperor came to London the correspondence doubled."[31]

Of these letters, "Trinidad and Grenada were foremost in the West Indies," while "Jamaica showed the smallest part of sympathy."

For Marson, this is not a source of pride, but shame. All over the world, Black people recognized the injustice of Italy's invasion as "a new form of white imperialism," with the League of Nations' refusal to "carry out the covenant" on Ethiopia's behalf indicating how fully "Italy is not alone to blame." Jamaica's disengagement marked a failure to recognize what the rest of the world saw clearly. Marson acknowledges the internal tensions and domestic problems of Ethiopia. (Slavery was only abolished there in 1942, and Selassie, like many Ethiopians—and many Jamaicans—was reluctant to call himself "Black" or, in the terms of the day, "a Negro.") However, she adds, "when people are in trouble, we do not dwell on their faults."[32]

Having established her central contribution in contrast to Jamaica's overwhelming indifference, Marson spends the second half of her editorial castigating Jamaicans for their lack of racial solidarity. "Educated Jamaicans spend their whole lives thinking they are not coloured," she writes, "and it is an insult to call them 'Negro' because one or two generations back they had some white ancestor of the male sex." Such colorism is not unique to Jamaica, but "in Jamaica it reaches its zenith. . . . In nearly all shops and offices . . . only light skinned people are seen . . . advertisements are continually appearing for workers (fair), (very fair), (or white) in brackets." Marson proposes an alternative vision of Black Jamaican unity, one that echoes her very first editorial in *The Cosmopolitan*: "If by some miracle all the people in Jamaica including those with one drop of coloured blood could be made to realise that they are a racial entity and all their first loyalties lie within the race, then in the next twenty years Jamaica would make more progress than she has done in the past hundred years." Rather than boasting of strong interracial relations that only perpetuate inequality, and a colorism that pretends an allegiance with white people who "won't own us as belonging to the same category with them," Jamaicans should regard "themselves as being bound by blood ties to coloured peoples throughout the world"; then "there would have been some such spontaneous evidence of sympathy when the fortunes of the last great Black Empire were at stake." Her closing exhortation is a rallying cry for Pan-African solidarity: "Let us not be ashamed to be a link in the great chain of dark-skinned peoples. History has shown us, and is showing us today that there is as much barbarity among white races as among the black races."[33]

Marson's is a powerful voice for racial justice. In expressing her views and sharing her experiences, she plays with gender expectations—conceding ground to her interlocutor only to immediately establish her powerful experience. Her openness to learning about African history and culture and her firsthand witness of the political challenges faced by African leaders transformed her thinking. In traveling to London, she discovered what Africa meant to her. In sharing her discoveries, she proved herself the most generous of explorers.

A writer of direct, accessible poetry, mostly ballads, all her life, Marson's early poetry resembled the English verse she had studied in school. Only during her first trip to England did her style shift to include some more notably modern and modernist influences, especially from African American poets. While the poems in her first collection resemble the *Lyrical Ballads* of Wordsworth, her strongest collection, *The Moth and the Star*, adds blues, jazz, dialect, and references to contemporary politics and culture to that Romantic tradition. In her poetry, Marson is topical and direct, writing as explorer and guide to the inner and outer experiences of a Black Jamaican woman at home and abroad.

In the poem "In Jamaica," the language of tourism alternates with social commentary, creating a sharp and disorienting satire. Each of the five stanzas begins with a joyful expostulation to Jamaica, but the first three stanzas end with an admission of social problems. Thus, "O! It's a glorious life in Jamaica" contrasts with

"But the darker set are striving / And facing a very stiff fight."[34] The penultimate stanza celebrates the tourists, but, given what we have heard of poverty, the roughness of the slums, and colorism in the first three stanzas, the bright final two lines of that stanza ring hollow: "And they say on the while sands of Mo. Bay / They get such a wonderful tan!" In the context of the poem, then, Marson's final expression of affection for Jamaica makes for a surprising turn:

> Should I leave these fair shores for another,
> Be that land yet the fairest of all,
> I should pine for the hills of Jamaica,
> And hasten to answer her call.

Leaving sarcasm aside, Marson returns to joyful expostulation, but now we hear it as fully mature allegiance to a home that is both beloved and struggling, allegiance that insists on Jamaica as a place, not merely a tourist destination or a social problem. This clever twist within the poem is utterly consistent with Marson's work elsewhere. She is a partisan for Jamaica and always insistent on acknowledging her country's flaws and its strengths.

Marson inverts the tourist narrative in "Quashie Comes to London" and "Little Brown Girl," two poems about Jamaicans in London. The derogatory nickname "Quashie" borrows from Akan, a West African language; as Kwasi was a common boy's name, Quashie became a generic term for any Black boy and, later, for a simple person.[35] In this dialect poem, Marson makes comic use of the credulous Jamaican tourist to show London back to Londoners. His London is a frank but uncomfortable mix of delights and racist affronts, ending with an unsatisfactory trip to a Lyons tea shop, where British food "look like pigeon feed," making Quashie long for home and "me good ole rice an' peas."[36]

The poem "Little Brown Girl," originally called "The Autobiography of a Brown Girl" in homage to her mentor and correspondent James Weldon Johnson, takes the perspective of a white Londoner peppering the girl of the title with questions: "What are you seeking? / What would you have?"; "Wouldn't you like a coat / With a fifty pound tag on it?"; and, most pointedly, "How is it you speak / English as though it belonged / To you?"[37] The poem's perspective, that of a white person observing a Black person in London, creates rich texture. As Marson scholar Anna Snaith writes, "The narrator gropes towards a position of empathy and understanding of the 'brown girl's' simultaneous alienation and racial pride, but this is undercut by her construction of the girl."[38] In this pair of poems, Marson defamiliarizes London for white readers and affirms the difficult and unpleasant experiences of Black residents and visitors.

Marson's exploration is not only external. In several of her best poems, she explores the pain of trying to think oneself beautiful in a world that deluges Black women with images of white beauty. In London, Quashie loves the concerts, musicals, and plays, but he avoids the movies because "I see so much back home."[39] The ubiquity of Hollywood is ordinary for Quashie, but, in "Cinema Eyes," Hollywood is a source of danger. The speaker is a mother, forbidding her daughter to go to the movies even though she is eighteen. The mother recounts her own struggles, growing up "with a cinema mind": "My ideal man would be a Cinema type— / No kinky haired man for me, / No black face, no black children for me."[40] What follows is a melodrama worthy of Hollywood: she rejects a dark suitor and marries a cruel, lighter-skinned man. Their daughter is born, and she is dark, reminding the speaker of her first suitor. Years later, when that first suitor returns, her husband, "in fury and in drink," shoots him dead. A second shot, from an unnamed shooter, kills the husband, and so, the mother concludes: "I will let you go / When black beauties / Are chosen for the screen."[41]

While the tragic speaker in "Cinema Eyes" cannot imagine her way out of the overwhelming beauty discourse of whiteness, the speaker in "'Black is Fancy'" (the title phrase is rendered in quotation marks), figures out a way to think past such images:

I used to feel
I was so ugly
Because I am black,
But now I am glad I am black,
There is something about me
That has a dash in it
Especially when I put on
My bandana.[42]

The simplicity of these affirmations speak to their necessity: Marson is living in a world where Black is not yet beautiful. The overwhelming message she has received is racist and colorist, and it takes conscious work for her to see her own beauty. The bandana, a typical Jamaican accessory, is a particularly nice touch, especially considering Marson's love for colorful clothes and her long natural hair. The speaker here grows to like the way she looks in the mirror and dislike the picture of the pretty white woman on her wall, eventually taking it down and even coming to believe that "my John" genuinely finds her beautiful.[43]

These explorations, internal and external, culminate and combine in her blistering poem, which takes the worst racial epithet as its title. "Nigger," published in the first issue of *The Keys*, the official organ of the League of Coloured Peoples, in 1933, painstakingly anatomizes the experience of being called the N-word on the street:

What made me keep my fingers
From choking the words in their throats?
What made my face grow hot,
The blood boil in my veins
And tears spring to my eyes?[44]

Marson details how her rage inhabits and overwhelms her body—first with the desire to hurt the children who "flung it at me," then with shame and anguish. The surprise of it all is part of the potency of the attack: one moment she is passing children on the street, the next she is restraining herself from violence and holding back tears. Moving to half rhyme, she asks: "What is there in a word / That should strike like a dagger"? In the fourth stanza, Marson's speaker addresses white people, explaining

> why 'tis a sin to tell
> Your offspring Coloured folks are queer,
> Black men are bogies and inferior far
> To any creature with a skin made white.
> You who feel that you are "sprung
> Of earth's first blood," your eyes
> Are blinded now with arrogance.[45]

With exemplary patience, the speaker takes the "urchins" epithet back to the parents who taught those children to be racist. Quoting Wordsworth's 1802 sonnet "It Is Not to Be Thought Of," Marson invokes his idea that the very notion of freedom is profoundly English. Wordsworth wrote:

> We must be free or die, who speak the tongue
> That Shakespeare spake; the faith and morals hold
> Which Milton held.—In every thing we are sprung
> Of Earth's first blood, have titles manifold.[46]

His paean to British freedom might be read as an affirmation of the freedom of all humanity, or at least all English-speaking humanity, but Marson's quotation of it in "Nigger" calls into question the confidence of the white person who claims this is a "universal" value. Wordsworth asserts the endurance of British freedom as long as people still speak the language of Shakespeare and Milton. But

Marson knows firsthand that many are unaware that Jamaicans, too, speak English, while others mock the Jamaican accent and disparage the Jamaican language, and still others profess surprise that any person of color can speak "English as though it belonged to you." She understands that many who take pride in including themselves in the number of those "sprung of earth's first blood" could never imagine that a Black person might share that distinction.[47]

Appealing to the noble qualities of Englishness, including the imperative to "be free or die," Marson returns to the pain of the epithet, refusing it: "Since this was the favorite curse / Of those that drove the Negroes / To their death in days of slavery." Surely, the implicit argument goes, people who believe it unthinkable that the "Flood of British freedom . . . should perish" can understand why an insult that dates back to the time of enslavement and persists through minstrelsy would be abhorrent to any free person with dignity. "Nigger" ends with a prayer, the speaker beseeching God for the strength not to hate the racists but to remember that those sinners who hurl hatred are committing the sin "of hurting human hearts that live / And think and feel in unison / With all humanity."[48]

Marson published this painful poem on a difficult but familiar topic not in a paper for white readers, despite the direct address to white adults, but in first issue of *The Keys*, the organ of the League of Coloured Peoples. As such, it would have reached several thousand subscribers committed to the cause of people of the African diaspora. In it, she addresses the most painful aspects of being a Black person in a London that was still overwhelmingly white and openly racist. Her direct address, the careful and detailed description of the feeling of being called "Nigger" by strangers on the street, the history of the word's use to dehumanize Black people dating back to the earliest moment of the slave trade, the allusion to Wordsworth, and the closing prayer to be delivered from hatred make this one of her most eloquent statements against racism.

Knowing the discrimination Marson faced makes her participation in the 1944 wartime propaganda film *West Indies Calling* more poignant. *West Indies Calling* inverts the title of Marson's BBC program: this is not London calling the West Indies, but the West Indies calling London, offering its help in the war effort. The film presents a multiracial group of men and women war workers from the West Indies dedicated to doing their part to defeat "Hitler and his gang."[49] The film that survives on YouTube is a fifteen-minute edit for British audiences of a longer film made for audiences overseas. Marson is the host, interviewing a succession of military officers and war workers. The script reflects the dual nature of the audience: some of the narration presumes white viewers with little knowledge of or experience with people of color, while other moments speak to the postwar aspirations of people of color. It opens with an off-screen male narrator addressing a presumptively white audience, confidingly acknowledging that "we know the Indian by his turban"—but where are these people from? As he speaks, we see a smartly dressed Una Marson with several others, including the cricketer and activist Learie Constantine, converging on BBC headquarters. Later, Constantine suggests that wartime skills "will mean a lot during reconstruction after the war when plans for a new era of life in the West Indies must be put into effect."

From the street, we cut to an assembly room, where a multiracial jazz band is playing. The conductor brings them to a stop, the BBC light goes on, and we hear "Ready, Miss Marson?" She approaches the large 1940s stand microphone. From there, the film moves between Marson talking with service members, and stock footage of West Indians in England and abroad contributing to the war effort. As little has survived of scripts or recordings of her radio work, this short film offers a rare chance to see her talent and command. In her gentle coaxing of the men, some of them quite nervous and stiff, we get a taste of her skill as a broadcaster.

The first man she interviews is the Trinidadian cricketer, barrister, and civil rights activist Constantine. He originally moved to

England in hopes of better opportunities as an athlete but turned to social welfare work during the war. Denied hotel accommodations, he successfully sued for housing discrimination in 1944, and, from then on, his career was focused on improving conditions for West Indians, work for which he was knighted in 1962. Next, she interviews Ulric Cross, an Air Force officer who was shot over Germany and returned to England flying "on one engine at just 7,000 feet at a reduced speed."[50] Cross, like Constantine, became a barrister after the war; he served in several nations in Africa before returning to serve in Trinidad. The third man interviewed is Carlton Fairweather, a lumberjack from British Honduras.

Each brief conversation is followed by an interlude of stock footage. First, we see men and women in a factory working at various intricate machines while the voice-over explains the value these skills in mechanical engineering will hold after the war. In the second interlude, we see a range of war work, with an emphasis on women and civilians, including nurses, drivers, traffic wardens, and officials who stamp passports. The third interlude presents the thesis of the film:

> West Indians are fighting for the new world that we all want to see. In Hyde Squadron, there are pilots from New Zealand, Poland, Britain, and Canada. Friendships are being made between people who before the war knew little or nothing about each other and we find it impossible to believe that these friendships will just fade out when the war is won. The Allied Nations will get together to ensure the future peace of the world, but you know and I know that it's when we meet in a canteen or on a job, then, for the first time, we try to understand each other, and real friendship begins.[51]

As the narrator speaks, we see Cross enter a barracks, still wearing a safety vest over his flight suit. Smiling, he greets a group of white Air Force men, and one lights a cigarette for him as they make small talk. After a few moments, we cut to a scene of three women, two white and one Black, in jumpsuits, cheerfully filling their trays at the canteen before playing ping-pong. These are happy aspirational images of interracial harmony, far from what Marson experienced day to day. The film cuts to an even more surprising scene: a tea dance in the studio in which Marson joins the others. Interracial couples crowd the floor, as well as several pairs of women, dancing together in acknowledgment of the shortage of male partners. Making such a film would have been impossible in the United States at this time. And, indeed, it was barely possible in England.

Marson's participation in this film testifies to her hopes for more. The persistence of this hope—despite her experience otherwise—damaged her mental health and cost her dearly. After the war, it took her several years to recover from her exhaustion. As a brave explorer, Marson went further than most. Her career is hard to define in part not only because she was so successful in so many arenas, but also because, as she ran up against obstacles, she changed course. Do we remember her as the founder of a magazine, or as the most prominent Black feminist in interwar England? As the author of the first Black play in the West End and of a series of incisive poems about racial injustice, or as the first Black producer at the BBC? She was all of these things.

PART 4

Mentors

The term "mentor" is an ancient one with overwhelmingly positive associations. In Homer's *Odyssey*, Odysseus's young son, Telemachus, has two key figures who assist him on his smaller journey to find what became of his father. The first is an elderly man named Mentor, whose role it is to guide him safely on his first journey away from home. The word "mentor" comes from him; Mentor's actions made his name synonymous with the supportive guidance of an elder. Later, the goddess Athena assumes Mentor's form and continues to guide young Telemachus with her divine powers. Given the help Telemachus receives, both human and divine, with no strings attached, it is no wonder that so many of us seek mentors. Athena's role, helping a young man attain full manhood, and her disguise, in the shape of an elderly man, point to one of the challenges a mentor faces. Mentors do not act for themselves; they foster the actions of others. Women, socialized as caretakers, often make wonderful mentors, but being perceived as a mentor means your ambitions, your career, your dreams are secondary to the younger person whom you help.

People seek mentors in parental figures, in teachers, and in books. Each has its advantages and challenges. Since Athena, many mentors have crossed gender to advise young people. Virginia Woolf offered mentorship to young men and women in her world, and both of the women in the next section, Jessie Fauset and

Dorothy Arzner, mentored men. Even so, there is something special in finding a mentor who faces similar challenges and obstacles, especially in a society like our own, with inequality along gendered lines. In *A Room of One's Own*, Woolf asserts that "we think back through our mothers if we are women," positing that our sense of who we are and who we can become is connected to our gender.[1] Woolf's mother died when she was thirteen. The context of her mother's death lends special poignancy to the idea of "thinking back through our mothers." When mentorship is absent, the loss can be profound.

In the aftermath of this tragic loss, Woolf (then Virginia Stephen) was fortunate enough to have several older women take an interest in her and foster her education, her intellect, and her aspirations. Her Greek tutors Clara Pater and Janet Case helped her as a teenager, and both Madge Vaughan and (most prominently) Violet Dickinson encouraged her writing. For a vulnerable, brilliant young woman, these relationships were priceless. Woolf honored her friendship with Dickinson in a series of early short stories. In them, she depicts Violet's curiosity as a force of revolutionary disruption. Visiting a country house in "The Magic Garden," Violet asks how the house is managed, what the drainage system is, and who cares for the roses. When her hosts reveal their ignorance—"No one could tell her how the drains were managed, for no one remembered that there were drains"—Violet obeys "some native instinct that was certainly not polite" and shares what she has learned about these practicalities.[2] So inconvenient is this candor that she sets out "to have a cottage of one's own."[3]

Thus, in 1907, more than twenty years before *A Room of One's Own*, Woolf celebrated how her older friend found the courage to strike out and live independently, something Woolf herself had just recently done, moving to Bloomsbury with her siblings after their father's death in 1904. While Dickinson disapproved of Woolf's move from respectable Kensington to bohemian Bloomsbury, Woolf overlooked that friction, focusing instead on their shared insistence on independence. Violet's move to a cottage of her own was "the beginning of a great revolution which is making England a very different place from what it was."[4] Virginia Stephen, decades before writing *A Room of One's Own*, recognized "Violet's cottage for a symbol of many things."[5]

Dickinson read Woolf's early writings, recognized her talent, and introduced her to the wider world, including Margaret Lyttleton, the editor of the women's supplement of a clerical newspaper called *The Guardian* that published many of her early essays, becoming Woolf's first paid publications. For all of this practical support, Dickinson's literary taste remained Victorian, something Woolf satirizes: "I should do my heroine a horrid injustice if I allowed it to be thought that she indulged literature any further than she indulged children."[6] As Woolf teases, Dickinson judged fictional characters as if they were real people; if a character lacked admirable virtues, she condemned the art. Woolf quickly outgrew her mentor's limited aesthetic vision, but she never discounted the centrality of Dickinson's support. Years later, in a letter, Woolf wrote to her: "It was certainly your doing that I ever survived to write at all."[7] The right mentor can make art possible; she can save a life.

From the beginning, Woolf looked to her reading for models and mentors. In *A Room of One's Own*, she offers her fullest articulation of how books shape us and of the importance of developing and understanding a tradition of women's literature. In it, she proposes the importance of reading women writers. When Woolf writes, "We think back through our mothers if we are women," she is saying much more than that women relate to other women.[8] She is making an argument that is economic, social, and aesthetic. She takes us back to Aphra Behn (1640–1689), the first English woman who made her living by writing. That example mattered to women writers who followed, because it meant that "writing became not merely a sign of folly and a distracted mind, but was of practical importance. A husband might die, or some disaster overtake the family," and women could "come to the rescue of their families by making translations or writing the innumerable bad novels."[9] Woolf's economic point matters as much as the aesthetic one: in this world, money matters to power and independence. Woolf's maxim, that "money dignifies what is frivolous if unpaid for," has been useful to me on several occasions, in salary negotiations and in conversations with men who call my passion for writing and teaching a "calling" as justification for underpayment.[10]

Woolf's ambition was to earn a living by writing *and* to write great literature. She argues that the emergence of a cohort of middle-class women writers in the late 1800s and early 1900s marked a cultural change

> of greater importance than the Crusades or the Wars of the Roses. The middle-class woman began to write. For if *Pride and Prejudice* matters, and *Middlemarch* and *Villette* and *Wuthering Heights* matter, then it matters . . . that women generally, and not merely the lonely aristocrat . . . took to writing. Without those forerunners, Jane Austen and the Brontës and George Eliot could no more have written than Shakespeare could have written without Marlowe, or Marlowe without Chaucer, or Chaucer without those forgotten poets who paved the ways and tamed the natural savagery of the tongue. For masterpieces are not single and solitary births; they are the outcome of many years of thinking in common.[11]

Woolf's powerfully simple claim has become so familiar that we can overlook its radical nature. Masterpieces emerge out of a culture; forerunners and pioneers make innovation possible. For women—so long shut out of education, so long denied the opportunity to study a foreign language or travel—reading about women precursors who defied convention is not only heartening; it can become crucial fodder in an argument with a family member who opposes a woman's ambition. When living mentors are unavailable or lacking, a book acts as a guide.

For all the importance of mentors in Woolf's life, her fiction depicts only a few, and the ones that are present range from the ineffective to the poisonous. She is particularly savage in her depiction of mothers and mother figures who conspire to quash any unconventionality in a young woman. In *To the Lighthouse*, Mrs. Ramsay's main aim for Lily Briscoe is that she marry, something Lily expresses less than no interest in doing. Lily is a painter; she wants to paint. These matronly mentors are not listening to their charges but simply replicating the social structures they inherited. As deeply as Woolf adored her mother, in adulthood she could see the ways in which Mrs. Ramsay, the fictional character most closely based on Woolf's mother, is driven to marry people off, sometimes without regard to their desires. Across Woolf's fiction, older women mentors work to take remarkable girls and turn them into marriageable women.

Tutors and teachers, too, when present in Woolf's fiction, are ineffective, jealous, or mere ghostly presences. She observes scholars entering the chapel at Oxbridge and reflects that the professors are "rare types which would soon be obsolete if left to fight for existence on the pavement of the Strand."[12] In *Mrs. Dalloway*, Miss Kilman is consumed by her frustrated desire for Elizabeth Dalloway, and Miss Isabel Pole inspires Septimus Warren Smith to enlist in World War I. Isabel Pole is a mouthpiece for the misplaced patriotism that led to widespread disillusionment with the war and government in general, and, in Septimus's case, indirectly responsible for the shell shock that costs him his life. Characters in *Jacob's Room* and *The Waves* attend university, but there are no significant professors or mentors in those novels. Nick Greene's interest in Orlando's writing career is almost entirely cynical.

Books, too, though balms for the lonely soul, can be bad mentors. Woolf rails against the legacy of John Milton, who has poisoned her imagination by blocking the sky from her view, interposing instead the image of God as "a gentleman, which Milton recommended for my perpetual adoration."[13] In *A Room of One's Own*,

Woolf's narrator goes to the British Library to research the history of women and fiction. There, she becomes overwhelmed by the mountains of misogynist literature. Rather than learning anything about women—the books are "worthless for my purposes"—she learns instead something about the relationship between anger and power.[14] She marvels at first that "a man with all this power should be angry. Or is anger, I wondered, somehow, the familiar, the attendant sprite on power?"[15]

Decades later, Alice Walker called out the limitations of Woolf's praise for the genius of nineteenth-century English women writers, showing Black women a way to honor their ancestors' genius outside of the literary tradition that excluded them. (It is tantalizing to imagine Walker encountering *A Room of One's Own* in one of Muriel Rukeyser's classes. Rukeyser often taught Woolf, and Walker was an esteemed student of hers.) Woolf's emphasis on the revolution that came about when women could earn money for writing of necessity excluded Black women, who for much of the nineteenth century in the United States were barred from learning to read, let alone to write. In "In Search of Our Mothers' Gardens," Walker identifies genius in gardens, cookpots, and quilts, showing a way to think about creativity beyond Woolf's narrower imagination. For Walker, Woolf was a salutary literary mentor to outgrow, as important as an antagonist as she had been as a model. In outgrowing Woolf, she turned to Zora Neale Hurston, and her study of Hurston's works and celebration of Hurston's legacy helped make Walker's novel *The Color Purple* a masterpiece and increased the readership for Hurston's *Their Eyes Were Watching God*.

These fictional representations of mothers, mother figures, mentors, and books as mentors suggest some of the downsides to being a mentor. Woolf had an ambivalent relationship to the younger generations. She referred to some of the young women in her circle as "crop heads," dismissing them with a reference to their short hair, but she could be generous with her time, as she was in letters to the World War I veteran and writer Gerald Brenan, or in person with Winifred Holtby when Holtby was writing one of the first book-length studies of Woolf's work.[16]

To be a mentor can mean admitting that the apex of your career is behind you. When the role is imposed too soon, before a person has achieved their own potential, the anger can be intense. We see the mentor's barely stifled rage in *Mrs. Dalloway*. When Miss Kilman remarks to Elizabeth Dalloway, "All professions are open to women of your generation," she is being truthful.[17] The Sex Disqualification (Removal) Act of 1919 made it illegal to enforce blanket prohibitions on women from the professions. Crucially, Woolf allows us to see all the unfulfilled hopes of Miss Kilman's life. She cannot resist adding, "But for herself, her career was absolutely ruined and was it her fault?"[18] Fired from her teaching job during World War I for refusing to condemn Germany, she has been reduced to work as a private tutor and only has her job with the Dalloways because of Richard's kindness. Angry as Miss Kilman is, at least she encourages Elizabeth to consider a profession.

Despite these drawbacks, mentoring remains valuable as a strategy for navigating the modern world. It can keep a woman in a room that might otherwise exclude her. A woman who makes her presence felt as a mentor may be allowed to stay at or near the center of power, even if her counsel always must go through a male intermediary. Thus, Lady Bruton, who "should have been a general of dragoons herself," enlists Richard Dalloway and Hugh Whitbread's help to write a letter to the editor of *The Times*.[19] But Lady Bruton is jealous of other women. The women in this book did not, for the most part, seek to be the only woman in their field: they sought out other women. Mentoring matters because it is good to journey together, to be friends with each other, and to each clear the path for those coming beside and behind. While Woolf's fiction depicts few mentors, it abounds with friendships, including those between St. John Hirst and Terence Hewet in *The Voyage Out*, Mary Datchet and Katherine Hilbery in *Night and Day*, Mr. and Mrs. Ramsay's eccentric and cherished houseguests in *To the Lighthouse*, all six central characters in *The Waves*, Chloe and Olivia in *A Room of One's Own*, and, most famously of all, Clarissa Dalloway, Sally Seton, and Peter Walsh in *Mrs. Dalloway*.

As literary editor of *The Crisis*, the magazine of the NAACP, Jessie Fauset (1882–1961) could simultaneously be a mentor to the greatest literary talent of the Harlem Renaissance and, in her work with W. E. B. Du Bois, his mentee and closest collaborator. In both roles she was at the center of mainstream civil rights leadership. Fauset did not come from money, and editing relieved her from the need to teach. Unattached to the classroom, she could take pleasure in offering her talents as a mentor only to those eager young writers seeking advice. As a mentor, Fauset had a keen eye for talent. Her encouragement of individuals shaped an entire movement, creating the Harlem Renaissance in literature. But, when it came to her own novels, she was persistently overlooked, diminished, and dismissed. People gladly accepted her mentorship but rarely reciprocated to help her as an artist in her own right.

Dorothy Arzner (1897–1979) started her career in films at the bottom, as a typist, and worked her way up to editor (where she made several field-defining innovations), and then to director. Along the way, she had the mentorship and support of others in the film business and was, by all accounts, equally generous with her colleagues. Filmmaking is a collaborative business, and Arzner thrived working with others. A product of the studio system, despite spending much of her career as a freelancer, Arzner directed with a firm hand while valuing the expertise of those around her. Once, when an actress was struggling with a performance, Arzner took her to the editing room to show her what she, as director, was seeing. But, when Arzner fell ill with pleurisy during a production, and her movie had to be finished by another director, she never made another one. Although she was only in her forties and at the height of her career, she had to turn to other work. Eventually, she became a teacher—and a great one— at UCLA, mentoring many of the great directors, producers, and editors of the late twentieth century, including most famously, Francis Ford Coppola. When Hollywood had no more use for her as a director, others saw her value as a mentor, and she embraced the role, having little other choice.

Mentors save lives and make art possible, but when a mentor is young and mortal (as opposed to elderly or divine as in *The Odyssey*), the help she offers comes at the sacrifice of working for herself. Still, mentors recognize more vividly than many the extent to which all of our lives are intertwined—that, in working with and for others, we advance a larger cause and a bigger story. A writer and publisher, Virginia Woolf had the financial and artistic independence to be a mentor occasionally as she kept her art first. Imagine the world in which more women artists had such freedom.

Jessie Redmon Fauset
1882–1961

FROM MENTOR TO ARTIST

Jessie Redmon Fauset's career as a novelist nearly ended the night it began. On March 21, 1924, she was the guest of honor at a party to celebrate the publication of her first novel, *There Is Confusion*, but, on this night, which some scholars mark as the beginning of the Harlem Renaissance, the men in charge made sure to diminish her achievements and give her no chance to enjoy her hard-won success. Fauset may have been announced as the honoree, but everything in the evening conspired to dismiss her project as already passé.

The evening was hosted by Charles Johnson, editor of *Opportunity: A Magazine of Negro Life*. Johnson's magazine was a direct competitor of *The Crisis*, where Fauset served as literary editor. At the time, *Opportunity* was just a year old while *The Crisis* had been around since 1910.[1] Fauset had published her first story there in 1912 and held the position of literary editor from 1919 to 1926. During those years, she often stepped in as editor, occasionally writing editorials in the name of her mentor, W. E. B. Du Bois. Despite her stature, Johnson took an evening billed as a celebration of Fauset and made it into what he called, in an editorial describing the night, "The Debut of the Younger School of Negro Writers." Fauset was forty-two; Johnson's declaration excluded her.

The rest of the evening unfolded in a manner calculated to make any protest from Fauset impossible. Charles Johnson opened the evening, presenting Alain Locke as the evening's host. Horace Liveright, Fauset's publisher, spoke next, but, instead of praising Fauset, he lamented the poor sales of another book on his list, Jean Toomer's *Cane*. Then, Locke introduced Du Bois, "as a representative of the 'older school,'" and he "explained the shortcomings of earlier Black writers who 'were of necessity pioneers.'"[2] Instead of focusing on Fauset's success, Locke framed the evening as a celebration of male writers from two generations. He verbally escorted Du Bois and James Weldon Johnson offstage with the faint praise reserved for those pioneers whose work we deem passé. Then, her publisher used his platform to usher in the next generation, represented by Toomer. Fauset's publisher's choice to harp on Toomer's book instead of praising—or even mentioning—Fauset's was gratuitously cruel. These stories of generational struggle among male writers, editors, and publishers have little room for women, as Fauset perceived. In the face of these public dismissals of the "older school," as embodied by Du Bois, her boss, friend, and mentor, and with the cascade of enthusiasm for young men, Fauset could hardly express her objection. Instead, "Miss Fauset performed as her hosts expected. She thanked her friends for their assistance, and, after singling out Dr. DuBois as her 'best friend and severest critic,' she sat down."[3] No one had praised her, and she could hardly praise herself. Johnson and the others counted on her silence, the reliable self-control of a woman of Fauset's professionalism. It cost her dearly, but her silence was by no means a signal of acceptance.

Her relationships with both Du Bois and, especially, Locke soon deteriorated. She recalled the evening in a 1933 letter to Locke, after he published a tepid review of her fourth novel: "I have always disliked your attitude to my work dating from the time years ago when you went out of your way to tell my brother that the dinner given at the Civic Club for 'There is Confusion' wasn't for me. . . . And

I still remember the consummate cleverness with which you that night as toastmaster strove to keep speech and comment away from the person for whom the occasion was meant."[4] Locke and Johnson conspired to make a night in her honor into an announcement of a younger generation's arrival on the scene. The impression of Fauset as a woman behind her times has persisted ever since.

Jessie Redmon Fauset was born in Camden County, New Jersey, on April 27, 1882, into an educated family, although not a wealthy one. She was her parents' seventh child, and her mother died when she was seven. Fauset's father, Redmon, grew up attending the AME Union Church in Philadelphia and became a minister and a vocal advocate for civil rights, especially for educational access.[5]

On November 20, 1883, when Fauset was still a baby, Reverend Fauset served as secretary for a meeting of Black civil rights activists in Camden, New Jersey. The civil rights cases of 1883 were a combined Supreme Court ruling that severely limited the reach of the Thirteenth and Fourteenth amendments and paved the way for discriminatory Jim Crow laws.[6] (*Plessy v. Ferguson*, which codified separate but equal, was not decided until 1896.) That night in Camden, those present advocated for the continued right of Black children to attend integrated public schools, a right that the court had thrown in doubt. They strategized about the best way to sound the growing alarm at the threat of excluding Black students, and Reverend Jeremiah H. Pierce affirmed that "an education placed in the brains of our children is worth more than all the dollars and cents we can get."[7] Pierce noted that Black schools were too small to have separate grades, and that they never sent children on to university. As the meeting closed, the attendees adopted the resolution, which protested any unequal treatment based on race. This advocacy did not sit well with the teachers at the Black school, one of whom wrote to the newspaper the following week, complaining that he had been called "a traitor to the race . . . I thought it very unjust for Redman [*sic*] Fauset to attempt to force his children into the white school. . . . I do not think men like him are fit to carry the gospel. I also think he must have a brick out in the upper story."[8] Before Jessie Fauset could walk or speak, her father was known as an advocate for civil rights, unafraid to disagree with others in public.

When she was young, her family left the all-Black hamlet of Lawnside, New Jersey, and moved to a white neighborhood in nearby Philadelphia. After her mother's early death, her father married a widow, Bella Huff, who had three children of her own. They had several more children, including her half-brother, the writer Arthur Huff Fauset (1899–1983). In Philadelphia, Fauset was able to access the college preparatory education that her father sought for his children. She graduated with honors from the Philadelphia High School for Girls in 1900, likely the only Black student there. She hoped to go on to the local women's college, Bryn Mawr. However, Bryn Mawr's president, M. Carey Thomas, refused to admit Black students. Instead, she raised money for Fauset to attend Cornell University.

To have the president of the college you hope to attend intervene to prevent your attendance speaks to the extent of racism at the time. To have that intervention include fundraising on your behalf to attend a school as good, if not better, is testament to your ability. Such contradictions are woven into the fabric of racism. The experience shaped Fauset's life and career. Each of her four novels includes scenes of bewildered, talented young people absorbing the unequal match between their undeniable talents and the meager opportunities available to them. The recognition of Fauset's talents was accompanied by a powerful impulse to exclude her from the easiest, most obvious paths to nurture that talent: an elite women's college in her hometown excludes her, but she can go to university in Ithaca, New York, where the dormitories will be closed to her on account of her race. Every door that opens reveals a new obstacle, another part of the structures of privilege that have not quite opened. The obstacles themselves are an admission of white supremacy's determination to keep the playing field uneven.

So, Fauset left Philadelphia for Ithaca and enrolled at Cornell, where she pursued a classical education, with an emphasis on Latin, English, and French. Her father died in 1903, and, that same year, she wrote Du Bois a letter of admiration that included a request for his help in finding work to uplift her race. "I want to work in the South," she explained. "I know only one class of my people well and I want to become acquainted with the rest."[9] With the help of Du Bois and her Cornell professors, she got a summer position teaching English at Du Bois's alma mater, Fisk University, in Nashville. In 1905, Fauset graduated at the top of her class with Phi Beta Kappa honors, and, although Cornell did not keep track of the race of recipients, she was one of their first Black Phi Beta Kappa recipients. Her achievement was noted in *The Afro-American* newspaper: "Competing with one thousand students in her course, Miss Jessye [*sic*] R. Fauset, the only Afro-American in her class carried off the highest honors in her class of arts at Cornell University."[10]

After graduation, Fauset did not want to be a teacher. Du Bois encouraged her to find ways to support her talent outside the high school classroom, professing it a shame that someone of her talents had to teach.[11] Even so, jobs were scarce for educated Black women in the early twentieth century. In the 1917 story "There Was One Time," she describes a dispiriting job search:

> Perhaps for the first time she began to realize the handicap of color. Her grade on graduation had been "meritorious." She had not shone, but neither had she been stupid. . . . Perhaps it was because at eighteen one is still idealistic that she answered advertisement after advertisement without apprehension. The result, of course, was always the same; always the faint shock of surprise in the would-be employer's voice, the faint stare, the faint emphasis—"You! Oh no, the position is not open to—er—you." At first

> she did not understand, but even when she did she kept futilely on—she could not, she would not teach—and why does one graduate from a Business High School, if one is not to be employed by a business firm?
>
> That summer her father, a silent, black man, died and her decisions against teaching fled.[12]

Mirroring her own life's choices, the heroine's father's death makes it impossible to decide *against* teaching. In *The Crisis*, Fauset had no need to explain the racism implicit in the inarticulate denial of the employer's "er—you" when faced with a job applicant, qualified on paper, who turns out to be Black. For all the promise of education, Fauset is clear on the limits of opportunity.

After graduation, Fauset was denied work as a teacher in the segregated Philadelphia schools; she taught in Baltimore for a year before moving to Washington, DC, where she taught French at the M Street High School (later the Dunbar School) for fourteen years. There, she met writers, poets, and activists including Georgia Douglas Johnson and, eventually, Du Bois himself. In 1912, she published her first poems and stories in *The Crisis* and began contributing regular columns on books. She also started doing activist work with the NAACP. In 1913, she helped a Black student at Smith College find housing, helping solve a problem she herself had faced at Cornell, where she was not allowed in the dormitories and had to board with a professor's family.[13] Fauset visited France in the summers, including a memorable trip in the summer of 1914, where she witnessed the lead-up to World War I.[14] While teaching, she pursued a master's degree at the University of Pennsylvania in the summers, and, in 1919 began working as the literary editor of *The Crisis*. After a year of editing from Washington, she moved to New York to be the magazine's full-time literary editor.

Fauset's tenure as literary editor of *The Crisis* (1919–26) is unparalleled for her discovery and promotion of some of the greatest African American writers of the twentieth century, including

Gwendolyn Bennett, Marita Bonner, Arna Bontemps, Countee Cullen, Arthur Huff Fauset (her half brother), Langston Hughes, Zora Neale Hurston, Claude McKay, Effie Lee Newsome, Jean Toomer, and Walter White.

Her faith in Langston Hughes, especially, was a powerful spur to his confidence: she was the first to publish him, and she never wavered in her belief in his talent. When Arna Bontemps submitted his poem to *The Crisis* in 1924, he was a college graduate working the night shift for the post office in Los Angeles, and Fauset's acceptance of his work gave him the courage to resign from his job and move to New York. He went on to a prolific career as poet, novelist, editor, and librarian, including many collaborations with Hughes. In these years of her literary editorship, Fauset often stepped in to serve as managing editor of *The Crisis* during Du Bois's absences, and during this time she also started an innovative magazine for Black children, *The Brownies' Book* (1920–21). Full of photographs of elegantly dressed children (in party attire, seated on ponies, dressed as little soldiers), poems, illustrations, and inspirational stories, *The Brownies' Book* was a joyful celebration of aspirational Black childhood. She contributed essays, columns, stories, and poems to the magazine while serving as editor, and, in this role, she attended the 1921 Pan-African Congress with Du Bois.

In the summer of 1924, Fauset took an extended trip to France and attended classes at the Sorbonne. She reveled in an independence and freedom greater than she had ever known. Upon her return to New York, her relationship with Du Bois having cooled, her attempts to find a new position—either in the nonprofit sector or as a publisher's reader—went nowhere. With no family wealth and none of her many colleagues willing or able to help her, she returned to teaching. Fauset taught at DeWitt Clinton High School in New York from 1927 to 1944.

In 1928, Fauset published her second and best-known novel, *Plum Bun*, a story of sisters who relocate from Philadelphia to New York. One moves to Harlem and experiences all the vibrancy of a booming Black city within the city; the other passes for white and lives in the Village among artists and activists. The following year, Fauset married Herbert Harris, a businessman and World War I veteran. She was forty-seven. She continued teaching and wrote her final two novels during her summer breaks: *The Chinaberry Tree* (1931), a story of incest narrowly averted, set in a small, Black New Jersey town like the one of her earliest childhood; and *Comedy, American Style* (1933), a satire of the poisonous effects of a mother's avid desire for her children to be able to pass for white. In 1944, Fauset retired from teaching and moved with her husband to Montclair, New Jersey. There, she participated actively in civic life, speaking at schools and book clubs. She spent a delightful term as a visiting professor of creative writing at Hampton University in Virginia. A newspaper article that year announced her plans for a new novel, but it never appeared.[15] She remained in Montclair until her husband's death in 1958, when she moved back to Philadelphia to be with family for the final years of her life. She died there from heart failure in 1961.

In his autobiography, *The Big Sea*, Langston Hughes calls Fauset and two other men, Charles Johnson and Alain Locke, the "midwives" of the Harlem Renaissance. It is a dubious honor. As Deborah McDowell quips, "Langston Hughes's famous statement . . . might well be said to have served as [Fauset's] epitaph."[16] And the label of midwife persists: in his history of Harlem in this period, David Levering Lewis adds James Weldon Johnson, Casper Holstein, and Walter White to the list. The unexamined metaphor of "midwife" to describe the literary and cultural work of five men and one woman, particularly when the five men resisted supporting Fauset, suggests the persistent refusal to recognize the challenges faced by Black women writers. The work of a midwife is essential, often misunderstood, and semiprofessional; a midwife assists at the birth and is expected to step aside afterward. Midwives help; they are not supposed to need help. When Fauset needed help, those around her could not and did not offer her a position that matched her talents and her desires. Even recasting that idea of midwifery as the less freighted one of mentor is not without complications.

As literary editor of *The Crisis*, Fauset was a mentor for Langston Hughes, Countee Cullen, Jean Toomer, and others. To these young men especially, Fauset must have seemed like an older woman who would selflessly, seemingly from a different plane, organize, help, and wish well for their careers. They would have had little reason to consider her career, her ambitions, or her needs. Indeed, in the role of mentor, she is plainly proud to be helpful to them; she is hopeful for them; she wants them to do well; she wants them to succeed and thrive, and not just for themselves, but for everyone—for the race, for society, for the cause of letters and poetry. But Fauset was no Mentor: in 1920, when she accepted Langston Hughes's first submissions to *The Crisis*, she was still four years away from publishing her first novel and in her late thirties—not a child, but hardly an elderly woman, either. She had high ideals that emerged from her upbringing, her faith in the ideals of Du Bois, and the purpose and mission of the NAACP and *The Crisis*. As seriously as she took her work as editor, she herself wanted to be mentored, helped, and recognized as an artist.

Her letters to Langston Hughes, which span from 1920 until 1950, begin with her enthusiastic solicitation of material for *The Brownies' Book* ("At the risk of being considered insatiable," she writes, asking for more), but, as soon as 1923, she is thanking him for "his kind words" about her own writing.[17] In a 1923 letter to Countee Cullen, we see her hunger to be considered a peer of the younger men whom she mentored: "No, 'There is Confusion' still isn't placed but it is with Boni and Liveright and I am supposed to receive a verdict from them next week. You are a minister's son; pray for me."[18] In Fauset's correspondence with these writers, she expresses a persistent desire for mutual support. They often offered it, but it never seemed to be quite enough. At several key moments—in 1924, when her first novel came out, and in 1926, when she left *The Crisis* for good—her friends were unwilling or unable to secure for her the kind of support, whether through a fellowship or a job, that allowed her time to write. By the 1940s, Hughes's career had eclipsed hers, the dynamic was completely reversed, and her letters seeking help were pleading.

As a literary editor, Fauset could be flattering, but she could also be sharp and dismissive. To one poor contributor in 1926 she wrote:

> It is the business of a literary editor to select for publication such articles as seem worthy according to his judgment and standards. . . . From my point of view your work, as yet, lacks distinction either or form or of subject. I am afraid that comment will wound you but I wonder if it won't put you on your mettle and I'm wondering too if you're not trusting too completely in the judgment of people who themselves may not be too well equipped.[19]

At the same time, she encourages Langston Hughes to finish college; she urges Jean Toomer to learn French and read the classics; she counsels a novice writer anxious about their first submission; she scolds a Southerner whose work has been rejected; she apologizes that *The Brownies' Book* cannot pay for submissions; she finds a way to send Claude McKay money when he is in Paris. In short, she does all the work any good editor does to maintain the standards of the journal, encouraging the promising, and discouraging those less so. During this time, Du Bois intervened on her behalf as well: securing her membership at the Civic Club—one of the few racially integrated clubs in the city, and located near the NAACP offices, so perfect for entertaining authors and others—and working with Boni and Liveright to bring *There Is Confusion* back into print in 1927, despite the publisher's lack of enthusiasm. Even so, what she did for others vastly outweighed what the powerful and influential men in her life did for her. The busiest years of her work as a mentor came before her first novel was published.

Fauset's dislike of teaching in the classroom and her pleasure in mentoring underscore the difference between the two kinds of help. A classroom teacher faces an assortment of students and an equal obligation to each, despite their various interests, talents, and purposes. Moreover, very few of the children in any one classroom are bound for university, and, if they are, they may not be gifted in French or English, the fields that mattered to Fauset. Such teaching, noble as it is, scatters the attention and distracts from the pursuit of one's own art and the development of one's talent. Mentorship, by contrast, entails working with a single person who has sought out your specific, hard-won expertise. The give and take of a good conversation between mentor and student offers something nourishing to the artistic practice of both.

The protagonist of the 1917 short story "There Was One Time" shows Fauset's familiarity with the drudgery of uninspired teaching. Toward the end of the story, the main character, whom we meet playing hooky from a teaching job she dislikes, has a surprisingly good day in the classroom: young Tim Reynolds seems to have learned some French. However, it soon becomes clear that Tim has not done his homework—his uncle did it. Even better, that uncle turns out to be the very man she has been pining for. This revelation reunites the lovers, joined together in their hope of moving to France once the war ends, with her pledging to work as a draughtsman in support of his architectural dreams. Despite the happy ending, Fauset allows us to share a snicker at the revelation that the heroine never did become a good teacher.

In her 1922 essay "Some Notes on Color," Fauset returns in nonfiction to the dispiriting toll of constant wariness on race. She describes always going to the same restaurant rather than risking poor service or worse: "I want food, not a law-suit."[20] Hughes, noting that her parties—and she threw many—tended to have no white people in attendance, explains: "At Miss Fauset's, a good time was shared by talking literature and reading poetry aloud and perhaps enjoying some conversation in French. White people were seldom present there unless they were very distinguished white people, because Jessie Fauset did not feel like opening her home to mere sightseers, or faddists momentarily in love with Negro life."[21] Where many Black writers of the Harlem Renaissance cultivated relationships with white patrons (including Hughes and the prominent women writers Nella Larsen and Zora Neale Hurston), Fauset retained a deep skepticism of white do-gooders.

Her 1922 essay on the death of the actor Bert Williams makes clear her familiarity with the compromises that come with being a Black artist. She recast this essay in 1925 as "The Gift of Laughter," one of two essays she contributed to Alain Locke's *The New Negro* anthology.[22] Williams (1847–1922) was born in the Bahamas and raised in California. His family could not afford the university education he desired, so he turned to another love: acting. In that profession, he faced the racial barriers of his day and adjusted again. He began performing in blackface roles, learning the vernacular of an American South that he had never known and developing an act with the veteran performer George Walker. Williams and Walker's success as Black performers in blackface was controversial, but it also helped the long, slow process of integrating the theater. As Fauset would note, the success of 1920s Broadway shows featuring jazz music and Black performers, notably *Shuffle Along*, owed a debt to Williams and Walker. As Fauset put it, "With that fundamental characteristic of true genius he took up the task of making the most of his restricted opportunities."[23]

Fauset knew a lot about making the most of restricted opportunities from attending Cornell rather than Bryn Mawr, teaching in Washington rather than Philadelphia, and returning from her study in France in August 1914 to finish her studies at the University of Pennsylvania. As Fauset wrote later, "This gift of ours [of laughter] has its rise, I am convinced, in the very woes which beset us."[24] The observation that adversity can be a spur to creativity, and, more specifically, that authentic joy in art depends on a knowledge of pain and sorrow is not original to Fauset. Nevertheless, framing her appreciation in terms of laughter captures something about her determination, despite her many setbacks. She knew, better than most, the pain behind both the act and the actor whose public role is to play the fool. She ends her tribute with an account of a bit in which Williams, as the rube, is tricked once again. He confirms his loss, but "as he reaches the exit he straightens up and thunders in that wonderful voice of his: 'But I shall return.' It was pitiful, it was funny, it was life."[25] The compromises that Fauset details in Williams's career indict American racism and prove his genius as an exemplar of Black artistry. These same compromises lie at the heart of the artistic ambitions and experiences of her characters, especially in her first two novels, *There Is Confusion* and *Plum Bun.*

There Is Confusion tells the story of two families: the Marshalls of New York and the Byes of Philadelphia, contrasting the Marshalls' pride in work with the Byes' reliance on their heritage as freedmen. At the heart of the novel is talented but snobbish Joanna Marshall, who interferes disastrously in her brother's love affair with Maggie, the daughter of a woman who keeps a boardinghouse. They reunite and marry, but he is killed in World War I. Joanna pursues a career as a dancer, inspired by children's street games in the Hell's Kitchen neighborhood of New York City as much as by classical dance, but she struggles to find teachers. Eventually, a teacher agrees to take her on as a student in his off hours, since his white students refuse to learn alongside a Black dancer. She wins a part in an off-Broadway review, dancing the Black and Indigenous American parts in a sequence of dances of the nations. When the dancer portraying white America quits in a racist pique, Joanna gets the finale, dancing "America" in a mask. Her unmasking at the demand of a rapt audience creates a *succès de scandale*, and the show comes to Broadway. Her persistence and her sense of her own exceptional talent pay off, and she seems on the brink of stardom, despite the considerable obstacles of race and racism. During this time, she is conducting an affair with Peter Bye, who loves her but is lazy. Only after the war does he learn the meaning of work and prove himself worthy of Joanna. At the novel's end, she leaves her career to marry and make a home with him. Despite the turn to marriage, *There Is Confusion* charts Joanna's precarious, dependent progress through her education, marking the obstacles and happy chances each step of the way, forcing a happy ending while charting the many types of racism young Black artists face.

In October 1924, a few months after her novel came out, Fauset took an extended leave from the offices of *The Crisis* and traveled to France for six months. She was full of hopeful enthusiasm—and some nerves. Before she left, she wrote a long cheerful letter to Langston Hughes, urging him to extend his stay to overlap with her own and meet her ship in Le Havre to help with the stressful and tiresome train journey to Paris. She proposed: "You can take me to all the dangerous places and I can take you to all the beautiful ones."[26] Although Hughes returned to the United States before she arrived, she luxuriated in the chance to be in France, free of cares and responsibilities, still riding high on the achievement of her book, despite the mixed reviews and ambiguous celebration of the party in her honor. At forty, Fauset was finally enjoying the kind of trip abroad that many young men take at twenty, a redo of the one that, ten years earlier, had been cut short by the war.

Still, it can be lonely to be in Paris. Fauset was accustomed to living with—or very near to—her sister, Helen Fauset Lanning, and conducting a busy social life in New York. A January 1925 letter to Hughes thanks him for a Christmas note that cheered her immensely. That letter came to play a key role in her second and best novel, *Plum Bun*.

Plum Bun is a novel of race passing, and in this it bears some resemblance to Nella Larsen's 1929 novella, *Passing*, a modernist masterpiece. *Plum Bun* has a more complex plot that owes more to literary realism than to the modernism of the moment. Both Larsen's Clare Kendry and Fauset's Angela Murray find, in passing, the ease of dating and being cared for by a wealthy white man. Du Bois, in comments on an early draft, found "the reasons for passing in a certain pleasure and comfort loving girl" to be the heart of the book.[27] However, Angela's initial reasons for passing are not only—or even primarily—about love and ease: she has to leave Philadelphia for New York if she is going to pursue her dream of becoming a painter.

As *Plum Bun* opens, we meet the Murray family: Mattie and Junius are happily married with two young adult daughters. Angela, a painter, is light-skinned like her mother, and Virginia, a musician, is dark like her father. On many Saturdays, they have fallen into the habit of separating, with Junius taking Virginia on long walks while Mattie and Angela go shopping, a pleasure that "would have been impossible with a dark skin."[28] But the seemingly harmless pleasure ends up teaching Angela a deeper lesson: "that the great rewards of life—riches, glamour, pleasure,—are for white skinned people only."[29]

Young Angela absorbs this lesson, but Fauset takes pains to undo it for her readers. In a flashback we learn that, while working as a lady's maid, Angela's mother was assaulted by a man who was attracted to light-skinned women. She turned to Junius, the dark-skinned coachman, for protection, and they married. Mattie attributes her happiness "to her black husband whom she had been glad and proud to marry" and knows, from bitter experience, that white people merely see her as a "white nigger."[30] Later, when Mattie faints on a shopping trip, they go to the hospital, and Junius has to pretend to be her chauffeur in order to visit her. Mattie embraces her husband and calls him by his first name, leaving the intern "raging about these damn white women and their nigger servants."[31] In both passages, Fauset is unflinching: racism extends to all Black people, regardless of skin tone. The hatred, exclusion, and sense of entitlement to control Black bodies may take different forms, but there is no escaping its reach. Both parents die shortly thereafter, too soon to undo the unintentional lesson that Angela has learned.

In grammar school, Angela is cut off by a friend who discovers she is "colored." In consequence, Angela finds herself increasingly isolated. The girls will not sit with her, and "little groups toward which she drifted during lunch, inexplicably dissolved to re-form in another portion of the room."[32] As Fauset writes, Angela "did not need such a hint more than once, but she was bewildered and hurt," so she gets into the habit of carrying a book to recess or drifting into the art room to perfect her drawings: "Miss Barrington thought her an unusually industrious student."[33]

This frustrating experience of childhood racism pulls Angela toward art and study, but in art school one of the same girls who snubbed her as a child exposes her again. In a life drawing class, the model spots Angela among the students and flounces out mid-class in indignation: "I haven't got to the point yet where I'm going to lower myself to pose for a coloured girl."[34] The art teacher confronts her, miserably, noting, "You never told me you were coloured."[35] Exposed by the model, Angela has to discontinue her lessons, thereby threatening her professional hopes. She puts the family house up for sale, cashes out her half, and moves to New York. There, passing for white, she intends to pursue her career as a painter, taking classes and having access to the museums, galleries, and fellowships from which she is barred: "Why should I shut myself off from all the things I want most,—clever people, people who do things, Art,—" her voice spelt it with a capital, "travel and a lot of things which are in the world for everybody really but which only white people, as far as I can see, get their hands on. I mean scholarships and special funds, patronage."[36]

Her arrival on Fourteenth Street in Manhattan is all exhilaration: she thinks "for the first time she would be seen, would be met against her new background or rather, against no background. No boyish stowaway on a ship had a greater exuberance in going forth to meet the unknown than had Angela as she entered her class that first afternoon."[37] The analogy to a "boyish stowaway" resonates strangely here. The intention of the sentence, its vocabulary and tone, would seem point toward adventure ("boyish stowaway," "exuberance," "going forth"). However, travel by ship has an evil history for African Americans. The distance that separates this naive, middle-class young Black woman from an exuberant stowaway of any race is less than the distance between either of those figures and that of the men and women stolen into incarceration whose Atlantic crossings were under conditions of slavery. The resonance of that history in Angela's desire to be carefree indicts both Angela herself, who knows that she is "being unconscionably idle," and the society that places a greater burden of responsibility on the descendants of slaves than it does on the descendants of slave owners and others who profited from an economy based on unpaid labor.

Angela's first hesitation comes when she visits Harlem for the first time, "amazed and impressed at this bustling, frolicking, busy, laughing great city within a greater one."[38] Passing, she sees for the first time how Harlem accommodates Black people of all classes, skin tones, types, and professions, and when she thinks to herself, "No, she was not sorry that she had chosen as she had," we hear the tinge of regret.[39]

If Harlem suggests that another path had been possible all along, Penn Station offers a keen reminder of what she has lost. There, in a climactic scene, Angela runs into her white boyfriend, Roger, just as her sister, who cannot pass, is getting off the train. Jinny, too, has decided to try her luck in New York, but she cannot pass and will live in Harlem. Frantic to avoid her sister and thus "out" herself to her white boyfriend, Angela is totally helpless and shuts her eyes. When her sister, recalling an old game of playing "lady," greets her by saying, "I beg your pardon, but isn't this Mrs. Henrietta Jones?," Angela seizes the opportunity to rebuff her sister rather than lose her chance at snagging a white husband.[40] This public denial of a darker-skinned sister determines the rest of the book.

But Fauset is not writing a tragedy. She is attempting something more unusual: a story of a woman who changes her mind and is not fatally punished. Her attempt to make a game of marriage to a rich man does not stick. In fact, immediately after her sister leaves, bewildered and incredulous, but with her "head high," Angela "began to waver. Surely no ambition, no pinnacle of safety was supposed to call for the sacrifice of a sister."[41] This moment, about a third of the way into the novel, intensifies the inner conflict that drives Angela to find a way to have the full life of an artist without losing touch with her Blackness and her sister. Matured by the rift with Jinny and the love affair that also eventually falters, Angela finds that her desire to be an artist persists. She uses her lunch hour to return to Fourteenth Street, remembering how she had found inspiration in the men idling in Union Square, in the pedestrians who would stop to listen to a player piano in the open window of a music store. She spends her evenings working "at the idea of a picture which she intended for a masterpiece" based on the homesick faces of the men in Union Square.[42] At first, homesickness is alien to Angela. When she first sees the look, she does not realize that "all unaware her face took on the wistfulness of the men gazing in the music store. She wished she knew some of these pleasant people."[43]

As in *There Is Confusion*, Fauset focuses us on the process, setbacks and all, and she keeps our eye on the ambition that remains as circumstances change. Even as Fauset sometimes shoehorns her plots into coincidence and happy endings, even as she has her women continually protest about the pleasure they take in homemaking, she also draws attention to the commitment to a career, to access to the opportunities—travel, privacy, fellowships, advanced classes—that allow a talent to develop. In *Plum Bun*, when Angela arrives in New York, the city unfolds its magic for her, and Fauset makes us see the glee with which she tastes that freedom. At one point, she thinks: "She remembered an expression 'free, white, and twenty-one,' this was what it meant then, this sense of owning the world, this realization that other things being equal, all things were possible. 'If I were a man,' she said, 'I could be president,' and laughed at herself for the 'if' itself proclaimed a limitation."[44] What might have seemed ridiculous in 1929 resonates differently nearly a century later. The ambition and hunger with which Angela seizes this moment confirm her hunger to become an artist. Her dismissal of ambition in the next sentence has contributed to the relative neglect of Fauset's work: There is little vogue among readers for women who extoll the virtues of wifedom. Angela pulls back, thinking, "Power, greatness, and authority, these were fitting, and proper for men; but there were sweeter, more beautiful gifts for women, and power of a certain kind too."[45]

Once in New York, Angela thrives in the racially integrated classes at Cooper Union, enjoying new friendships, especially one with Anthony Cross, a Spanish art student who has changed his name from Cruz. (This, as readers of novels about race passing will note, is a clue: a common way to pass is to claim Spanish heritage, and, yes, he turns out to be passing, too, but Angela takes a long time to figure that out.) At the same time, Angela watches the progress of a very talented Black painter, Rachel Powell. This girl, who is almost always referred to formally as Miss Powell, holds herself aloof from the others, just as Angela had done in school as a girl: she "lent her belongings, borrowed nothing, and spoke only when she was spoken to."[46] In an overture of friendship, Angela proposes lunch but rejects Miss Powell's favored Automat for a tea-room. When Angela is late, she finds Miss Powell waiting outside, unsure of her reception in an unfamiliar place: "Angela could not pretend to misunderstand her," after all, as Fauset herself wrote of her own lunches, one wants a meal, "not a law suit," and the meal forces Angela into a shocked recognition at how blithely she had allowed herself to forget the uncertainties of life as a Black person.[47] Later, a happy Miss Powell puts her hand on Angela's arm, but Angela brusquely shakes her off for fear that her white lover will see their intimacy.

Proud and wise, Miss Powell thanks Angela with a bunch of jonquils, but she makes no more attempts at friendship and treats her only with a "remote and frozen" courtesy.[48] Miss Powell wins a fellowship to France, but it is revoked when the agency learns she is Black, as had happened to so many other Black artists and writers of Fauset's acquaintance, as had happened to Fauset herself when she wanted to attend Bryn Mawr. The committee writes Miss Powell to say "they were sure the enforced contact on the boat would be unpleasant to many of the students, garnered as they would be from all parts of the United States. Furthermore, they couldn't help but think that such contact would be embarrassing to Miss Powell too."[49] Fauset devastatingly captures the absolutely correct language of bureaucratic racism, the certainty that no one, including Miss Powell, would want to be "embarrassed," the cruel way that those in authority count on supplicants not raising a fuss. Miss Powell's experience is drawn most directly from that of the sculptor Augusta Savage (1892–1962) who studied at Cooper Union, sculpted a bust of Du Bois, and, in 1923, had a fellowship to the Palace of Fontainebleau withdrawn after having been accepted. Savage's case was the subject of much conversation and activism at *The Crisis*, and she eloquently defended herself in an editorial in the *New York World*: Savage did *not* behave as was expected, but not everyone possesses such bravery.[50] In a 1926 essay, Du Bois imagined a different, more cautious artist: "There is in New York tonight a black woman molding clay by herself in a little bare room, because there is not a single school of sculpture in New York where she is welcome. Surely there are doors she might burst through but when God makes a sculptor He does not always make a pushing sort of person who beats his way through doors thrust in his face."[51]

Du Bois's picture of an artist who is not "a pushing sort of person" may well have been describing Miss Powell or Fauset herself. Who will push when the artist cannot push for herself? Even Savage, with all her pushing, did not get to France for several more years, and, although she is celebrated today, much of her greatest work has been lost or destroyed. If, like Fauset, the artist is reluctant to mix with white folks and suspicious of white patronage, and if, even in Du Bois, she has a champion who is notoriously bad with money, who borrows from her rather than lending to her (as Du Bois did), then what opportunities are there for her to work uninterrupted?

In *Plum Bun*, Miss Powell's crushing disappointment stirs Angela into action: as much as her betrayal of her sister, and, more urgently, her classmate's inability to secure the education she seeks persuades Angela to be honest about her own race. She visits Miss Powell at home and tells a pack of reporters that she, too, is Black. Hearkening back to the meeting on school segregation that Fauset's father had attended back in 1883 in Camden, New Jersey, Angela faces a choice between acknowledging her heritage and seizing an educational opportunity. Belatedly, but with fierce pride, she tells a reporter that "it's a great deal better to be coloured and to miss—oh—scholarships and honours and preferments, than to be the contemptible things which you've all shown yourselves to be this morning," even though Miss Powell's mother pronounces her a fool for giving up her chance.[52] As Angela finally discovers that passing for white is not a clear path to happiness, she thinks: "Jinny had changed her life and been successful. Angela had changed hers and had found pain and unhappiness. Where did the fault lie?"[53] In the ensuing pages, Fauset tries to answer that question, shifting the fault away from the woman who chooses to pass and onto the racist society.

Fauset's novels attempt to do something that few understood at the time—and that few have understood since. Working in a tradition of women's novels, informed by realism and sentimentalism, Fauset was caught in a moment in which the market for books by Black writers was dominated by modernism, and the market for traditional fiction was for whites only. Her writing looks strange next to the spare brilliance of Nella Larsen or the rural exuberance of Zora Neale Hurston. She is embarking on a different project entirely. And, like nearly every Black woman novelist before her, she faces criticism for perceived failures of representation. If Hurston is too earthy and uses dialect in ways that raise objections, then Fauset is too genteel. There is no winning.

On the final page of *Plum Bun*, Fauset gives her heroine the fairy-tale ending that she herself never achieved. Having given up her white lover, defended Miss Powell, and renounced passing, Angela has found her way to Paris to paint. Alone on Christmas Day, she looks for the present her sister has promised when she finds Anthony Cruz himself on her doorstep, teasing: "There ought to be a tag on me somewhere . . . but anyhow Virginia and Matthew sent me with their love."[54] It is a Hollywood ending: the two artists, both of whom can pass for white but who each have determined to pass no longer, are reunited in Paris, where they can paint beyond the reaches of American racism.

Plum Bun is centrally about a young woman's search for a mentor, for a fitting lover and teacher. She finally gets that in Paris with her lover. The letter from Hughes that Fauset received on Christmas Day in Paris in 1924 provides the spark for the end of *Plum Bun*. From that welcome letter, Fauset develops a story in which, instead of a letter coming on Christmas Day, she receives the special delivery of the boyfriend with a sister's blessing. Fauset lived much of her adult life with her sister, but, in *Plum Bun*, she imagines a cruel alternative in which an artist denies her sister's centrality. Angela needs three things: she needs family, she needs love, and she needs her career. In that climactic moment in Penn Station, it seems to her that she can sacrifice family for love. In that, she explores the intensity of wanting something so badly that you will betray your family.

It is tempting to end Fauset's story of mentoring and emerging into her own as an artist with this triumphant moment: the happy ending of her second novel. This conclusion combines her joy in Paris with the joy she imagines for Jean Toomer, who, as she points out in a 1922 letter, should enjoy Europe as he has "no prejudicing appearances."[55] It makes the words of Hughes's welcome Christmas letter to her turn flesh, in the person not just of a friend but a lover. To end here, however, would be to miss the last acts of Fauset's life, in which she finally had the chance to serve as a mentor to college students, and in which she turned, fruitless, back to Hughes in search of help.

When *There Is Confusion* came out, Fauset described herself to Hughes as finally embarking on her career, but the path was not as direct as she seems to have hoped. She left *The Crisis* in 1926 but could not find employment as an editor or a publisher's reader, despite her willingness to work from home (out of consideration for racist coworkers). In 1927, she appealed to Du Bois once more for help securing a position teaching high school. Even that was not easy, but she eventually got a job at DeWitt-Clinton High School, where she taught until 1944.

Plum Bun came out in 1928, and in 1929, at the age of forty-seven, she married Herbert Harris, a World War I veteran and insurance broker. They continued living with her sister Helen in New York until Helen's death in 1938. The marriage seems not to have been ideal, and some sources suggest that they separated for a time in the early 1930s. During these years, Fauset published her final two novels and, in the 1940s, she and her husband retired to Montclair, New Jersey. There, she returned to the civil rights activism of her earliest years, writing a long and fiery rebuttal in the *Montclair Times* to a racist editorial. "Roger W. Babson's comments on colored people," it begins, "are so superficial and inadequate to the situation that his advices become ineffectual."[56] She also participated extensively in public life, setting up a library fund in her sister's memory; speaking at local schools, women's clubs, and the teacher's college (now Montclair State University); teaching classes on African American history and literature at the local adult school; and contributing to the annual women's college book fair. Up until 1960, Fauset still hosted parties in New York (at the apartment of a sister and brother-in-law), especially in honor of visiting African artists and dignitaries, including Nana N'Ketsia IV of Ghana, Dr. Njoroge Mungai of Kenya, and the great South African singer and activist Miriam Makeba.

In 1948, Hughes asked Fauset for some poems to include in an anthology he and Arna Bontemps were editing. Their back and forth over this project, while still friendly, is exasperating. Fauset sends "fourteen poems" for consideration along with "love and constant pride in all your undertakings."[57] She expresses her frustration at their selection of only a few previously published poems: "Certainly my readers will think I have not advanced."[58] As they are finalizing the contributor biographies, she writes a tart note about hers:

> I thought it very strange of Mr. Bontemps to speak only of my teaching at Dunbar, when it really means something for a colored person to have taught at DeWitt Clinton which was then the largest High School in the world. I noticed Mr. B. stressed everything possible in his own somewhat unremarkable career. Also Langston for obvious reasons—NO dates. Please don't think me bitter about Mr. B. but I've suffered a good deal from colored men writers from Locke down to Bontemps—you know
> "Without sneering teach the rest to sneer," sort of thing.
> Only you and Gloster have been fair.[59]

Getting the life right mattered to Fauset. Many of her letters while at *The Crisis* concern biography: providing them for Du Bois's hosts in advance of a speaking engagement, requesting and correcting them. In the 1920s, Du Bois wrote a sharp note to Roscoe Bruce: "I want to say to you in confidence that if any biography has got to be written by Mr. Locke I would much prefer it to be left out of your book."[60] The mistrust of Locke was deep. After retirement, Fauset applied for fellowship money to write a curriculum of biographies of notable African Americans, and Hughes corresponded several times with Mary McLeod Bethune to see if Fauset might work with her, either as assistant, ghost writer, or biographer. As a teacher, Fauset understood the value of a well-written curriculum, and, as a writer and mentor to others, she knew the power of a biographical note for preserving the record of Black achievement in the face of racist obstacles.

One of the great joys of these years was a year as a visiting professor of creative writing at Hampton University in Virginia. "Dear Langston," she wrote Hughes. "I love Hampton! Of course, tho; since I am a person whose middle name is 'Nostalgia,' I am happy to be going home tomorrow."[61] While frustrated as a full-time high school teacher, Fauset reveled in the chance to work with young writers. One wonders what her life might have been like if college teaching had not been closed to her.

Fauset writes candidly to Hughes of her frustrations, and how much she depended on her sister's unflagging faith in her. As films with racial themes came into vogue in the late 1940s, Fauset tried, one more time, to insert herself into the conversation, begging Hughes more than once to help her find a Hollywood agent: "I think I shall die if I don't succeed in getting THE CHINABERRY TREE and COMEDY: AMERICAN STYLE accepted in Hollywood."[62] Ever positive, ever patient, Hughes shared with her his own inability to get a footing in Hollywood and his sense of how difficult this ambition was.

With all this activity, it hardly seems fair to call the years after *Plum Bun* empty, or to dismiss them as a time of sad decline. With two additional novels and abundant civic activity, Fauset's late middle age was not merely sad. And, while it is a pity that she never had the professional success she wished for, this is, after all, a common fate. Her ability to retain the friendship and affection of her most famous discovery forty years later is a tribute to her generosity and their mutual esteem.

Dorothy Arzner
1897–1979

HOLLYWOOD'S DIFFIDENT PIONEER

Dorothy Arzner was the only woman film director to successfully make the transition from silent to sound film. She invented the boom mic and gave Katharine Hepburn her first starring role, but, when she got pleurisy on the set of the World War II drama *First Comes Courage*, she was forced to leave directing. Though she was only in her forties, Arzner's career as a director was over. Ultimately, her main involvement with movies would be as a teacher, a role in which she excelled.

In that last film, *First Comes Courage* (1943), Merle Oberon plays Nicole Larsen, a resistance fighter who becomes engaged to a Nazi officer in occupied Norway so she can pass battle plan information to the Allies, and who endures the contempt of her fellow villagers so she can gather war secrets. When the Nazi, Major Dichter (played by Carl Esmond), begins to suspect her, she informs her contacts, and they send a team to assassinate him. The team is led by a British officer and her former lover, Captain Allan Lowell (Brian Aherne). As Dichter confronts Nicole, she bravely admits to working for the resistance; Allan appears from behind a curtain and shoots and kills him. They trundle Dichter's body into his waiting car, and Allan says, "Nick, you have to come back to England with me now. Don't you see? Von Elser [Dichter's commanding officer] will suspect you. It'll be suicide for you to stay."[1] Allan's assertion is ominous. Up to this point, he and Nicole, whom he calls "Nick," have had a companionable and equal relationship, sharing information and plans, consulting each other, and, in every way, behaving as colleagues. However, with the mission complete, Allan is eager to get her to safety.

With the Nazi's body in the back seat, Allan and Nick must get to the coast before the bomb on the booby-trapped roadway detonates. Their time is tight, and, what is more, they are being pursued by Colonel Von Elser and several other Nazis. By a hair's breadth, they reach safety in time to see the bomb explode, killing the Colonel and everyone in his car. As they scramble from their vehicle to the boat that will take them to safety, Nick keeps looking back over her shoulder. Thinking she is upset, Allan soothingly urges her on, but Nick has another idea: "Allan . . . I'm the widow of a German hero. Do you realize what that means? . . . It's too good of an opportunity to miss. Von Elser dead, too. There'll be a new commandant. He'll respect me. I'll have his confidence. I must go back." It is a brave plan, and a good one, but Allan objects. "I won't have it," he says. "You've done more than your share. More than any woman could be expected to do." With a magnificent toss of her head, Nick shoots back: "I'll quit when you quit." Allan pivots from her contribution as a woman and makes a case for the primacy of love, but Nick objects: "Ah, but, Darling, it isn't that kind of a world anymore. People don't dance and laugh and ski as we once used to." Their back and forth continues, as a stretcher passes with soldiers carrying a wounded man. Urgently, Nick demands a kiss. Allan returns the embrace, making her promise to stop talking of going back. Hailed by another wounded soldier, Allan's attention turns from Nick just long enough for her to run toward the danger. The film ends with a shot of Allan on a transport boat, looking mournfully back at Nick, as Nick, tears in her eyes, stands between Norwegian pines, watching her lover as he departs for safety without her, flames from the explosion roaring behind her head.

Nick still loves Allan, but it is she who carries the message that *all* must persist in the fight, putting personal cares aside until the war is over. *First Comes Courage* was made in 1943, *during* World War II, which makes it even more thrilling as propaganda. It was meant to inspirit the audience to persist in the fight, and it has as its centerpiece a woman who not only understands the mission but also takes it more seriously than her lover. The film, Arzner's twentieth feature as a director, was a departure for Arzner, who had not made an action movie before, and it ought to have been the beginning of a new phase in her career. Unfortunately, she got pleurisy while shooting and could not finish the film. For a while, she was not even given a director's credit; the film was finished by Charles Vidor. Arzner never directed another feature.

In the years after she left Hollywood, moving to the desert and working as a film instructor at the Pasadena Playhouse and UCLA, Arzner refused to complain, insisting that it was time for a new chapter. She behaved with the dignity and courage of Oberon's character. But no one in Hollywood successfully advocated for her. She appealed to Preston Sturges and Howard Hughes for work at their new studio, but they did not offer her anything. In the prime of her career, at forty-six, Arzner, one of the few women directors in Hollywood, was unable to find anyone to hire her to direct again. She became a beloved mentor to many and made a powerful impact on the history of film, but the role of mentor was not one she sought. Circumstances made mentoring her best option, and she put her intelligence and her heart into the work.

Dorothy Arzner liked to say she was born with the century, and, since her original birth certificate was destroyed in the San Francisco earthquake of 1906, few could contradict her. This fib was not to shave years off her age but to make her success in the movies seem inevitable: a child of the century, she and the movies grew up together. She was, in fact, born in 1897, the second child and only daughter of Ludwig and Janet Arzner. Both of her parents were immigrants, her father from Germany and her mother from Scotland. The proud child of immigrants, Arzner wrote that she liked to imagine herself as "a citizen of the world," something that briefly got her in trouble during World War II:

> In 1942, when all Americans had to prove their birthright as American citizens, there was no proof that I had been born. The record had been destroyed in the devastating fire and earthquake of April 18, 1906. My pride of birthplace was now being tested by questions. My last name, originally Artzner, was German. I had earlier responded when I heard the phrase "a citizen of the world." I liked the phrase. I liked the idea of belonging to the whole instead of being a limited person. However, school records and a bank record satisfied the inquiries—had I been in America for more than twenty years? All was well. I was not a German enemy. But I cherished the idea that I was a citizen of the world.[2]

She loved her mother, remembering that "there was something about [her] that was always exciting."[3] However, when she was five, her parents divorced, and her father got sole custody of the children. Young Dorothy was taken downtown to the Palace Hotel, where she saw her mother, "dressed in a sealskin jacket and wearing violets. I rushed toward her—my face was crushed into the violets and fur. She started to cry, and so did I. Then a pulling apart. That was the last time I saw my mother, except for one brief glimpse a few years later. I was five years old. Now my brother and I were 'children of divorce.'"[4]

Ludwig Arzner moved from San Francisco to Los Angeles in search of work and eventually came to own Hoffman's, a German restaurant associated with the Grand Opera House, one of the first live theaters in Los Angeles.[5] For several years, while he was looking for work, he put Dorothy and her brother in a series of homes, both as paid boarders and with family members. It was a tumultuous and traumatic beginning. At one point, a beloved aunt got cancer and died while Arzner lived with her. Once, wanting to have her desk in her room, she moved it from the basement. When she got in trouble for it, she told her brother, and, defending her, he threatened to get his gun and kill their caretaker. Her brother was soon sent to live with a relative in Ohio—another family member she lost.[6] In 1905, Dorothy's father married a woman named Mabel Mills, and Arzner went to live with her new stepmother's mother in Oakland. There, she experienced the great San Francisco earthquake firsthand. Reflecting on these early years, Arzner would be characteristically generous and philosophical. Of course she was shocked and hostile to a new stepmother—"Hard on her and hard on me"—and she wrote of her father: "I now have the deepest sympathy for [him] and what he must have gone through—trying to find a place for his children."[7] Arzner practiced the same powerful empathy on her own story that she brought to her movies.

Years after the divorce, Arzner had "a longing for my mother and an inner secret dream that I would leave home like the Alger boys and go looking for her."[8] In fact, one day, Arzner's mother did come looking for her, but she was not allowed downstairs to see her. Here is how Arzner would remember what must have been an achingly distressing, cruel experience:

> Apparently, there had been the warning that my mother would try to take us away. Even at my aunt's, there was a day the doorbell rang, and instead of opening the door, my aunt rushed to all of the windows and drew the blinds. Then I heard my mother's voice calling my name. Of course, I wanted to go to her, but I was held with a hand placed over my mouth as I tried to cry out to her. All around the outside of the house, I heard her voice calling me, but no sound was allowed to go out to her. She soon went away. There may have been a reason for not letting her see me, but it all seemed wrong and mysterious then, and no one ever said anything against her, and there were no explanations.[9]

At this time, she was no more than nine years old. The matter-of-fact narrative cannot hide the horror of the moment. After relaying it, Arzner mentions that this experience "played a reprise" in her directing life when she made Ruth Chatterton's first starring picture, "*Sarah and Son*. It was the story of a mother who had been separated from her baby son. After she had attained wealth in a career, she searched for her son and found him. Pretty fundamental plot—it was an enormous success. By that time, I thought I was sophisticated and was afraid the story might be too 'corny' but I knew the story down to the ground as far as emotional content."[10]

Arzner's memoir moves swiftly on. In the following paragraph, she expresses her gratitude for her step-grandmother's kindness. Arzner brushes away her own pain, but we can linger on *Sarah and Son* (1930) and its significance. The movie is a remarkably affecting melodrama adapted into a screenplay by Zoë Atkins from a novel of the same name by Timothy Shea. The movie twists its biblical allusion in a new direction: instead of centering on faithful Abraham, who is willing to put God ahead of his much-wanted son, our focus is on Sarah: What would it be like to be the mother of a much-loved child married to a man who unilaterally decides he knows what's best? Sarah's husband is no Abraham; he is a shiftless alcoholic, a performer of uncertain talent and no ambition. When Sarah and her husband have a marriage-ending argument, he, in a fit of anger, vengeance, and desperation, kidnaps the baby and gives it up for adoption to a wealthy man. He then enlists in the Army and shifts off to Europe as a volunteer in World War I.

Sarah is desperate, but she has no way of finding her son. She continues singing and finds success, and even stardom. Eventually, she is in Europe, performing for wounded soldiers. In a hospital ward, she is reunited with her dying, repentant husband, and he tells her the name of the wealthy family who is raising their child. Knowing where to find her son is just the beginning of Sarah's struggle: it is not the same as a reunification. In fact, the adoptive parents are fantastically wealthy, and they have a lawyer working to protect their right to raise the boy. (The lawyer later becomes Sarah's love interest and turns against the older couple.) They argue that the boy is better off with all the riches they can provide. In the end, Sarah does reunite with her son and proves herself to be the boy's true mother. The little boy, now twelve or thirteen, chafes at his coddled upbringing. He longs to drive a motorboat, to be active, but his older conservative parents are petrified that he might come to harm. He runs away to his grandfather's country house on Long Island—not a very daring escape, but even that is part of the film's tenderness toward the boy. Sarah finds him there, and her normal, calm, and loving reaction to when he recklessly steals a motorboat proves that she is his genuine, understanding mother. In *Sarah and Son*, Arzner imagined a heroic mother, successful in her quest to rescue her child and to recognize his right to a little fun, a little danger. And the boy himself is a wonderful stand-in for Arzner: his struggles to be normal in the face of coddling parents are not that different from what Arzner faced as a tomboy who grew up to be an out lesbian at a time when few queer people were open about their sexuality.

By the time she finished grade school, her father and stepmother had Arzner and her step-grandmother Mam join them in Los Angeles. This is where all Arzner's official biographies begin: with Arzner hanging out in Hoffman's, her father's restaurant, meeting the movie and theater people who patronized it. including D. W. Griffith, Mary Pickford, James Cruze, Mabel Normand, and Charlie Chaplin. These facts are alternately treated either as central or irrelevant to her eventual career: either she grew up hanging on all the stories around these tables or she was too young to properly comprehend what was going on. Either way, the early traumas and losses—the years of moving home, the divorce and traumatic separation from her mother, the death of her aunt, the separation from her brother, the San Francisco earthquake—are almost never mentioned.

In multiple interviews in the 1970s, Arzner declared that she would never write an autobiography, without mentioning that she had already written one. The Arzner archives at UCLA include a fifty-seven-page typescript, covering the first twenty years of her life, up to her start in the movies. In a 1973 interview, Francine Parker records that "the young, friendly waiter who had evidently served her similar lunches leaned over to ask, 'Miss Arzner, when are you going to write your life story?' 'Never,' she said," and Judith Mayne's *Directed by Dorothy Arzner* (1995), the only full-length biography, does not mention it.[11] (It has been recently reprinted in Martin Norden's collection of interviews.) In addition to this autobiographical fragment of childhood, the archives are full of interviews, several essays, press releases, and brief studio biographies. These documents all participate in Hollywood mythmaking.

Her parents were concerned by her boyish ways—she liked to dress in boy's clothes and play stick ball—and they enrolled her in the fashionable Westlake School for Girls. She would recall that those days "have always made me think of Jack London's *White Fang*. . . . I thought all the girls at school were such 'sissies.' I would stand at a distance and throw rocks while they greeted each other in the morning."[12] After Westlake, Arzner went to the University of Southern California for a while, but when the United States entered World War I in 1917, she volunteered as an ambulance driver. Because she was only twenty, she was never sent overseas and drove for the Army in California instead.

After the independence she experienced during the war, Arzner no longer wanted to be in school, and the long road of medicine, which had initially interested her, was not as appealing. She took a studio tour with an old friend and decided to try the movie industry. Her father promised to match her salary, dollar for dollar, so, with his support, she knew she could make it.[13] She began as a typist, then worked as a screenwriter before being promoted to editor. Here is where the fragment of her autobiography ends; she never wrote about her life in Hollywood.

Editing *Blood and Sand* (1922), a Rudolph Valentino bullfighting vehicle, Arzner figured out how to splice in stock footage of bullfights from Madrid, saving the production a lot of money and making things much safer for their star. A precise, exacting editor, Arzner cut shots of a giant crowd from Madrid with close-ups of the box seats and Valentino in the ring, giving an effective impression that the star himself was really there. Arzner invented this film technique, which is still widely used today. One day, the actor and director James Cruze was walking through the Paramount lot and passed Arzner while she was editing. Impressed by what he saw, and surprised to see that the editor was the same little girl he used to see at Hoffman's, he hired her to edit *Covered Wagon* (1923), a silent epic.[14]

This was a major break in Arzner's career, and it elevated her profile. *Covered Wagon* was a grueling location shoot with a huge, multiracial cast. Arzner remembered working with the Indigenous extras, some of whom were badly treated by the white actresses:

> We were very friendly with the Indians, but we had a problem with some of the girls we brought out from Hollywood. They were fascinated by the beautiful silver bracelets and ornaments, and the girls would all casually walk into the Indian tents. Then one night, an Indian decided to walk into the girls' tent. I heard these screams and whatnot, and the girls were going to tie up the Indian or chase him out of camp. I defended him. I said, "What can you expect?" I told Jim Cruze, "This is wrong. The girls have been walking in and out of his tent. What's wrong about the Indian walking in and out of theirs?"[15]

Cruze agreed and the incident blew over. Arzner's defense of the Indigenous actor was repaid mightily. He saddled her horse for her every day, and one night, in the snow, he came and tightened the canvas on her tent and Cruze's so they would not collapse under the weight of the snow: "The next morning all the tents were down but ours."[16]

Around this time, Arzner began a relationship with Marion Morgan, a dancer and choreographer who would be her partner until Morgan's death in 1971. Morgan's experience as a dancer informed Arzner's films, most notably *Dance, Girl, Dance* (1940), but also many others, which include formal and informal choreography. The two women were an acknowledged couple in Hollywood at a time when open lesbianism was rare, and gay marriage did not exist. Arzner never conformed to expectations for women at the time, wearing skirt suits and little to no makeup and keeping her hair short and brushed back off her forehead. Interviewers often commented on her androgynous looks before reassuring readers of her kind eyes and feminine qualities. Mayme Peak's 1928 description is typical: "Here's a woman who could run the studio if she had a mind to! Not that there is anything aggressive about Dorothy Arzner's manner. She isn't masculine. Neither is she especially feminine. Just one of those modern college girl types with a certain air of boyishness and an awful lot of confidence."[17] Somehow, Arzner had found a way to navigate Hollywood while being herself.

In 1927, after much persistence, Arzner was given her chance to direct. Paramount gave her a script and two weeks to fix it, and she turned in *Fashions for Women* ahead of schedule and under budget. Two years later, when Paramount wanted to put Clara Bow in her first sound film, they asked Arzner to direct. Bow was so nervous about the sound equipment that she was struggling. Arzner asked for a fishing pole and some line and rigged up the first boom microphone to capture Bow's first sound performance: the boom mic was invented. *The Wild Party* (1929), about a college girl who falls in love with her professor, was Arzner's fifth feature (and her earliest surviving movie) and a big success for Arzner and Paramount. Arzner was a great editor, a skill that informed her directing and taught her to respect the many roles on set. She valued her screenwriters, often inviting them to sit with her during filming, and while other directors often worked out of view, calling directions from an overhead microphone, Arzner insisted on directing on the soundstage floor, next to the cameras and in clear view of the actors, giving them a person to perform for.

After her success with Bow, she became known for her ability to elicit the best from her actors. *Sarah and Son* made Ruth Chatterton a star. In giving Katharine Hepburn her first starring role in *Christopher Strong* (1930), she knew right away that Hepburn's supple, athletic body would be equally great in trousers and slender, body-skimming gowns. In *Craig's Wife* (1936), she gave Rosalind Russell a chance to show her unique screen presence, showcasing Russell's absolutely gorgeous erect carriage, her radiating intelligence, and her ability to turn what might be the villainous role of a demanding wife into the sympathetic part of a woman desperate to control her domestic sphere. In *The Bride Wore Red* (1937), she shows us how Joan Crawford can be sexy and commanding but also vulnerable and open to love. Arzner got a wonderful performance from Maureen O'Hara in *Dance, Girl, Dance*: "O'Hara got tired of being typecast as spirited fiery lasses. . . . *Dance, Girl, Dance* allows her to call forth all kinds of qualities she wasn't often asked to utilize: tenderness, innocence, vulnerability, shame. In O'Hara's capable hands, a character who could have been a simplistic ingenue is not an ingenue at all."[18] Arzner did not do this only for O'Hara: In *Dance, Girl, Dance*, Lucille Ball is both gorgeous and hilarious, demonstrating all the comic genius she is known for while flashing real star power. And Merle Oberon is smoky, beautiful, controlled, and utterly believable as an undercover agent in *First Comes Courage* (1943), Arzner's last feature film.

Arzner was only forty-six and at the height of her powers when her directing career ended. *First Comes Courage* is an action film, something of a departure for her, but, like all her other films, it has a strong woman at its heart. In a 1975 interview, while Arzner was giving Mary Murphy, a journalist from the *Los Angeles Times,* a tour of her garden, the subject of Charlie Chaplin came up: "Yes, it was so unfortunate that he was blackballed, but then we were all blackballed at some time."[19] In what sense was Arzner blackballed? She was not particularly political, but Murphy surmises that "her vision of women and how they should be portrayed on screen and treated in the studio classed with the dictates of Louis B. Mayer, whom she calls 'the great dictator.'"[20] This clash on gender, combined with the wartime atmosphere and suspicion that might hover around the daughter of a German immigrant with no birth certificate, would certainly give studios reasons not to hire her. As Arzner told another interviewer, "The true reason I retired from Hollywood may forever remain a secret, and I'd rather it does."[21]

Whatever the cause, Arzner's efforts to get other directing jobs, including an appeal to Preston Sturges to work for his newly founded (and ultimately not very successful) studio, failed. She was the inventor of a crucial editing technique and the boom mic, and was the first woman to join the Directors Guild of America (in 1938), but she could not get hired by any studio. She had been signed on to make a film with an African American cast in 1940 that—like many Hollywood projects—never got made, and, in 1944, she was attached to a film starring the African American dancer and choreographer Katherine Dunham that also never got off the ground. She made some training films for the Women's Army Auxiliary Corps (WAACS) during the war and taught filmmaking to the WAACS as well. She and Morgan moved to La Quinta, a desert town over a hundred miles from Hollywood, in 1951, marking the end of her efforts to get back into directing. She gardened, painted, and drew. She wrote her fragmentary autobiography and hosted a radio show.

In 1952, Arzner was appointed head of the television and motion picture department at the Pasadena College of Theatre Arts. She directed Billie Burke, who had starred in several of her movies (and is best remembered today as Glinda the Good Witch from *The Wizard of Oz*) in a stage play there in 1954. During the 1950s, she reunited with Joan Crawford, making dozens of television commercials for Pepsi. (Crawford was then married to a Pepsi executive.) In 1959, she became a lecturer at UCLA, where she taught until her retirement in 1965, having supervised over fifty student films, including Francis Ford Coppola's. Morgan died in 1971. The final years of Arzner's life were marked by celebrations and requests for interviews as the feminist film revival screened her work. The Directors Guild of America hosted a tribute to her in 1975, and the Second International Festival of Women's Films featured a four-film retrospective of Arzner movies in 1976. Arzner died in 1979. She received a posthumous star on the Hollywood Walk of Fame in 1986, and in 2018, at Coppola's urging, Paramount named a studio building after her.

Dorothy Arzner's 1933 movie, *Christopher Strong*, opens with a heedless group of bright young things in evening dress piling out of several taxis. It is the middle of the night, and they are returning to a London townhouse with the spoils from a scavenger hunt. They dump their miscellaneous findings on the ground, and the hostess gives a knowing laugh. They have gotten too good at the game; they need a harder task. She challenges them to bring back a woman over twenty who has never had a love affair and a man who has been happily and faithfully married for more than five years. Soon, the young people return. Monica Strong (Helen Chandler) brings her father, Christopher (Colin Clive), and her married boyfriend brings the aviator Cynthia Darrington (Katharine Hepburn), who has just beaten him in an impromptu drag race earlier in the evening. Asked to prove her bona fides, Cynthia, in a flight suit and cap, leans back against a grand piano, her elbows cocked behind her like wings, legs thrust out before her, filling the screen with angular power. She shoves her hands in her pockets and speaks to the assembled: "I'm exhibit B, I suppose. I've never had a love affair or been married—in any sense of the word. I've always wanted to fly, and moreover as my flights were usually alone, that may be the reason I never met the man I might be in love with. It certainly is the reason I've got to keep fit. You've not gone to bed yet and I've just got up! And now I'm off!"[22] With that, she pushes off; she is due at the airfield. Her apparently unnecessary "in any sense of the word" winks at anyone in the audience imagining queer possibilities. But that is subtext. The overt result of this speech is that the affair between Cynthia and Christopher Strong, the only two sensible people in the room, is set in motion.

Also set in motion is a pattern of people turning to Cynthia, asking her for advice. Her command of the room makes Christopher fall in love with her. Simply by telling the partygoers how she has managed to achieve something impressive where they have just been partying, she gives everyone a lesson in how to be, in how to pursue goals. Both Christopher and his daughter, Monica, turn to Cynthia for guidance. Impressed by Cynthia's independence, Monica confides the challenges she faces in her affair with the married Harry Rawlinson (Ralph Forbes) and her misery when her parents force her to break contact after she returns home drunk. Later, when Harry has honored the Strongs' demand, stayed away, *and* procured a divorce, he rejects Monica because she had a fling while they were separated. Desperate and threatening suicide, Monica again turns to Cynthia, who prevents her from acting rashly and intervenes with Harry on her behalf. The two marry, and Monica is soon pregnant.

Early in the film, Christopher, on the pretext of asking for advice, stops at Cynthia's apartment unannounced. Having decided that maybe she should have more fun, on this night she is getting ready for a fancy dress party. With her offscreen, they launch into conversation, companionable and professional. Suddenly, she emerges dressed as a sparkling moth, in an incredible hooded metallic lamé gown, with antennae sticking out of her head. Hepburn looks impossibly long and slender in this gorgeous shiny outfit; you cannot keep your eyes off her—she is sparkling, she is glowing, she is unmissable. At the same time, she is forthright, honest, willing to listen to what he has to say. Christopher is in the position of everyone in the audience: dazzled by her beauty, and amazed that a creature so magical and fun is also speaking practically, earnestly listening to him, and trying to offer the advice he sought.

Cynthia's crew respects her, too, and the film takes care to show her at work as an aviator. Several times, we see Cynthia poring over maps and charts, consulting with her flight crew. They treat her as an equal; in fact, they treat her exactly as Arzner says a *director* should be treated. The cinematographer Stephen Burum, best known for his work with Brian De Palma and Francis Ford Coppola, was Arzner's student at UCLA. He credited her with an important lesson in offering advice to someone of a higher rank:

> As a graduate student, Burum was the permanent cinematographer in Arzner's intermediate workshop. 'She probably taught me more than anybody else,' he says . . . 'If the director was about to make a misstep, she'd say, "Steve, you know that's wrong; don't let him do that." So I'd tell the director what he should do, and she'd come over and say, "You can't say that, he's the director." She taught you from the beginning where your place was and how far you could go.'[23]

The director is in charge, but the responsibility is to the film. If the cinematographer (or anyone else) notices something wrong, they need to find a way to tell the director without disrupting the hierarchy. This is the kind of set that Arzner seems to have run. She often brushes off interviewers who want to imply that she is an auteur; she does not believe in that theory of directing. She understands Hollywood filmmaking as an intensely collaborative process, but she also has a very clear understanding of the role and relation of each person or each job to every other job. She is not in any doubt that she is the director, and as the director she has the final cut, but she is unwilling to take credit for the whole film, because she also knows it has been a collaborative process. Thus, in filming these scenes of collaboration in which a group of men accept a woman as their collaborator and their leader, Arzner offers us a version of the kind of workplace she created.

Christopher Strong, named for the male lead, was Hepburn's second film and her first starring role. Hepburn, who started onstage, had had unexpected success in her first film: "As the fan letters, the exhibitors' reports, the columns of newspaper praise poured in, David Selznick, then head of Radio Pictures, realized that here was a girl who might be one of that small group of really great stars. . . . Whether she achieved that great place . . . or whether she joined those who have made one great hit and then drifted into mediocrity, depended largely upon her second picture. . . . What should they do to ensure her future? They sent for Dorothy Arzner."[24] Of their collaboration, Hepburn said simply, "She wore pants. So did I. We had a good time working together."[25] Made before the Hays Code in 1934, which imposed moral strictures on film, *Christopher Strong* includes open discussion of sex and pregnancy and has an extramarital affair at its heart. (It is the only time Hepburn played a mistress.)

The movie's double plot exposes the hypocrisy of sexual mores. Christopher, whose last name becomes increasingly ironic as the movie progresses, presents himself smugly as a paragon of moral virtue: he and his wife, Elaine (the magnificent Billie Burke), wonder if they are the only nice people left. They are shocked at their daughter's affair with a married man and take her off on a vacation in Cannes to get her mind off him. Yet, at the same time, Christopher is pursuing his relationship with Cynthia, under his wife's nose. After a separation, they consummate their affair. In an extraordinary and justly celebrated close-up, we see Cynthia's hand, her wrist englobed by an elaborate bracelet, reaching to turn out the bedside light. The two, now clearly lovers, are talking. Christopher asks her to give up flying for him. She does. As Pauline Kael says, "It's the intelligent woman's primal post-coital scene."[26]

Now Cynthia is a mere mistress: bored, waiting, and robbed of her career. The situation reaches a crisis when Monica, now happily married and pregnant, encounters Christopher and Cynthia in a village pub. Monica is shocked and judgmental, and demands condemnation, but Elaine refuses, insisting that she is a "brave girl—not cheap." Rather than make the wife a rival or a victim, Arzner directs Burke to show the pain of betrayal without hatred toward another woman. This refusal to pit women against each other—and the simultaneous exposure of Monica as small-minded for pursuing revenge—is an Arzner hallmark.

In this moment of crisis, Cynthia, whose advice has been sought on everything from flight patterns to how to conduct a love affair, has no one to turn to. Moreover, she has just learned she is pregnant: she has a new reason to keep from flying. Tentatively, she tries to tell Christopher, saying that her doctor does not want her to fly, but "it's not because of my heart."[27] He misses the clue that her shining face makes plain. Instead, he delivers yet another morally upstanding speech about duty, leaving love unmentioned, and it is vividly apparent that he will indeed never leave his wife. With Monica angry and Christopher weak, Cynthia is a mentor with no one to help her. She decides to fly one last time. Perhaps she can break the altitude record. On the eve of her flight, as she is leaving a party, a woman asks for her autograph: "You were our hero at school. . . . You gave us courage for everything."[28] Even in despair, Cynthia pauses to offer a kind word and an autograph. One last time, she gets into her airplane, breaks the altitude record at thirty-four thousand feet, and takes off her mask, committing suicide. The film ends on a shot of a statue erected in her honor. It is not a satisfying ending, but it is a bleakly realistic one.

It is easy to speak sop about being a mentor, about how satisfying it can be to help young people find their way, but one of the insidious workings of patriarchy is to slot women in their prime into mentorship roles. After all, a mentor is no threat; a mentor is not even a professional anymore. In *Christopher Strong*, Arzner gives us a portrait of three women affected by an affair: the conventional Monica, unselfconsciously reverting to tradition once her own messy affair conforms; the wife, Elaine, pained by her husband's betrayal, but choosing to remain in the marriage nevertheless; and Cynthia, the daring aviator, whose first love affair asks her to give up her career and then, her life. In Arzner's hands, each of these women face a complicated circumstance; none is simple.

At the climax of *Dance, Girl, Dance* (1940), Judy (Maureen O'Hara) breaks the fourth wall, confronting the audience in the theater, both on-screen and off. This scene exemplifies how Arzner puts women at the center of movies that still adhere to the rules of Hollywood at the time. *Dance, Girl, Dance* follows the sharply differing ambition and fates of two dancers, Judy and Bubbles (Lucille Ball), members of a struggling dance troupe. Classically trained Judy longs to be a professional dancer and dreams of the chance to audition for a modern dance company.

Witnessing one of their rehearsals, in which a multiracial company dances, in a style inflected by George Balanchine and Martha Graham, in front of a set of stylized skyscrapers, Judy is both enraptured and intimidated. (Ernst Matray was the film's choreographer, and Arzner was assisted by her knowledge of dance through her partner, Marion Morgan.) Bubbles, by contrast, wants success on the stage and enthusiastically seizes her chance to become a burlesque star and a character in the gossip columns. While Judy looks to the morning star, praying that God may make her a dancer, Bubbles assures a producer, "I ain't got an ounce of class, sugar, honest."[29]

Remarkably, the movie doesn't choose between them. Bubbles's lack of class, her "oomph," her talent, and her ambition land her a job, and she quickly becomes a burlesque star. Soon, she has enough pull to offer Judy a job, but the catch is that Judy will perform her serious dance as the stooge in Bubbles's act, the comedic dupe that the audience boos off to summon Bubbles on-stage. Humiliating as this is, Judy is happy to be dancing, and the two reach an uneasy truce as Bubbles's act grows into a phenomenon.

The movie reaches its climax one night when Judy has finally had enough. Moping over a romantic misunderstanding (the two women are interested in the same wealthy playboy), she almost misses her cue. On-stage, she is professional as ever, but a strap on her tulle gown has come loose, and every time she tries to tuck it into her bodice, it falls back out. Her increasing discomfort only eggs on the hecklers, who shout, "Don't mind us, we can take it!" Then, as she makes to leave the stage, another heckles: "She's going home to Mama." This stops her—and the orchestra quiets to only an insistent drumbeat. Judy turns around and steps onto the passerelle, the gangway that passes from one side of the stage to the other in front of the orchestra, to address the audience. As she prepares to speak, Arzner cuts to Steve Adams (Ralph Bellamy), the head of the company she most wants to dance for, and his assistant, Miss Olmstead (Katherine Alexander). They, too, have come to see Bubbles's show. In short, the stakes are high for Judy: heartbroken, frustrated, and angry, she has just danced for the audience she most desires. In this moment, she delivers a blistering speech, addressed both to the people in the theater and those of us watching the film:

> Go ahead and stare. I'm not ashamed. Go on, laugh. Get your money's worth. Nobody's going to hurt you. I know you want me to tear my clothes off so as you can look your fifty cents worth. Fifty cents for the privilege of staring at a girl the way your wives won't let you. What do you suppose we think of you up here, with your silly smirks your mothers would be ashamed of? And we know it's the thing of the moment for the dress suits to come and laugh at us, too. We'd laugh right back at the lot of you, only we're paid to let you sit there and roll your eyes and make your screamingly clever remarks. What's it for? So's you can go home when the show's over and strut before your wives and sweethearts

> and play at being the stronger sex for a minute? I'm sure they see through you just like we do.[30]

Shocking and sobering, Judy's speech calls out the audience for leering. When she finishes, Miss Olmstead, clad in a stylish skirt suit much like those Arzner herself usually wore, stands to give her an enthusiastic ovation. Steve joins in, as does the orchestra leader, a small man with wild hair and a jaunty foulard; soon, the whole auditorium is cheering. Judy takes a stand. She addresses the audience, and, in doing so, she breaks the compact between audience and performer that, in this context, allows the audience to rest easy in their superiority to Judy's earnest ballet, confident her lovely dance is "stupid" and worthless, a sucker's pastime.

The directors push her back out to take another bow, but Bubbles is livid. She accuses Judy of crowding her act, calls her a "jealous little pig," and slaps her. A full-on fight ensues, with Bubbles in her slim metallic lamé gown and Judy in her tulle confection slapping, pulling, and rolling on the ground, in full view of the audience and increasingly entangled in the velvet curtain.

The whole scene is a searing critique of the crowd's hunger for spectacle. However, earlier, we have witnessed Bubbles's dance, and the movie has encouraged us to delight in her burlesque performance. As Sheila O'Malley puts it, "Judy feels victimized by the leers. Bubbles doesn't. Is Bubbles lying to herself? Can both women be right? Judy loses power on the stage, Bubbles gains it."[31] When Judy's impromptu speech gets an ovation, the men in the wings are delighted because they measure their success in applause. Bubbles's values are more aligned with the men's, but, crucially, the movie does not decide. Instead, it invites us to be aware of our status as spectators, while the sympathetic gaze of those who admire Judy offers us a way to imagine an ethical version of spectatorship. *Dance, Girl, Dance* tells a story of women in relationship to each other—women as rivals, and even as allies. They are prickly at first, but ultimately supportive of each other in their different dreams.

So many of Arzner's public comments about being a woman director dismiss easy generalizations, even dismiss entirely the idea that being a woman matters at all. In some moments, especially early in her career, she offers journalists easy conclusions about women's greater understanding of emotions or the need to make decisions with the confidence of a man. Later, especially in the 1970s, when journalists were turning to her for her memories of Golden Age Hollywood, her impatience is palpable.

Molly Haskell wrote an influential appreciation of *Dance, Girl, Dance* called "Women in Pairs," in which she observes how "Arzner bridges the gap between the different kinds of women she depicts and the different worlds they life in. Like Ouspenskaya [the dance troupe leader], she [Arzner] loves both Bubbles and O'Hara, and never views them as opposites of a judgemental virgin-versus-whore dichotomy as most men would."[32] Haskell's judgment, both deft and accurate, was memorable enough that in 1976, a Barnard undergraduate quoted another passage from Haskell in her thesis: "Arzner's films move forward with the jerky unpredictability of a vision not quite resolved into a style. Without rationalization, I think we might see this as an expression of the discomfort of a woman who feels herself an artist in an alien land, but is nevertheless trying, always, to bridge the gap: between Hollywood and her artistic aspirations; between the romantic conventions and her own feminist sensibility."[33] This Barnard student sent her thesis to Arzner, who not only read it, but marked it up with her commentary, writing, "Not true" and "I never had women weeping" next to an offhand characterization of her films as "weepies." But, along the margin next to the Haskell quote, in blue ballpoint pen, Arzner has drawn a bold, curvy line marking out Haskell's language and has written "TRUE" in letters bigger than her usual script.

Arzner's typical combination of respect for Hollywood and impatience with those she deemed inaccurate or sloppy makes her marginal "TRUE" next to Haskell's observation remarkable. Arzner loved Hollywood and was proud to have succeeded, largely as a freelance director, in the studio era. Within these rules, she consistently found ways to tell stories about women, and often, as in *Working Girls* (1931) and *Dance, Girl, Dance*, giving audiences a vivid illustration of the many ways of being a woman and taking charge of your life. For a generation of moviegoers still relatively new to the idea that women, like men, had the ability—and the responsibility—to decide what they wanted to make of their lives, *Dance, Girl, Dance* offered something new. Moreover, Arzner insisted on showing how the complicated mix of talent, opportunity, ambitions, and constraints mean that there are many paths to many different outcomes. At the end of *Dance, Girl, Dance*, both women get a happy ending, both are a success, and neither is married or engaged (though Judy melts suggestively into Steve Adams's embrace). When, thirty years after the fact, audiences and critics took note, Arzner had the satisfaction of seeing that the power and truth of her message had gotten through.

Arzner never sought out teaching. An indifferent student, she was an avid learner, telling an interviewer in 1936, "I enjoyed reading, and right now am reading Plato; only don't mention this, for I will be put down as a highbrow."[34] When the door to directing closed on her in her forties, she turned to teaching and was by all counts an incredible, generous, loving, and thoughtful mentor. Really, from the start of her career, she took the time to mentor others. As early as 1927, she was candid about the fears she had to overcome while directing. An interviewer asked her if she had been frightened to make her debut as a director:

> "Just scared stiff," confessed Miss Arzner. "Nobody ever suffered from stage fright as I did, I'm sure. But I kept going doggedly. I grew thin and got a cough. I felt like a rat in a trap. I would be figuring out speeches of resignation to make to Mr. Lasky and

> Mr. Schulberg. But, strangely enough, it seemed to me, the rushes came out all right. I was really putting on the screen just what I meant to. That is the oddest sensation, I believe, a director can ever have, seeing himself, as it were, coming to life on the screen, his own mental attitude and philosophy of life."[35]

Arzner's confidence extends to admitting her fear, but it also lies in her ability to look at her work and judge it good enough. Moreover, her editing experience meant that she could see that she was "really putting on the screen just what I meant to." When actress Bebe Daniels was having trouble understanding why a scene was not working, Arzner called her to the cutting room:

> Dorothy used to hold the film up to the light and cut it in the hand. I remember my first lesson; she held the film up and said, "Well, now, look—this is dead from here to here—we're going to put this close-up in here—so we'll go to here. We don't need this—wait a minute, we can come in here." Gradually I began to understand, and learnt to cut film myself. We used to mark the frame with a wax pencil, scrape the emulsion off with a razor blade, apply the glue, then put the other piece of film on top and press it down hard. Then we'd check our sprocket holes, and examine the cut under the magnifying glass.[36]

Always thinking about the entire crew, Arzner knew that Daniels's performance would improve if she understood more about camerawork, editing, and film. There is a fundamental patience and respect in stories about working with and for Arzner. She liked actors, writers, editors, and extras. She understood their contributions. Never taking credit for a film's success, she insisted that a director must be held accountable if a film fails.

So many young women wrote to her, seeking advice on how to break into the business, that she wrote and published an open letter of her stock advice in the *Hollywood Reporter* in 1932: "There is only one way to become a woman director. You have to be a woman. Then you must get your chance."[37] That twinkle, that impatient humility, the brisk deflection of the question from the challenges of directing to the condition of sex, all conspire to discourage idle seekers, dreamers with no intention of putting in the work. No-nonsense and slightly impatient, this remark suggests less warmth and encouragement than Arzner offers elsewhere. Elsewhere, she offers her reflections on the adage "Ask and ye shall receive," noting that you need to "keep on asking. . . . Don't give up! Ask is the only active part of that message."[38] Unfortunately, all her talent and persistence could not secure her any more directing work, and the many interviews she gave in the 1920s and 1930s dry up to nothing until silent film historian Kevin Brownlow sought her out in 1970, ushering in the beginning of a rediscovery.

Arzner describes to Brownlow her initial diffidence about teaching and her gradual turn from lecturing to an active, experimental teaching style. Arzner recognized that her film students, like she herself, would learn best and most quickly if she built a classroom that replicated a controlled version of a movie set. She turned her classes into a studio for filmmaking:

> Finally, I said, I just don't want to go on unless we really make pictures. You have a camera right here and a few lights—now do it like matinee theater. Just no sets—furniture and drapes. So, they draped the whole thing, and we started that way, and then bit by bit the students began building little sets, and finally, we were ending up with real pictures with sets and furniture and everything in them, and a cast. They began casting professional actors from Hollywood, and the actors were delighted to be helpful to the students. So, they brought in professional actors from outside, cast any way they wanted, wherever they could get them, and we ended up winning awards.[39]

In the early 1960s, this hands-on method, so familiar to us today, would have been extraordinarily innovative. It inspired her students to work late into the night on their projects, and they began winning awards for their films. In this, Arzner's teaching was at the vanguard of the transition toward college-educated filmmakers. But a collaborative teaching style is unlikely to gain the teacher a cult following, precisely because it puts students first and camouflages the mentor's expertise. In her mentoring, as in her filmmaking, Arzner stayed behind the camera. Her students included cinematographer Stephen Burum, who won an Oscar for *Hoffa* and worked with Brian De Palma on *The Untouchables* and Francis Ford Coppola on *The Outsiders*; Daisy Gerber, the only woman enrolled in UCLA's directing program, and an assistant director on *Annie Hall* and dozens of other films; Jack Hill, director of *Foxy Brown* and other blaxploitation films; Donald Shebib, one of Canada's most significant independent filmmakers; and, most famously, director Francis Ford Coppola, best known for *The Godfather* trilogy and *Apocalypse Now*.[40]

Arzner's teaching emerged out of her deep regard for the roles and hierarchies of a movie set. She began her career as a typist and grew into the best editor in the business, "the only editor from the entire silent period to be officially remembered."[41] Perhaps the best tribute to Arzner as a mentor is the way she assured her students of her belief in them. Her confidence in their ability was sustaining, as Coppola remembers. When he was a student at UCLA, not everyone saw his promise. One day, he was sitting on the steps outside a classroom building and Arzner walked by. He recalled: "She stopped and she handed me a box of crackers that she always had with her for her hungry students and she said to me, 'You'll make it, I know, I've been around and I know.' Then she disappeared into the shadows like the ending of one of her movies."[42]

AFTERWORD

When I tell friends about this book, a common reaction is "Why haven't I heard of these women? Why didn't I learn these stories?" The stories of women's lives are still stories we have to seek out; they are not the stories that a casual reader just happens upon. That means it can be easy to overlook how much has changed. It has only been a century since women have been able to imagine the room of one's own and the control of finances that, in 1929, Virginia Woolf posited as the first necessity of a creative life. Even then, the twin advantages of privacy and financial independence were partial and unevenly distributed. A woman in the United States could not rent an apartment or get a checking account without a man as her guarantor until the 1970s. Despite many gains, that room of one's own, that financial independence, remained out of reach for fifty years after Woolf's essay. At the time of this writing, another fifty years later, many are working to take away the privileges women have won, suggesting that perhaps women should not vote, that a woman's main purpose in life is to bear children. Uneven as these developments have been, uncertain as their future may be, the change to women's lives is recent; it crosses nations and continents. The opportunities that have opened for women and the resistances that have arisen in their wake mark a massive social change that we have yet to fully comprehend.

I began this book as an entirely hopeful project: a collection of stories of obstacles overcome and success against the odds.

Optimism is my nature, but I have wonderful friends in my life whom I credit with helping steady me, listening, and asking good questions. Instead of telling unnuanced stories of triumph—which I almost did—I am happy to say that this book is composed of real stories of women's lives. That includes the disappointments, setbacks, and obstacles these women faced, as well as all the moments when success arrived despite challenges, or belatedly, or in a minor key. Too often, we oversimplify what a woman's life in the past was or could be, but a collection of eight very different women, with appearances by Virginia Woolf, prevents easy answers.

I want to clarify, too, that my commitment to representing women artists includes an expansive and inclusive understanding of the word "woman." All women, including transgender women, are women. A hundred years ago, the category of woman was less fractious than it is today, and I have used "woman" throughout this book because it is what these writers used. A hundred years ago, the category of a nonbinary person was not widely known, but it is now, and many of the challenges and obstacles faced by the women in this book may feel relevant to feminine-presenting nonbinary people today. My focus on the category of "woman" stems from a deep commitment to naming, describing, and addressing the specific obstacles that all people who may be included under the umbrella of "woman" face.

As I tried to narrow down the list of women writers I wanted to include in this book, I was helped, again, by a friend. Together, at a Mexican restaurant in a remodeled garage in the Village, we pored over my list of neglected women writers. We sorted out those that interested me most. What qualities did they share? All of my women were determined to speak in their own voice, and each of them changed her mind, and, in doing so, the life she lived and the art she made changed, too. In that moment I understood that, as various as this list is, these women share a crucial interest in documenting what it was like to be part of the first generation of women who seized the chance to speak in their own voices.

Not so long ago, it was fashionable to tell young people that they could be anything they wanted to be. Such unbridled optimism is harder to access today. Economic stressors, the threat of climate disasters, a global pandemic, and political unrest have made the facts of precarity and constraint vivid to even the sunniest optimist. It is tempting to concede that the sky, in fact, may not be the limit, that we may reach the limit long before then. The fact is, constraints have always affected our ability to pursue dreams, and designing a life, speaking up for ourselves in our own voices, requires negotiating between reality and the sky, between what Woolf called "that queer amalgamation of dream and reality, that perpetual marriage of granite and rainbow."[1] As we negotiate these poles of granite and rainbow, it is helpful to have models of how women before us faced parallel challenges. Did they give themselves time to wander before settling on a path? Did they follow their strong moral instinct to rebel? Were they able to chart a new course when their explorations hit a snag? Did they work to bring others along with them, mentoring the next generation of artists? And how did their art fare in pursuing these strategies?

At the end of *A Room of One's Own*, Virginia Woolf speaks for the first time in her own voice, dropping the fictional narrator. In doing so, she speaks to her audience as a community of women. It is a reminder that *A Room of One's Own* started as lectures at the women's colleges of Oxford and Cambridge. While, for most of the book, Woolf has offered the history of women working alone, she looks up and marvels at the fact of a roomful of women students. The sight inspires her hopeful conclusion: "If we live another century or so . . . then the opportunity will come and the dead poet who was Shakespeare's sister . . . shall find it possible to live and write her poetry."[2] Even in this hopeful mood, Woolf reminds us that Shakespeare's sister will not come "without that preparation, without that effort on our part, without that determination. . . . But I maintain that she would come if we worked for her, and that so to work, even in poverty in obscurity, is worth while."[3] For Woolf, working together is essential for creating the masterpieces she longs for. Sylvia Townsend Warner continues this idea in a 1959 lecture, noting that "early women writers caused so little alarm [because] they only went off one at a time."[4] Once many women could read and write, any literate woman "must be kept in bounds: she must subserve."[5] For Woolf and Warner, women write with a complex awareness: of the forces wanting to keep them in bounds, and of the company of women, from the past, in the present, and into the future, who break those boundaries.

The women in this book were creating new kinds of lives, and they were doing so in a world full of other women doing the same. This created opposition, but it also created community. None of the women in this book imagined herself as the only woman pursuing a different kind of life, a new way of making art. In fact, each of these women had friends who, like them, were asking what they wanted from life. While the eight women in this book might not recognize the pattern of their life in a taxonomy of wanderers, rebels, explorers, and mentors, that list has power for us readers a century later, looking back. The simple act of naming a range of approaches to building a life may enable us to shift strategies when necessary. Wanderers, rebels, explorers, and mentors: these are all roles that a woman can inhabit while remaining in community with others.

So often women are socialized to care for others. They are taught that their happiness will arrive in the shape of a life with care for others at its center. A "happy" life, in the eyes of many, especially those seeking to curtail a woman with bigger dreams, means becoming a wife and mother, serving as a partner to a man and caregiver to children. These are formidable roles, labors of love and intensity and a source of pride, in my own life as they are in the lives of many. However, there are other things to do, other paths to take, and women have the right to decide, for themselves and in their own voice, how they want to shape their lives. As women pursued new opportunities and discovered that they could fulfill their desires and ambitions in other ways, they found ways to turn that habit of care in new directions—toward friends, partners, mentees, other artists, and themselves. They also found other talents, other parts to speak, other paths to choose distinct from care. The wanderers, rebels, explorers, and mentors in this book understood the feeling of wanting more from life, of wanting to change art. Their lives and their art show us the hard granite reality of opposition, but they also show us rainbows.

ACKNOWLEDGMENTS

Many people and institutions helped me in completing this book. Looking back over the long years of researching, teaching, and writing, I am humbled by the debts that I have accrued and grateful for the support shown to me and this project. It is an honor to acknowledge that help here. This book would not have been possible without a summer travel grant, sabbatical, research assistantships, and conference funding from Fordham University's English Department and Office of Research. I would also like to thank my agent, Laura Blake Peterson; my editor Haley Lynch; and the wonderful, attentive editorial staff at Beacon.

For permission to reprint copyrighted material, I am grateful to the Literary Executors of the Vera Brittain Will Trust (1970); the Estate of Muriel Rukeyser; Peepal Tree Press and Blue Banyan Books for permission to quote Una Marson; the Countee Cullen papers at the Amistad Research Center in New Orleans; the W. E. B. Du Bois Papers at the Robert S. Cox Special Collections and University Archives Research Center, UMass Amherst, and the librarians who digitized those papers and made them available online. Portions of chapter 1 were published in a different form online at *Public Books*.

Librarians and archivists played a vital role in helping me. In particular, I would like to thank the New York Public Library, especially the Wertheim Room in the Stephen A. Schwarzman Building, where much of the research for this book was conducted. Also helpful were the Mills Library at McMaster University in

Hamilton, Ontario, and the wonderful and enthusiastic archivists there who shared Vera Brittain's papers with me; the librarian in the New Jersey Room of the Montclair (New Jersey) Public Library; Special Collections at the University of California, Los Angeles; Special Collections at the University of Southern California; the Bank Street College Archives; and the Beinecke Library at Yale University, especially the digitized files in the James Weldon Johnson Collection.

Colleagues around the world afforded me the chance to test out my ideas at conferences, public talks, and invited lectures. I learn best in conversation, so the increasingly rare chance to travel and exchange ideas made this book markedly better. Thank you to Laura Sims and the South Orange Public Library; Faye Hammill and the faculty and graduate students at the University of Glasgow; Urmila Seshagiri and the University of Tennessee Humanities Center; and Nan Zhang and Nicole Huang of Hong Kong University. My deepest gratitude to Michael Whitworth and Merton College, Oxford University, for hosting me on a Visiting Research Fellowship for a term. During those magical months, I wrote much of this book. Amidst a warm Merton College faculty and staff, Laura Ludtke stood out as especially welcoming. While at Oxford, I participated in weekly seminars at the Oxford Centre for Life Writing (OCLW). I thank OCLW for including me in the seminar where I learned so much and made lasting connections: it was a pleasure. Ava Chin knows how much better the book is thanks to her brilliant and incisive feedback.

Before this book was a thought, John Duvall gave me the opportunity to edit a special issue of *MFS: Modern Fiction Studies*. I am grateful to him and to Sara Bryant and Rowena Kennedy-Epstein, whose articles introduced me to Dorothy Arzner and Muriel Rukeyser.

Many colleagues not yet mentioned have helped me refine my ideas and sustained me intellectually and otherwise through the years of writing: Kim Arin, Jay Barksdale, Natalia Cecire, Debra

Rae Cohen, Sarah Cole, Sarah Cornish, Amy Elkins, Eric Gardner, Anna Girling, Mark Hussey, Ane Thon Knutsen, Doug Mao, Adam McKible, Kate Nash, Jacqueline Norton, Beth Rosenberg, Paul Saint-Amour, Urmila Seshagiri, Anna Snaith, Alice Staveley, Janine Utell, Julie Vandivere, and many more. Colleagues at Fordham, especially Mary Bly, Steve D'Augustino, Shonni Enelow, the late Anne Hoffman, Julie Kim, Jordan Alexander Stein, Keri Walsh, and Sarah Zimmerman, have helped me over the years. I would like to thank my New Jersey writing group—Marcy Dermansky, the late Joanne Fisher, Karen Gevirtz, Corey Mead, Jon Michaud, Karen Shelby, Laura Sims, Nicole Rudick, and Helen Wan—for consultation and good cheer. My weekly coffees with Karen Gevirtz sustain me more than she knows. My life is enriched beyond measure thanks to the daily friendship of Melissa Bradshaw, Jane Garrity, Tamar Katz, Celia Marshik, and Allison Pease.

This book owes much of its existence to my students, for listening, asking great questions, and showing me where readers are enthusiastic, bored, and confused. Among the many wonderful students over the years, I want to especially thank Faye Arthurs, Alin Haberle, Aurora Hegarty, Hector Maccise, Alana Murphy, Jordan Smith, Lizzy Sobiesk, and all those in my spring 2025 graduate class, who so enthusiastically helped me refine my ideas. Thanks to Jaisa Pinnock for helping research agents, publishers, and fellowships. My former student from DePauw, Shavonne Johnson, showed up, twenty years later, to offer some vital research assistance on the Fauset chapter, just for the love of it. Participants in my reading groups at the Center for Fiction in Brooklyn have read and discussed so many of these texts with me over the years. I am so grateful that this wonderful nonprofit exists as a space to gather and talk about books.

My family has been unwavering in their support. My parents, Greta and Graham, fostered a love of reading, history, and a strong sense that *Girls Can Too*, as my childhood poetry anthology had it. My sister Sarah is always there for me. My wonderful children,

Olivia and Izzy Morgan, made me want to make this book better: their creativity, curiosity, passion for social justice, and support of me and my writing sustained me. I love them more than I can say. My husband, Bill Morgan, has stood beside me every step of the way, cheering me on, picking up the slack, and being a loving and thoughtful sounding board. I love you.

NOTES

INTRODUCTION

1. Virginia Woolf, *A Room of One's Own* (Mariner, 1989), 48.
2. Virginia Woolf, *Three Guineas* (Harvest, 1966), 14.
3. Jessie Redmon Fauset, *Plum Bun: A Novel Without a Moral* (Beacon, 1999), 82–83.
4. Mark Granovetter, "Threshold Models of Collective Behavior," *American Journal of Sociology* 83, no. 6 (1978): 1422.
5. Una Marson, *Una Marson: Selected Poems* (Peepal Tree, 2011), 128.
6. Sylvia Townsend Warner, *Lolly Willowes, or, The Loving Huntsman* (New York Review, 1999), 91.
7. Eileen Chang, *Love in a Fallen City*, trans. Karen S. Kingsbury (New York Review, 2006), 69.
8. Virginia Woolf, *The Letters, 1929–31*, vol. 4, ed. Nigel Nicholson (Harvest, 1981), 106.

PART 1: WANDERERS

1. Rebecca Solnit, *Wanderlust: A History of Walking* (Penguin, 2001), 234.
2. Solnit, *Wanderlust*, 234.
3. Virginia Woolf, *A Room of One's Own* (Mariner, 1989), 5.
4. Woolf, *A Room of One's Own*, 5.
5. Virginia Woolf, *Moments of Being*, ed. Jeanne Schulkind (Harcourt, 1985), 97–98.
6. Virginia Woolf, *The Essays, 1925–1928*, vol. 4, ed. Andrew McNeillie (Harcourt, 1994), 480.
7. Woolf, *The Essays*, 4:480.
8. Virginia Woolf, *The Essays, 1933–1941, and Additional Essays, 1906–1924*, vol. 6, ed. Stuart Clarke (Hogarth, 2011), 480–81.
9. Woolf, *The Essays*, 6:480.
10. Sara Ahmed, *The Promise of Happiness* (Duke, 2010), 53.
11. Woolf, *The Essays*, 6:482.

12. Woolf, *The Essays*, 6:482–83.
13. Sara Ahmed, *The Feminist Killjoy Handbook: The Radical Potential of Getting in the Way* (Seal, 2023), 263.
14. Margaret Wise Brown, *The Sailor Dog* (Western, 1992), n.p.

MARGARET WISE BROWN

1. Bruce Bliven, "Child's Best Seller," *Life*, December 2, 1946, 59.
2. John Fleischman, "Shakespeare of the Sandbox Set," *Parents*, July 1988, 92.
3. Leonard S. Marcus, *Margaret Wise Brown: Awakened By the Moon* (William Morrow, 1999), 3.
4. Aimee Bender, "What Writers Can Learn from 'Goodnight Moon,'" *New York Times*, July 19, 2014, https://archive.nytimes.com/opinionator.blogs.nytimes.com/author/aimee-bender/.
5. Gertrude Stein, *Writings, 1903–1932* (Library of America, 1998), 313.
6. Margaret Wise Brown, *Goodnight Moon* (Harper Collins, 1991).
7. Stein, *Writings*, 313.
8. Marcus, *Margaret Wise Brown*, 12.
9. Marcus, *Margaret Wise Brown*, 12, 16.
10. Marcus, *Margaret Wise Brown*, 25–26.
11. Marcus, *Margaret Wise Brown*, 29–30.
12. Margaret Wise Brown, 1935–1936, RG5 Graduate Programs (bsc.05.08.C.062, Box: 42), Bank Street College Archives, New York, NY, https://bankstreetarchives.libraryhost.com/repositories/2/archival_objects/5462.
13. Margaret Wise Brown, Teachers Reports (December 10, 1935), Bank Street College Archives.
14. Margaret Wise Brown, 1935–1936, RG5 Graduate Programs.
15. Margaret Wise Brown, 1935–1936, RG5 Graduate Programs.
16. Quoted in Marcus, *Margaret Wise Brown*, 79.
17. Margaret Wise Brown, *Seven Little Postmen* (Golden, 2010).
18. Margaret Wise Brown, *The Color Kittens* (Golden, 2000).
19. Margaret Wise Brown, "Writing for Five-Year-Olds," 1939, Barbara Biber Papers (bsc.10.03.E.03.026, Box 21), Bank Street College Archives, New York, NY, https://educate.bankstreet.edu/centennialbooks/1.
20. Brown, "Writing for Five-Year-Olds," 7.
21. Brown, "Writing for Five-Year-Olds," 7–8.
22. Marcus, *Margaret Wise Brown*, 92.
23. Margaret Wise Brown, *The Important Book* (Harper, 1949).
24. Quoted Marcus, *Margaret Wise Brown*, 225.
25. Marcus, *Margaret Wise Brown*, 199–200.

26. Marcus, *Margaret Wise Brown*, 112.
27. Gertrude Stein, *The World Is Round* (Harper, 2013).
28. Charles Gounod and Fréderic Mistral, "Mireille," *Opera Guide*, https://opera-guide.ch/operas/mireille/, accessed August 31, 2025
29. Brown, "Writing for Five-Year-Olds," 7–8.
30. Margaret Wise Brown, *Little Fur Family* (HarperCollins, 1984).
31. Margaret Wise Brown, *The Sailor Dog* (Golden, 1953).
32. Diane Zahler, via Twitter, March 12, 2014 (no longer available).
33. Stein, *The World Is Round*, 345.
34. Bender, "What Writers Can Learn from *Goodnight Moon*"; Elisabeth Egan, "The Enduring Wisdom of *Goodnight Moon*," *New York Times*, September 20, 2022 https://www.nytimes.com/2022/09/20/books/goodnight-moon-margaret-wise-brown.html; Anna Holmes, "The Radical Woman Behind *Goodnight Moon*," *New Yorker*, January 31, 2022. https://www.newyorker.com/magazine/2022/02/07/the-radical-woman-behind-goodnight-moon.
35. Quoted Marcus, *Margaret Wise Brown*, 285–86.

EILEEN CHANG

1. Eileen Chang, *Lust, Caution*, trans. Julia Lovell (Random House, 2007), 46.
2. Chang, *Lust, Caution*, 55.
3. Julia Lovell, "Foreword," in Chang, *Lust, Caution*, xv.
4. Chang, *Lust, Caution*, 19.
5. Chang, *Lust, Caution*, 20.
6. Chang, *Lust, Caution*, 24.
7. Chang, *Lust, Caution*, 14.
8. Chang, *Lust, Caution*, 43–44.
9. Chang, *Lust, Caution*, 39.
10. Chang, *Lust, Caution*, 44–45.
11. Chang, *Lust, Caution*, 15.
12. Chang, *Lust, Caution*, 43.
13. Chang, *Lust, Caution*, 45.
14. Chang, *Lust, Caution*, 46.
15. Eileen Chang, "'What Is Essential Is That Names Be Right,'" in *Written on Water*, ed. Andrew F. Jones and Nicole Huang (New York Review, 2023), 37.
16. Chang, "Whispers," in *Written on Water*, 165.
17. Chang, "Whispers," 165.
18. Chang, "Whispers," 166.

19. Eileen Chang, "Jasmine Tea," in *Love in a Fallen City*, trans. Karen S. Kingsbury (New York Review, 2006), 85.
20. Chang, "From the Ashes," in *Written on Water*, 47.
21. Chang, "From the Ashes," 47.
22. Chang, "From the Ashes," 51. *An Exposé of the Bureaucrats* is also translated as *Officialdom Unmasked*; 官场现形记; Guanchang Xiangxing Ji, by Li Boyuan, 1903.
23. Chang, "From the Ashes," 46.
24. Chang, "From the Ashes," 50.
25. Chang, "On the Second Edition of *Romances*," in *Written on Water*, 215.
26. David Der-wei Wang, *The Lyrical in Epic Time: Modern Chinese Intellectuals and Artists Through the 1949 Crisis* (Columbia University Press, 2015), 163.
27. Wang, *The Lyrical in Epic Time*, 180.
28. Peter J. Kalliney, *The Aesthetic Cold War: Decolonization and Global Literature* (Princeton University Press, 2022), 118.
29. Virginia Woolf, "Street-Haunting," in *The Essays*, 4.480.
30. Chang, "Seeing with the Streets," in *Written on Water*, 64.
31. Chang, "Seeing with the Streets," note, 249.
32. Chang, "Seeing with the Streets," 65.
33. Chang, "Seeing with the Streets," 66.
34. Chang, "Seeing with the Streets," 67.
35. Chang, "Seeing with the Streets," 67.
36. Chang, "Notes on Apartment Life," in *Written on Water*, 31.
37. Chang, "Notes on Apartment Life," 33.
38. Chang, "Writing of One's Own," in *Written on Water*, 22.
39. Chang, *Love in a Fallen City*, 66.
40. The film has been subtitled in English by Christopher Rea, a scholar of Chinese cinema, and is available on YouTube. https://chinesefilmclassics.org/.
41. Chang, "Let's Go! Let's Go Upstairs," in *Written on Water*, 105.
42. Chang, "Let's Go! Let's Go Upstairs," 105.
43. Nicole Huang, "Women, War, Domesticity: Shanghai Literature and Popular Culture of the 1940s," *China Studies* 6 (2005): 21.

PART 2: REBELS

1. Virginia Woolf, *Mrs. Dalloway: Authoritative Text, Contexts, Criticism*, ed. Anne E. Fernald (W. W. Norton, 2021), 118.
2. Woolf, *Mrs. Dalloway*, 7.
3. Woolf, *Mrs. Dalloway*, 49.

4. Virginia Woolf, *To the Lighthouse: A Norton Critical Edition*, ed. Margaret Homans (W. W. Norton, 2023), 91.
5. Woolf, *To the Lighthouse*, 91.
6. Woolf, *To the Lighthouse*, 91.
7. Woolf, *To the Lighthouse*, 91.
8. Woolf, *To the Lighthouse*, 93.
9. Woolf, *To the Lighthouse*, 50.
10. Woolf, *To the Lighthouse*, 50.
11. Woolf, *To the Lighthouse*, 50.
12. Woolf, *To the Lighthouse*, 66.
13. Woolf, *To the Lighthouse*, 17.
14. Virginia Woolf, *The Essays, 1933–1941, and Additional Essays, 1906–1924*, vol. 6, ed. Stuart N. Clarke (Hogarth, 2011), 242–43.
15. Woolf, *The Essays*, 6:244.
16. Virginia Woolf, *The Diary, 1936–1941*, vol. 5, ed. Anne Olivier Bell (Harcourt Brace Jovanovich, 1977), 189.
17. Virginia Woolf, *The Essays, 1929–1932*, vol. 5, ed. Stuart N. Clarke (Houghton Mifflin, 2010), 471.
18. Woolf, *The Essays*, 5:473.
19. Woolf, *The Essays*, 5:473.
20. Catherine Gander, *Muriel Rukeyser and Documentary: The Poetics of Connection* (Edinburgh University Press, 2013), 208.
21. Muriel Rukeyser, "Poem (I lived during the first century of world wars)," in *The Collected Poems of Muriel Rukeyser*, ed. Janet E. Kaufman, Anne F. Herzog, and Jan Heller Levi (University of Pittsburgh Press, 2006), 430.

VERA BRITTAIN

1. Virginia Woolf, *The Essays, 1933–1941, and Additional Essays, 1906–1924*, vol. 6, ed. Stuart N. Clarke (Hogarth, 2011), 244.
2. Vera Brittain, *Testament of Youth* (Penguin, 1995), 17.
3. Vera Brittain, "Semi-detached Marriage," *Evening News*, May 4, 1928, quoted in Deborah Gorham, *Vera Brittain: A Feminist Life* (Blackwell, 1996), 193.
4. George Eliot, *Middlemarch* (Penguin, 1988), 25.
5. Brittain, *Testament of Youth*, 45.
6. Brittain, *Testament of Youth*, 41.
7. Brittain, *Testament of Youth*, 32.
8. Brittain, *Testament of Youth*, 33.
9. Brittain, *Testament of Youth*, 52.

10. Brittain, *Testament of Youth*, 53.
11. Vera Brittain, *Chronicle of Youth: Vera Brittain's Great War Diary, 1913–1917*, ed. Alan Bishop (Phoenix, 2000), 28.
12. Brittain, *Testament of Youth*, 59.
13. Brittain, *Testament of Youth*, 60.
14. Brittain, *Testament of Youth*, 63.
15. Brittain, *Testament of Youth*, 91.
16. Brittain, *Chronicle of Youth*, 156.
17. Brittain, *Chronicle of Youth*, 156–57.
18. Quoted in *Testament of Youth*, 98; ellipses in original.
19. Quoted in Gorham, *Vera Brittain*, 173.
20. Quoted in Paul Berry and Mark Bostridge, *Vera Brittain: A Life*, 2nd ed. (Northeastern University Press, 2002), 83.
21. Virginia Woolf, *The Diary, 1915–1919*, vol. 1, ed. Anne Olivier Bell (Harcourt, 1977), 171.
22. Brittain, *Testament of Youth*, 155.
23. Brittain, *Testament of Youth*, 172.
24. Quoted in Berry and Bostridge, *Vera Brittain*, 89.
25. Brittain, *Testament of Youth*, 210.
26. Brittain, *Testament of Youth*, 210.
27. Brittain, *Testament of Youth*, 217.
28. Brittain, *Testament of Youth*, 291.
29. Virginia Woolf, *The Essays, 1933–1941, and Additional Essays, 1906–1924*, vol. 6, ed. Stuart N. Clarke (Hogarth, 2011), 244.
30. Brittain, *Testament of Youth*, 239.
31. Brittain, *Chronicle of Youth*, 301.
32. Brittain, *Testament of Youth*, 251.
33. Brittain, *Testament of Youth*, 343.
34. Brittain, *Testament of Youth*, 343–44.
35. Brittain, *Testament of Youth*, 373.
36. Brittain, *Testament of Youth*, 373–74.
37. Brittain, *Testament of Youth*, 374.
38. Quoted in Brittain, *Testament of Youth*, 377.
39. Brittain, *Testament of Youth*, 166.
40. Brittain, *Testament of Youth*, 374–75.
41. Brittain, *Testament of Youth*, 369–70.
42. Brittain, *Testament of Youth*, 423.
43. Vera Brittain and Winifred Holtby, *Testament of a Generation: The Journalism of Vera Brittain and Winifred Holtby*, ed. Paul Berry and Alan Bishop (Virago, 1985), 121.

44. Brittain and Holtby, *Testament of a Generation*, 121.
45. Berry and Bostridge, *Vera Brittain*, 130.
46. Berry and Bostridge, *Vera Brittain*, 133.
47. Woolf, *To the Lighthouse*, 139.
48. Brittain, *Testament of Youth*, 651.
49. Wilde, *The Importance of Being Earnest*, 2.1.
50. Woolf, *To the Lighthouse*, 74–75.
51. Vera Brittain, *Testament of Experience* (Seaview, 1981), 47.
52. Vera Brittain, Diaries, Vera Brittain Fonds, Section D, Box 51, Vol. 22, McMaster University Archives, Hamilton, Ontario.
53. Brittain, *Testament of Experience*, 216.
54. Brittain, *Testament of Experience*, 219.
55. Brittain, *Testament of Experience*, 253–54.
56. Brittain, *Testament of Experience*, 257.
57. Vera Brittain, *The Dark Tide* (Virago, 1999), 257.
58. Brittain, *The Dark Tide*, 257–58.

MURIEL RUKEYSER

1. Muriel Rukeyser, *Savage Coast: A Novel*, ed. Rowena Kennedy-Epstein (Feminist Press at CUNY, 2013), 184.
2. Quoted in Rowena Kennedy-Epstein, "Pillars of Process: Muriel Rukeyser, Franz Boas, and the Poetics of Birth," *Modernism/Modernity Print Plus* 6, no. 3 (March 10, 2022), https://modernismmodernity.org/articles/kennedy-epstein-pillars-process-rukeyser-boas-poetics-birth.
3. Muriel Rukeyser, *The Orgy: An Irish Journey of Passion and Transformation* (Coward-McCann, 1965), 105–6.
4. Rukeyser, *The Orgy*, 106.
5. Muriel Rukeyser, "Kathe Köllwitz," in *The Collected Poems of Muriel Rukeyser*, ed. Janet E. Kaufman, Anne F. Herzog, and Jan Heller Levi (University of Pittsburgh Press, 2006), 463.
6. Virginia Woolf, *The Essays, 1933–1941, and Additional Essays, 1906–1924*, vol. 6, ed. Stuart N. Clarke (Hogarth, 2011), 483.
7. Louise Kertesz, *The Poetic Vision of Muriel Rukeyser* (Louisiana State University Press, 1980), 268.
8. Rukeyser, "Letter to the Front," in *The Collected Poems of Muriel Rukeyser*, 243.
9. Rukeyser, "Poem Out of Childhood," in *The Collected Poems*, 3.
10. Muriel Rukeyser, "Author's Introduction," in *The Muriel Rukeyser Era: Selected Prose*, ed. Eric Keenaghan and Rowena Kennedy-Epstein (Cornell University Press, 2023), 30.

11. Rukeyser, "Author's Introduction," 31.
12. Weldon Kees, "Miss Rukeyser's Marine Poem," *Partisan Review* 9, no. 6 (December 1942): 540.
13. Rebecca Rukeyser, "If One Woman Told the Truth About Her Life," *The Believer* 141 (May 1, 2023), https://www.thebeliever.net/if-one-woman-told-the-truth-about-her-life/.
14. Emma Train, "A Queer Lesbian Feminist Ecopoetics: Muriel Rukeyser and the Beyond-Human," *GLQ: A Journal of Lesbian & Gay Studies* 28, no. 3 (June 1, 2022): 386–87.
15. Rukeyser, *Savage Coast*, 184.
16. Rukeyser, *Savage Coast*, 184.
17. Rukeyser, *Savage Coast*, 220.
18. Rukeyser, *Savage Coast*, 11.
19. Rukeyser, *Savage Coast*, 46.
20. Rukeyser, *Savage Coast*, 71.
21. Rukeyser, *Savage Coast*, 101.
22. Rukeyser, *Savage Coast*, 92.
23. Rukeyser, *Savage Coast*, 151.
24. Rukeyser, *Savage Coast*, 82.
25. Rukeyser, *Savage Coast*, 82.
26. Rukeyser, *Savage Coast*, 82.
27. Rukeyser, *Savage Coast*, 83.
28. Rukeyser, *Savage Coast*, 83.
29. Rukeyser, *Savage Coast*, 5.
30. Rukeyser, *Savage Coast*, 107.
31. Rukeyser, *Savage Coast*, 199.
32. Rukeyser, "Speech for the Assistant," from *Houdini*, in *The Collected Poems of Muriel Rukeyser*, 179.
33. Rukeyser, *Savage Coast*, 184–85.
34. Rukeyser, *Savage Coast*, 224.
35. Rukeyser, *Savage Coast*, 266.
36. Rukeyser, *Savage Coast*, 269.
37. Rukeyser, *Savage Coast*, 7.
38. Kennedy-Epstein, "Pillars of Process." Quotations from Louise Bogan, "Verse," *New Yorker*, November 3, 1951, 150–51; and Delmore Schwartz in James Brock, "The Perils of a 'Poster Girl': Rukeyser, *Partisan Review*, and Wake Island," in *How Shall We Tell Each of the Poet: The Life and Writing of Muriel Rukeyser*, ed. Anne F. Herzog and Janet E. Kaufman (Palgrave Macmillan, 1999), 258. For more information on Rukeyser and her readers, see Rowena Kennedy-Epstein,

"The Spirit of Revolt: Women Writers, Archives, and the Cold War," *Modernism/modernity Print+ 2* (2017), https://modernismmodernity.org/forums/posts/spirit-revolt-women-writers-archives-and-cold-war; and Rowena Kennedy-Epstein, *Unfinished Spirit: Muriel Rukeyser's Twentieth Century* (Cornell University Press, 2022).

39. Kertesz, *The Poetic Vision of Muriel Rukeyser*, 43.
40. Rukeyser, "Author's Introduction," 35.
41. Rukeyser, "Reading Time: 1 Minute 26 Seconds," in *The Collected Poems*, 155.
42. Muriel Rukeyser, *The Life of Poetry*, foreword by Jane Cooper (Paris Press, 1996), 14.
43. Rukeyser, "If One Woman Told the Truth About Her Life."
44. Rukeyser, "Waking This Morning," in *The Collected Poems*, 471.
45. Rukeyser, *The Collected Poems*, n626.
46. Rukeyser, *The Life of Poetry*, 20.
47. Rukeyser, *The Life of Poetry*, 139.
48. Rukeyser, *The Life of Poetry*, 85.
49. Rukeyser, *The Life of Poetry*, 137.
50. Rukeyser, *The Life of Poetry*, 3.
51. Rukeyser, *The Life of Poetry*, 1.
52. Rukeyser, *The Life of Poetry*, 213.
53. Kertesz, *The Poetic Vision of Muriel Rukeyser*, 373.
54. Virginia Woolf, *A Room of One's Own* (Harcourt, 1981), 98.
55. Virginia Woolf, *Orlando: Authoritative Text, Backgrounds and Contexts, Criticism*, ed. Madelyn Detloff (W. W. Norton, 2025), 10–11.
56. Virginia Woolf, *The Essays, 1925–1928*, vol. 4, ed. Andrew McNeillie (Harcourt, 1994), 160.
57. Elaine Edelman, "'Were We All Brave, but at Different Times?': A Student Remembers Muriel Rukeyser," in *How Shall We Tell Each Other of the Poet? The Life and Writing of Muriel Rukeyser*, ed. Anne F. Herzog and Janet E. Kaufman (St. Martin's, 1999), 78.
58. Rukeyser, "[Untitled]," in *The Collected Poems*, 397.
59. Edelman, "'Were We All Brave, but at Different Times?'" 78.
60. Edelman, "'Were We All Brave, but at Different Times?'" 78–79.
61. Rukeyser, "Foghorn in Horror," in *The Collected Poems*, 265.
62. This widely quoted sentiment was the blurb on the back of Muriel Rukeyser's poetry collection, *The Speed of Darkness* (Vintage, 1971).
63. Rukeyser, "Poem Out of Childhood," in *The Collected Poems*, 4.
64. Rukeyser, "Poem (I lived during the first century of world wars)," in *The Collected Poems*, 430.

PART 3: EXPLORERS

1. Virginia Woolf, *The Letters, 1888–1912 [Virginia Stephen]*, vol. 1, ed. Nigel Nicolson and Joanne Trautmann (Harcourt, 1975), 2.
2. Alan Bell, "Stephen, Sir Leslie (1832–1904), Author, Literary Critic, and First Editor of the Dictionary of National Biography," *Oxford Dictionary of National Biography*, https://doi.org/10.1093/ref:odnb/36271, accessed August 24, 2025.
3. Virginia Woolf, *The Letters, 1923–1928*, vol. 3, ed. Nigel Nicolson and Joanne Trautmann (Harcourt, 1978), 126.
4. Woolf, *The Letters*, 3:291.
5. Woolf, *The Letters*, 3:231, 250, 325.
6. Woolf, *The Letters*, 3:253.
7. Woolf, *The Letters*, 3:326.
8. Woolf, *The Letters*, 3:430.
9. Virginia Woolf, *The Voyage Out* (Harcourt, [1915] 1948), 88.
10. Alice Fox, *Virginia Woolf and the Literature of the English Renaissance* (Clarendon, 1990), 23.
11. Woolf, *The Voyage Out*, 292.
12. Woolf, *The Voyage Out*, 123.
13. Woolf, *The Voyage Out*, 85, 292.
14. Woolf, *The Voyage Out*, 83.
15. Woolf, *The Voyage Out*, 175.
16. Woolf, *The Voyage Out*, 326.

SYLVIA TOWNSEND WARNER

1. Sylvia Townsend Warner, *Lolly Willowes, or, The Loving Huntsman* (New York Review, 1999), 81–82.
2. Warner, *Lolly Willowes*, 103.
3. Warner, *Lolly Willowes*, 117–18.
4. Warner, *Lolly Willowes*, 117.
5. Warner, *Lolly Willowes*, 175.
6. Claire Harman, *Sylvia Townsend Warner: A Biography* (Minerva, 1991), 20; Michael Schmidt and Val Warner, "Sylvia Townsend Warner in Conversation" (1975), *PN Review Print and Online Poetry Magazine* 8, no. 3 (1982), https://www.pnreview.co.uk/archive/sylvia-townsend-warner-in-conversation/6978.
7. Harman, *Sylvia Townsend Warner*, 32.
8. Harman, *Sylvia Townsend Warner*, 41.
9. Harriet Baker, *Rural Hours: The Country Lives of Virginia Woolf, Sylvia Townsend Warner and Rosamond Lehmann* (Penguin, 2025), 112.

10. Quoted in Harman, *Sylvia Townsend Warner*, 100.
11. Quoted in Harman, *Sylvia Townsend Warner*, 242.
12. Karl Marx and Friedrich Engels, *Manifesto of the Communist Party*, 1848, https://www.marxists.org/archive/marx/works/1848/communist-manifesto/ch01.htm.
13. Sylvia Townsend Warner, *Summer Will Show* (New York Review, 2009), 327.
14. Warner, *Summer Will Show*, 237.
15. Warner, *Summer Will Show*, 137.
16. Warner, *Summer Will Show*, 117.
17. Warner, *Summer Will Show*, 131–32.
18. Warner, *Summer Will Show*, 143.
19. Warner, *Summer Will Show*, 82.
20. Warner, *Summer Will Show*, 83, 82.
21. Warner, *Summer Will Show*, 7.
22. Warner, *Summer Will Show*, 314.
23. Warner, *Summer Will Show*, 47.
24. Warner, *Summer Will Show*, 214.
25. Warner, *Summer Will Show*, 326.
26. Warner, *Summer Will Show*, 318.
27. Warner, *Summer Will Show*, 327.
28. Warner, *Summer Will Show*, 175.
29. Harman, *Sylvia Townsend Warner*, 125.
30. Warner, *Summer Will Show*, 282.
31. Quoted in Harman, *Sylvia Townsend Warner*, 308.
32. Warner, *Summer Will Show*, 227.
33. Sylvia Townsend Warner, *With the Hunted: Selected Writings*, ed. Peter Tolhurst (Black Dog, 2012), 115.
34. Heather Love, *Feeling Backward: Loss and the Politics of Queer History* (Harvard University Press, 2007), 143.
35. Stephen Spender, *World Within World: The Autobiography* (University of California Press, 1966), 244.
36. Quoted in Harman, *Sylvia Townsend Warner*, 216.
37. Sylvia Townsend Warner, *The Corner That Held Them* (New York Review, 2019), 110.
38. Sylvia Townsend Warner, "Behind the Firing Line. Some Experiences in a Munition Factory. By a Lady Worker." *Blackwood's*, no. 199 (February 1916): 194.
39. Sylvia Townsend Warner, "Women as Writers," in *The Gender of Modernism: A Critical Anthology*, ed. Bonnie Kime Scott (Indiana University Press, 1990), 544.

40. Sylvia Townsend Warner, *Scenes of Childhood* (New York: Viking, 1981), 129.
41. Warner, *The Corner That Held Them*, 343.
42. Warner, *The Corner That Held Them*, 111.
43. Warner, *The Corner That Held Them*, 220.
44. Warner, *The Corner That Held Them*, 248.
45. Warner, *The Corner That Held Them*, 398.
46. Warner, *The Corner That Held Them*, 399.
47. Sylvia Townsend Warner and William Maxwell, *The Element of Lavishness: Letters*, ed. Michael A. Steinman (Counterpoint, 2001), 319.

UNA MARSON

1. Delia Jarrett-Macauley, *The Life of Una Marson, 1905–1965* (Manchester University Press, 2009), 1.
2. Una Marson, *Pocomania and London Calling* (Blouse & Skirt, 2016), 10.
3. Marson, *Pocomania and London Calling*, 16–17
4. Marson, *Pocomania and London Calling*, 17.
5. Imaobong Umoren, *Race Women Internationalists: Activist-Intellectuals and Global Freedom Struggles* (University of California Press, 2018), 54.
6. Marson, *Pocomania and London Calling*, 33.
7. Marson, *Pocomania and London Calling*, 35.
8. Marson, *Pocomania and London Calling*, 43–44.
9. Marson, *Pocomania and London Calling*, 43.
10. Marson, *Pocomania and London Calling*, 43.
11. Marson, *Pocomania and London Calling*, 66.
12. Jarrett-Macauley, *The Life of Una Marson*, 101, 213.
13. Una Marson, "Our Debut," *Cosmopolitan*, May 1928, 4. The magazine, which only survived in a single print run, is now digitized and available at the Digital Library of the Caribbean (https://dloc.com/).
14. Jarrett-Macauley, *The Life of Una Marson*, 44.
15. Jarrett-Macauley, *The Life of Una Marson*, 54.
16. Jarrett-Macauley, *The Life of Una Marson*, 54.
17. Umoren, *Race Women Internationalists*, 28–29.
18. Quoted in Jarrett-Macauley, *The Life of Una Marson*, 77.
19. Jarrett-Macauley, *The Life of Una Marson*, 69.
20. Jarrett-Macauley, *The Life of Una Marson*, 69.
21. Jarrett-Macauley, *The Life of Una Marson*, 78.
22. Jarrett-Macauley, *The Life of Una Marson*, 88.
23. Umoren, *Race Women Internationalists*, 38.

24. Umoren, *Race Women Internationalists*, 44.
25. June Sarpong and Jennifer Obidike, *Calling Una Marson: The Extraordinary Life of a Forgotten Icon* (Akan, 2025), 146.
26. Sarpong and Obidike, *Calling Una Marson*, 202.
27. Sarpong and Obidike, *Calling Una Marson*, 222.
28. Sarpong and Obidike, *Calling Una Marson*, 195.
29. Umoren's *Race Women Internationalists* is a welcome exception.
30. Una Marson, "To Wed Or Not to Wed," in *Selected Poems*, ed. Alison Donnell (Peepal Tree, 2011), 63.
31. Una Marson, "Racial Feelings?" *Public Opinion*, July 17, 1937, http://contentdm64-srv.uwimona.edu.jm/cdm/ref/collection/publicopin/id/25, 3. Subsequent quotations from this editorial.
32. Marson, "Racial Feelings?"
33. Marson, "Racial Feelings?"
34. Marson, "In Jamaica," in *Selected Poems*, 78–79.
35. "Quashie (n.), Etymology," *Oxford English Dictionary*, June 2024, https://doi.org/10.1093/OED/7836876158.
36. Marson, "Quashie Comes to London," in *Selected Poems*, 104.
37. Marson, "Little Brown Girl," in *Selected Poems*, 92–95.
38. Anna Snaith, "'Little Brown Girl' in a 'White, White City': Una Marson and London," *Tulsa Studies in Women's Literature* 27, no. 1 (Spring 2008): 99.
39. Marson, "Quashie Comes to London," in *Selected Poems*, 104.
40. Marson, "Cinema Eyes," in *Selected Poems*, 139.
41. Marson, "Cinema Eyes," 141.
42. Marson, "'Black Is Fancy,'" in *Selected Poems*, 127.
43. Marson, "'Black Is Fancy,'" 127.
44. Marson, "Nigger," in *Selected Poems*, 85.
45. Marson, "Nigger," 85.
46. William Wordsworth, "It is not to be thought of," https://www.poetryfoundation.org/poems/45525/it-is-not-to-be-thought-of.
47. Marson, "Nigger," 86.
48. Marson, "Nigger," 85.
49. *West Indies Calling* (Paul Rotha Productions, 1943), YouTube video, 13:54, September 8, 2009, https://www.youtube.com/watch?v=ViGwxJloI7o; captions automatically generated by YouTube and edited by the author.
50. Stephen Bourne, "Cross, (Philip Louis) Ulric (1917–2013), Air Force Officer, Judge, and Diplomat," *Oxford Dictionary of National Biography*, January 1, 2017, https://www-oxforddnb-com.avoserv2.library

.fordham.edu/view/10.1093/ref:odnb/9780198614128.001.0001/odnb-9780198614128-e-109229.

51. *West Indies Calling*, 8:52.

PART 4: MENTORS

1. Virginia Woolf, *A Room of One's Own* (Mariner, 1989), 75.
2. Virginia Woolf, *The Life of Violet*, ed. Urmila Seshagiri (Princeton University Press, 2025), 21, 22.
3. Woolf, *The Life of Violet*, 22.
4. Woolf, *The Life of Violet*, 22.
5. Woolf, *The Life of Violet*, 22, 24.
6. Woolf, *The Life of Violet*, 26.
7. Virginia Woolf, *The Letters, 1912–1922*, vol. 2, ed. Nigel Nicolson and Joanne Trautmann (Harcourt, 1976), 402.
8. Woolf, *A Room of One's Own*, 75.
9. Woolf, *A Room of One's Own*, 64.
10. Woolf, *A Room of One's Own*, 64.
11. Woolf, *A Room of One's Own*, 64–65.
12. Woolf, *A Room of One's Own*, 8.
13. Woolf, *A Room of One's Own*, 39.
14. Woolf, *A Room of One's Own*, 32.
15. Woolf, *A Room of One's Own*, 34.
16. Woolf, *Letters*, 2.232.
17. Virginia Woolf, *Mrs. Dalloway: Authoritative Text, Contexts, Criticism*, ed. Anne E. Fernald, A Norton Critical Edition (W. W. Norton, 2021), 93.
18. Woolf, *Mrs. Dalloway*, 93.
19. Woolf, *Mrs. Dalloway*, 75.

JESSIE REDMON FAUSET

1. See David Levering Lewis, *When Harlem Was in Vogue* (Penguin, 1997), 157. Cheryl Wall comments, "Fauset was no prognosticator, but perhaps during the evening David Lewis calls 'the dress rehearsal of what was soon to be known as the 'Harlem Renaissance,' she divined: whatever she had done to produce it, Fauset would not have a starring role when the renaissance hit the big time." Cheryl A. Wall, *Women of the Harlem Renaissance* (Indiana University Press, 1995), 70–71. For a written version of Johnson's remarks, see Charles S. Johnson, "The Debut of the Younger School of Negro Writers," *Opportunity* (May 1924): 143–44.

2. Wall, *Women of the Harlem Renaissance*, 69–70.
3. Wall, *Women of the Harlem Renaissance*, 70.
4. Quoted in Jaime Harker, *America the Middlebrow: Women's Novels, Progressivism, and Middlebrow Authorship Between the Wars* (University of Massachusetts Press, 2007), 53. See also Wall, *Women of the Harlem Renaissance*, 70.
5. Joseph H. Morgan, *Morgan's History of the New Jersey Conference of the A.M.E. Church, from 1872 to 1887; and of the Several Churches, as Far as Possible, from Date of Organization, with Biographical Sketches of Members of the Conference*, 22–24, https://babel.hathitrust.org/cgi/pt?id=emu.010002588524&seq=1.
6. Civil Rights Cases, 109 U.S. 3 (1883). Five separate cases were combined into one 8-1 ruling, with Justice John Marshall Harlan offering the lone dissent.
7. "Civil Rights," *Camden (NJ) County Courier*, November 24, 1883.
8. "To the Editor," *Courier-Post* (Camden, NJ), November 27, 1883.
9. Jessie Redmon Fauset to W. E. B. Du Bois, December 26, 1903, W. E B. Du Bois Papers (MS 312), Special Collections and University Archives, University of Massachusetts Amherst Libraries.
10. *The Afro-American*, July 1, 1905.
11. W. E. B. Du Bois to Jessie Fauset, July 11, 1914, W. E. B. Du Bois Papers (MS 312), Special Collections and University Archives, University of Massachusetts Amherst Libraries.
12. Jessie Redmon Fauset, "There Was One Time," *The Crisis* 13, no. 6 (April 1971): 273.
13. Wall, *Women of the Harlem Renaissance*, 43; see also Sylvander, Carolyn Wedin, *Jessie Redmon Fauset, Black American Writer* (Whitson, 1981), 35–42.
14. See Jessie Redmon Fauset, "Tracing Shadows," *The Crisis* 10, no. 5 (September 1915): 247–51.
15. Samuel Hoskins, "Jessie Fauset to Write New Novel of American Culture," *The Afro-American*, August 5, 1944.
16. Deborah McDowell, "Introduction," in *Plum Bun* by Jessie Redmond Fauset (Beacon, 1990), ix.
17. Jessie Redmon Fauset to Langston Hughes, December 7, 1920; April 18, 1923, Langston Hughes Papers, James Weldon Johnson Collection, Yale Collection of American Literature, Beinecke Rare Book and Manuscript Library, Yale University.
18. Jessie Redmon Fauset to Countee Cullen, July 20, 1923, Correspondence: Fauset, Jessie Redmon, 1923–1932, Box 2, Folder 9, Countée Cullen Papers, 111, Amistad Research Center, Tulane University.

19. Thomas Jefferson Flanagan to Jessie Redmon Fauset, February 19, 1926, W. E. B. Du Bois Papers (MS 312), Special Collections and University Archives, University of Massachusetts Amherst Libraries.
20. Jessie Fauset, "Some Notes on Color," *World Tomorrow*, March 1922, 76.
21. Langston Hughes, *The Big Sea* (Knopf, 1940), 247.
22. Jessie Fauset, "The Gift of Laughter," in *The New Negro: An Interpretation*, ed. Alain Locke (Atheneum, 1925), 161–67. Even though the idea for *The New Negro* had arisen at the end of that fateful 1924 dinner party in her honor, Locke was slow to invite Fauset to contribute to the project and seems only to have done so when Du Bois threatened to withhold his own contribution if she were not included.
23. Jessie Fauset, "The Symbolism of Bert Williams," *The Crisis* 24, no. 1 (May 1922): 13.
24. Fauset, "The Gift of Laughter," 166.
25. Fauset, "The Symbolism of Bert Williams," 15.
26. Jessie Fauset to Langston Hughes, April 20, 1924, Langston Hughes Papers, James Weldon Johnson Collection, Yale Collection of American Literature, Beinecke Rare Book and Manuscript Library, Yale University.
27. W. E. B. Du Bois, Memorandum to Jessie Fauset, September 10, 1925, W. E. B. Du Bois Papers (MS 312), Special Collections and University Archives, University of Massachusetts Amherst Libraries, http://credo.library.umass.edu/view/full/mums312-b028-i339.
28. Fauset, *Plum Bun*, 16.
29. Fauset, *Plum Bun*, 17.
30. Fauset, *Plum Bun*, 14.
31. Fauset, *Plum Bun*, 60.
32. Fauset, *Plum Bun*, 39.
33. Fauset, *Plum Bun*, 40
34. Fauset, *Plum Bun*, 71.
35. Fauset, *Plum Bun*, 72.
36. Fauset, *Plum Bun*, 78.
37. Fauset, *Plum Bun*, 93.
38. Fauset, *Plum Bun*, 96.
39. Fauset, *Plum Bun*, 97.
40. Fauset, *Plum Bun*, 159.
41. Fauset, *Plum Bun*, 159.
42. Fauset, *Plum Bun*, 240.
43. Fauset, *Plum Bun*, 92–93.
44. Fauset, *Plum Bun*, 88.
45. Fauset, *Plum Bun*, 88.

46. Fauset, *Plum Bun*, 95.
47. Fauset, *Plum Bun*, 113.
48. Fauset, *Plum Bun*, 196.
49. Fauset, *Plum Bun*, 337.
50. Martin Kalfatovic, "Savage, Augusta (1892–1962), Sculptor," in *American National Biography* (Oxford University Press, 1999), https://www.anb.org/display/10.1093/anb/9780198606697.001.0001/anb-9780198606697-e-1700783.
51. W. E. B. Du Bois, "Criteria of Negro Art," *The Crisis* 32, no. 6 (October 1926): 294.
52. Fauset, *Plum Bun*, 349.
53. Fauset, *Plum Bun*, 243.
54. Fauset, *Plum Bun*, 379.
55. Jessie Fauset to Jean Toomer, February 4, 1922, *The Crisis*: Toomer, Jean, 1894–1967, 1922–32, Yale Collection of American Literature, Beinecke Rare Book and Manuscript Library, Yale University.
56. Jessie Fauset, letter to the editor, *Montclair Times*, April 13, 1944.
57. Jessie Fauset to Langston Hughes, January 23, 1948, Langston Hughes Papers, James Weldon Johnson Collection, Yale Collection of American Literature, Beinecke Rare Book and Manuscript Library, Yale University.
58. Jessie Fauset to Langston Hughes, March 3, 1948, Langston Hughes Papers, James Weldon Johnson Collection, Yale Collection of American Literature, Beinecke Rare Book and Manuscript Library, Yale University.
59. Jessie Fauset to Langston Hughes, June 9, 1949, Langston Hughes Papers, James Weldon Johnson Collection, Yale Collection of American Literature, Beinecke Rare Book and Manuscript Library, Yale University. The quotation is from Alexander Pope's "Epistle to Dr. Arbuthnot." Gloster is likely Hugh Gloster (1911–2002), who had been dean at Hampton College before becoming the seventh president of Morehouse. https://www.nytimes.com/2002/03/07/us/hugh-gloster-90-ex-president-of-morehouse.html.
60. W. E. B. Du Bois to Roscoe Conkling Bruce, December 11, 1925, W. E. B. Du Bois Papers (MS 312), Special Collections and University Archives, University of Massachusetts Amherst Libraries, http://credo.library.umass.edu/view/full/mums312-b031-i359.
61. Jessie Fauset to Langston Hughes, December 18, 1949, Langston Hughes Papers, James Weldon Johnson Collection, Yale Collection of American Literature, Beinecke Rare Book and Manuscript Library, Yale University.

62. Jessie Fauset to Langston Hughes, October 2, 1950, Langston Hughes Papers, James Weldon Johnson Collection, Yale Collection of American Literature, Beinecke Rare Book and Manuscript Library, Yale University.

DOROTHY ARZNER

1. *First Comes Courage*, dir. Dorothy Arzner (Columbia Pictures, 1943).
2. Dorothy Arzner, "The Unfinished Autobiography," in *Dorothy Arzner: Interviews*, ed. Martin F. Norden (University Press of Mississippi, 2024), 171.
3. Arzner, "The Unfinished Autobiography," 172.
4. Arzner, "The Unfinished Autobiography," 175.
5. Kevin Brownlow, "Interview with Director Dorothy Arzner," in Norden, *Dorothy Arzner*, 142.
6. Arzner, "The Unfinished Autobiography," 183.
7. Arzner, "The Unfinished Autobiography," 181, 184.
8. Arzner, "The Unfinished Autobiography," 186.
9. Arzner, "The Unfinished Autobiography," 186.
10. Arzner, "The Unfinished Autobiography," 186.
11. Francine Parker, "Approaching the Art of Arzner," in Norden, *Dorothy Arzner*, 117.
12. Arzner, "The Unfinished Autobiography," 191.
13. Arzner, "The Unfinished Autobiography," 195.
14. Mayme Ober Peak, "Only Woman Movie Director," in Norden, *Dorothy Arzner*, 19.
15. Kevin Brownlow, "Dorothy Arzner 1970 Interview," in Norden, *Dorothy Arzner*, 110–11.
16. Brownlow, "Dorothy Arzner 1970 Interview," 111.
17. Peak, "Only Woman Movie Director," 15.
18. Sheila O'Malley, "*Dance, Girl, Dance*: Gotta Dance," Criterion Collection, May 21, 2020, https://www.criterion.com/current/posts/6950-dance-girl-dance-gotta-dance.
19. Mary Murphy, "Film Director Dorothy Arzner: Tribute to an Unsung Pioneer," in Norden, *Dorothy Arzner*, 137.
20. Murphy, "Film Director Dorothy Arzner," 137.
21. Boze Hadleigh, "Dorothy Arzner," in Norden, *Dorothy Arzner*, 165.
22. *Christopher Strong*, dir. Dorothy Arzner (RKO Radio Pictures, 1933).
23. Rachael K. Bosley, "A Bulletproof Cinematographer," *American Cinematographer* 89, no. 1 (January 2008): 83.
24. Adela Rogers St. Johns, "'Get Me Dorothy Arzner!'—Samuel Goldwyn," in Norden, *Dorothy Arzner*, 57–58.

25. Katharine Hepburn, *Me: Stories of My Life* (Penguin, 1991), 113.
26. Pauline Kael, *5,001 Nights at the Movies* (Holt Rinehart, 1982), 108.
27. *Christopher Strong*, 1:02:15.
28. *Christopher Strong*, 1:05:14.
29. *Dance, Girl, Dance*, dir. Dorothy Arzner (RKO Radio Pictures, 1940).
30. *Dance, Girl, Dance*, 1:17:40.
31. O'Malley, "*Dance, Girl, Dance.*"
32. Molly Haskell, "Women in Pairs," *Village Voice*, April 28, 1975, 78.
33. Deborah Derow, "What Is This We Hear? —A Broad Is Gonna Direct," bachelor's thesis, Barnard College, 1976, 71; quoting Haskell, "Women in Pairs," 78.
34. Marguerite Tazelaar, "Meeting Miss Dorothy Arzner, Screen's Only Woman Director," in Norden, *Dorothy Arzner*, 39.
35. Grace Kingsley, "Leave Sex Out, Say Director," in Norden, *Dorothy Arzner*, 5.
36. Kevin Brownlow, *The Parade's Gone By . . .* (Abacus, 1973), 323, 326.
37. Dorothy Arzner, "How to Become a Woman Director," in Norden, *Dorothy Arzner*, 53.
38. Alice Tildesley, "Would You Be Master of Your Fate?" in Norden, *Dorothy Arzner*, 76.
39. Brownlow, "Dorothy Arzner 1970 Interview," in Norden, *Dorothy Arzner*, 98.
40. Martin F. Norden, "Exploring the Work of Dorothy Arzner as a Film-Making Teacher in Southern California," *Film Education Journal* 5, no. 2 (2022): 69.
41. Brownlow, *The Parade's Gone By . . .*, 327.
42. Kirsten Chuba, "Francis Coppola Helps Paramount Dedicate Building to Pioneer Director Dorothy Arzner," *Variety* (blog), March 2, 2018.

AFTERWORD

1. Virginia Woolf, *The Essays, 1925–1928*, vol. 4, ed. Andrew McNeillie (Harcourt, 1994), 478.
2. Virginia Woolf, *A Room of One's Own* (Mariner, 1989), 112.
3. Woolf, *A Room of One's Own*, 112.
4. Sylvia Townsend Warner, "Women as Writers," in *The Gender of Modernism: A Critical Anthology*, ed. Bonnie Kime Scott (Indiana University Press, 1990), 539.
5. Warner, "Women as Writers," 539.

CREDITS

MARGARET WISE BROWN

Excerpt(s) from THE SAILOR DOG by Margaret Wise Brown, illustrated by Garth Williams, copyright © 1953 and copyright renewed © 1981 by Penguin Random House LLC. Used by permission of Golden Books, an imprint of Random House Children's Books, a division of Penguin Random House LLC. All rights reserved.

Excerpt(s) from SEVEN LITTLE POSTMEN by Margaret Wise Brown, illustrated by Tibor Gergely, copyright © 1952, renewed 1980 by Random House, Inc. Used by permission of Golden Books, an imprint of Random House Children's Books, a division of Penguin Random House LLC. All rights reserved.

Excerpt(s) from THE COLOR KITTENS by Margaret Wise Brown, copyright © 1949, 1958, renewed 1986 by Penguin Random House LLC. Used by permission of Golden Books, an imprint of Random House Children's Books, a division of Penguin Random House LLC. All rights reserved.

Writing for 5-Year-Olds, copyright © Margaret Wise Brown, 1992. Used with permission from Hollins University.

Excerpts from THE IMPORTANT BOOK by Margaret Wise Brown, illustrated by Leonard Weisgard, copyright © 1949 by Margaret Wise Brown. Text copyright renewed © 1977 by Roberta Brown Rauch. Illustrations copyright renewed © 1977 by Leonard Weisgard. Used by permission of HarperCollins Publishers.

Excerpts from LITTLE FUR FAMILY by Margaret Wise Brown, illustrated by Garth Williams, copyright © 1946 by HarperCollins Publishers. Text copyright renewed © 1974 by Roberta Brown Rauch. Illustrations copyright renewed © 1974 by Garth Williams. Used by permission of HarperCollins Publishers.

Excerpts from GOODNIGHT MOON by Margaret Wise Brown, illustrated by Clement Hurd, copyright © 1947. Renewal copyright © 1975 Albert E. Clarke III Living Trust, dated April 4, 2013, and Peaceable Kingdom, LP. Used by permission of HarperCollins Publishers.

VERA BRITTAIN

Quotation from Vera Brittain's diary is © The Literary Executors of the Vera Brittain Will Trust (1970) and is reproduced with permission.

MURIEL RUKEYSER

Quotations from "Kathe Köllwitz," "Letter to the Front," "Speech for the Assistant," "Reading Time: 1 Minute 26 Seconds," "Poem Out of Childhood," and "Poem (I Lived during the first century of world wars)" copyright © 2005, Muriel Rukeyser, Janet E. Kaufman, and Anne F. Herzog. Reprinted by permission of the Estate of Muriel Rukeyser.

UNA MARSON

Una Marson, "To Wed or Not to Wed," "In Jamaica," "Quashie Comes to London," "Little Brown Girl," "Cinema Eyes," "Black is Fancy," and "Nigger" used with permission from *Una Marson: Selected Poems*, Peepal Tree Press, 2011.

Quotations from *Pocomania* used by permission from Blue Banyan Books Ltd., Kingston, Jamaica.

JESSIE REDMON FAUSET

Quotations from the Memorandum from W. E. B. Du Bois to Jessie Fauset, September 10, 1925, and the letter from W. E. B. Du Bois to Roscoe Conkling Bruce, December 11, 2025, printed courtesy of the Du Bois Literary Estates, Odell Murry, Trustee.

Letter from Jessie Fauset to Countee Cullen courtesy of the Countee Cullen Papers, Amistad Research Center, New Orleans, LA.

INDEX